Neighborhood of Fear

Neighborhood of Fear

The Suburban Crisis in American Culture, 1975–2001

Kyle Riismandel

Johns Hopkins University Press
Baltimore

Johns Hopkins University Press
2715 North Charles Street
Baltimore, Maryland 21218-4363
www.press.jhu.edu

Library of Congress Cataloging-in-Publication Data

Names: Riismandel, Kyle, 1978–author.
Title: Neighborhood of fear : the suburban crisis in American culture,
    1975–2001 / Kyle Riismandel.
Description: Baltimore : Johns Hopkins University Press, 2020. |
    Includes bibliographical references and index.
Identifiers: LCCN 2020006277 | ISBN 9781421439549 (hardcover ; alk.
    paper) | ISBN 9781421439556 (ebook)
Subjects: LCSH: Suburbs—United States—History—20th century. |
    Suburban life—United States—History—20th century. | Suburbanites—
    Political activity—United States. | Suburbs—Environmental aspects—
    United States. | Fear—Political aspects—United States. | Privilege
    (Social psychology)—United States. | Social values—Political aspects—
    United States. | United States—Civilization—20th century.
Classification: LCC HT352.U6 R55 2020 | DDC 307.740973/0904—dc23
LC record available at https://lccn.loc.gov/2020006277

A catalog record for this book is available from the British Library.

*Special discounts are available for bulk purchases of this book. For more
information, please contact Special Sales at specialsales@jh.edu.*

For Mom and Dad, Paul and Ellen,
Robert and Ruth Beers,
and Vaino and Elli Riismandel

Contents

Acknowledgments

All book acknowledgments should be books themselves. Beyond the work of the author, many people and their acts of kindness, generosity, and pure effort go into turning a good idea into a finished product. No one can cover them all, including me, but I want anyone reading this to know that many, many family members, friends, colleagues, and strangers helped make this book a reality. Its successes are theirs and flaws are mine.

The kernel of this project began while I was a master's student in the American Studies program at Penn State Harrisburg under the direction of Simon Bronner. Without him accepting me into the program and finding funding for my degree, I would not have gone on to a PhD or completed this book. And, as luck would have it, he is a great guy who provided timely advice and guidance about navigating academia. That opportunity also introduced me to John Gennari and Jessica Dorman, who were generous with their time and effort in helping me figure out just what it was I wanted to do. Jess directed my MA thesis on depictions of suburbs in film. She took great care in reading my work, gave valuable feedback, and was relentlessly supportive in getting me to study suburban culture in a more programmatic way. Since I left Middletown some time ago, she and John, like Simon, have continued to be resources. I am extremely thankful that they came into my life when they did and for all of their help along the way.

One pivotal and lucky moment, going to Penn State Harrisburg, led to another, one that was foundational in making this book possible. I started the PhD program in American Studies at George Washington University (GW) in fall 2002. My funding as a grad student supported the research and writing of much of this manuscript. There, I met a cohort of students and friends who changed my life. My writing group, the Brain Trust, kept me accountable, gave thoughtful feedback, and constantly reminded me that I could actually do it even when it seemed as if I might not. Laura Cook was a great editor and always had enthusiasm for mining the cultural texts in the manuscript. Similarly, Julie Passanante Elman showed me how to do better, more nuanced analysis of culture and media, and was unrelentingly sharp-eyed in helping me seize opportunities to make the dissertation better. Stephanie Ricker Schulte asked incisive questions that cut to the core of an issue, usually, "So what? Who gives a bleep?" and often in the same moment showed the way forward that saved hours of work. Laurel Clark Shire reminded me to not lose the broader historical thread and to think more cohesively about the manuscript. On top of that, our time working together was fun, funny, and engaging. Grad school can often be traumatic, but I always think about working with them wistfully. It was quite simply ideal.

The program at GW afforded the opportunity to meet and work with faculty who were influential on the thinking and analysis in this book. Chad Heap directed my dissertation and did yeoman's labor in helping me to better ground my work in the archives, refine my writing, and understand what it means to construct a whole, cohesive project. Learning those skills with his guidance made working on the book manuscript much more efficient and effective. Melani McAlister served on my dissertation committee and provided pointed and extremely useful advice that has fundamentally informed both my research and my teaching. Suleiman Osman arrived at GW just as I was beginning to work in earnest and joined the dissertation committee. His timely counsel helped me get over the hump and find my way to finishing.

Being part of GW's lively intellectual, academic, and social community enhanced my work and enriched my life. Cameron Logan has given consistent and brilliant feedback, including a crucial and timely critique of a full draft of the manuscript. Our conversations about this book and many other things shaped me and it for the better. Kevin Strait, too, has been a rock-solid presence in my life whose support and friendship helped make this book possible. Jeremy Hill was always ready to talk turkey and gave much good advice and practical guidance. Many others at GW and in Washington, DC, were helpful in getting through the work of grad school and providing a chance to blow off steam: Liz Breiseth, Kurtis Cooper, Jesse Gelwicks and Erin Brasell, Dave Elman, Andrew Hartman, Josh Fisher and Liz Snyder, Dave and Emma Kieran, Lars Lierow, Clare Monagle, Bret Schulte, Carolyn Shire, Jason and Ann Thompson, Matt and Ali Balus, Yusuke Torii, and Lauren Van Damme. Thanks, as well, to Sally Adee for her support during the writing of my dissertation.

I started work in the Federated History Department at the New Jersey Institute of Technology / Rutgers-Newark due to the timely intervention of Allison Perlman, who got me hired as an adjunct. Once again, I was incredibly lucky to find amazingly smart and supportive friends and colleagues. Their advice and encouragement helped me to finish the manuscript while teaching full-time. Neil Maher and Stephen Pemberton provided stellar examples of how to be academics who do great work and are great people. They did whatever they could to get me time and money to keep writing while providing priceless mentorship. This included research monies that allowed me to visit archives that were otherwise inaccessible. Maureen O'Rourke also continually supported my research and encouraged me to be ambitious while making my life so, so much easier. Rick Sher welcomed me as a colleague and showed genuine interest in me and this project while helping me find my footing as a member of the department. Alison Lefkovitz gave much of her time to read parts of the manuscript and to talk about the project and, more generally, how to do our work well. She is a sharp-eyed editor, a brilliant person, and a good friend. I am forever indebted to her. The administration of the College of Science and Liberal Arts was also supportive of this endeavor. Dean Kevin Belfield showed keen interest in my research, and Assistant Dean John Wolf volunteered much of his time to talk about research and writing and help me push through.

My colleagues at Rutgers-Newark were also essential to bringing this book to fruition. Mark Krasovic and Whit Strub gave thoughtful feedback on parts of the manuscript and provided essential guidance about the revision process. Mary Rizzo likewise provided a valuable critique and was a sounding board, helping me refine a number of things now in the book. She was always there with a crucial bit of insight or impeccable advice. Further, she connected me with Laura Davulis at Johns Hopkins University Press, which has proven to be a great match. Many others I met in Newark one way or another helped me finish the manuscript: Lauren Bell, Marybeth Boger, Karen Caplan, Jon Curley, Melissa Cooper, Rosanna Dent, Darshan Desai, Caroline DeVan, Jess and Jeff Dyer, Stephan Endicott, Lisa Gill, Carla Guerriero, Corey Heffernan, Amy Hoover, Theresa Hunt, Scott Kent, Elektra Kostopoulou, Audrey Le, Heather Lewis, Allison Love, N.K. Padala and Rosemary Joyce, Katia Passerini, Allison Perlman, Liz Petrick, Beryl Satter, Karl Schweizer, Maria Stanko, Tim Stewart-Winter, Christina Strasburger, and John Yarotsky.

At Johns Hopkins University Press, it has been an absolute pleasure working with Laura Davulis and Esther P. Rodriguez. Laura has been everything you need an editor to be—thoughtful, clear, and prompt. Esther, too, has always been on top of the process of getting the book to press, which I very much appreciate. I am also extremely appreciative for the effort that Juliana McCarthy put into producing the finished book. I am deeply thankful to two anonymous reviewers for taking great care in evaluating the manuscript. Their comments, thoughts, and suggestions helped me improve the book immensely.

I also want to thank the editors of *Environment, Space, Place* for their recommendations on an article that became chapter 4. Similarly, Paul Renfro greatly improved an earlier version of chapter 5 that appears in *Growing Up America: Youth in Politics since 1945*.

Being back in New Jersey has meant spending more time with old friends who have long supported me and this project. Michael and Sarah Miceli have given me unflinching confidence and essential friendship. Ken Newarksi quite literally made this book possible by giving me a place to live when I needed it. His friendship has helped me navigate tough times and have fun doing it.

Lastly, I cannot thank my family enough for all they have done up to and including their support for the writing of this book. All four of my grandparents never wavered in their encouragement of me and my work. Robert Beers, Ruth Beers, Vaino Riismandel, and Elli Riismandel were all people who started with virtually nothing and made better lives for my parents, me, and my brother. Their examples and ongoing support sustained me through this process and so many other things. I know they would be proud to see this book in print. Paul Riismandel and Ellen Knutson showed me how to live a life not defined by my work but enriched by it. They were always there when I needed to talk or to seek a refuge from the storm. I love you guys very much. Linda and John Riismandel have been my biggest supporters. From attending every Little League game to helping license images in this book, and providing every big and small thing in between, they loved and supported me unconditionally. It wasn't always easy, but they did it anyway. There is no thanks that can properly account for all they have done. Still, thanks, and I love you, Mom and Dad. Without my family, I know this book would not exist.

Neighborhood of Fear

Introduction

On June 7, 1982, the *New York Times* published homeowner Linda Saslow's contribution to "Speaking Personally," its series detailing the lives of ordinary Americans. Saslow described her experience of a home invasion to demonstrate how the suburbs had changed since her childhood. "Life in the suburbs has become a mass of contradictions," she wrote. "Many parents who chose a suburban life style in order to guarantee a comfortable and safe environment for children have been painfully disillusioned. We followed the promise of security, and one by one our plans were thwarted; our dreams were shattered. And we have sadly been forced to compromise on our ideals, as slowly we began to contradict our original plans."[1] Saslow's shattered dreams signified the shifting culture of suburban life at the end of the twentieth century. Promised safety, security, and a healthy environment by cultural visions of the postwar American dream, Saslow and her fellow suburbanites experienced a profound crisis of privilege as they found their expectation to escape or ignore danger unmet. In closing, she highlighted the emerging mindset of the American suburbanite in coping with a new era of hazard and its consequences: "Ultimately, we, who have wonderful memories of growing up in the suburbs, have been forced to lock our doors and increase our home security. We, who actively sought the suburbs for our own children, are quickly retreating behind a wall of distrust, fear and skepticism."

"Distrust, fear, and skepticism" were not unusual in the United States in the late 1970s and early 1980s, as the fog brought on by what Jimmy Carter called a "crisis of confidence" dissipated and the sun rose on morning (again) in America, as President Ronald Reagan's reelection campaign claimed in 1984. However, Saslow's lament symbolized the way suburbanites, in particular, newly saw their world after decades of peaceful associations. From nineteenth-century picturesque homes to sprawling housing tracts in the postwar era, the idea of suburbs as essentially pastoral havens of privilege prevailed as powerful forces throughout American life produced and cemented this notion. The federal government, advertisers, real estate agents, home builders, and the culture industries (mainstream news media and popular culture producers) emphasized home ownership, family life, and consumption of goods as essential to upward mobility and the health of the nation, particularly during the height of the Cold War.[2]

Through this vision, these historical actors marginalized conflict and danger, even though residents existentially feared integration as they policed racial borders and embraced other discriminatory practices. Instead, in the first decades after World War II, boosters and homeowners imagined suburbs as a refuge from crime, racial dissension, domestic strife, and environmental threats that most assuredly existed but remained largely invisible in culture and media.[3] Although the vision of a clean, safe, and uncontested suburb did not always match life on the ground, this powerful and dominant understanding of the suburban experience informed the expectations of the continuously increasing population of suburbanites.[4] For them, the privilege to not see, worry about, or confront local dangers was implicit in the act of moving to the suburbs.[5]

Yet the broad investments in infrastructure, industry, and consumerism that fueled postwar suburban growth also planted the seeds of local environmental, criminal, and moral dangers that took root and later blossomed. These new, homegrown hazards undermined suburban expectations by confronting residents with unexpected danger. They became apparent through a number of events that signaled material danger—posed by crime, toxic drinking water, and teen suicide, among other sources—while their depictions in popular culture produced and expanded the sense that threats were lurking in suburban homes and neighborhoods. As the threats emerged in the 1970s as consequences of suburban expansion, the broader cultural and political conditions of postwar America made it easier for suburbanites to recognize them not as anomalous but as persistent and dangerous. Environmentalism, second-wave feminism, "law and order" politics, the localism and antigovernment fervor of the New Right, the increasing prominence of Christian conservatives, and the emergence of the culture wars provided accepted and accessible ways for suburbanites to understand their world as endangered. They used these frames to make sense of their world at a time when the outcomes of more than two decades of suburban development proved more hazardous than expected. Together, the dangerous conditions wrought by expansion and these cultural and political frames not only made those dangers legible but justified suburbanites' responses.

These conditions marked a new era of the suburban past that historians have yet to identify and fully analyze. This book argues that a new era began in the mid-1970s. New, local threats undermined the expectations and understandings of suburban life as tranquil, safe, and family friendly; eroded the status of the suburb as a refuge from the conflict and discord often located in the city; and thereby created the neighborhood of fear.

On the physical landscape, the postwar deindustrialization of cities pushed manufacturing and corporate headquarters onto cheaper, undeveloped land closer to non-unionized workforces and expanding networks of highways outside the metropolis. By the 1960s, whether by design or as an accident of poorly planned, sprawling housing developments, these industrial parks were located in or abutted residential communities.[6] Soon thereafter, as deindustrialization and globalization affected the suburbs too, companies closed and abandoned sites, leaving behind toxic time bombs in and around adjacent bedroom communities. At that same moment, an ecological view of environmental protection became not just public policy but an accepted and widely available way to understand society as inescapably enmeshed in the natural world.

Suburban residents were essential to mainstreaming this view as they responded to the problems of development through the end of the 1960s.[7] In the 1970s, however, suburbanites found themselves increasingly surrounded by toxic threats more deadly than soapy tap water or improperly engineered greenfields. The tragedy of massive toxic poisoning of the community at Love Canal, the specter of nuclear meltdown at Three Mile Island, and the appearance of other severe environmental illnesses stemming from daily exposure to toxins in everyday products established the calamitous threats to the suburban environment, while news media narratives of toxic contamination and popular culture depictions like those in the movie *The China Syndrome* (1979) disseminated and enhanced this sense of hazard. Together, they showed that mortal environmental threats suffused suburbs and escalated the local peril to suburban families and neighborhoods. In this way, these narratives destabilized the presumed suburban privilege of good health and Arcadian natural surroundings and led suburbanites to act in their own defense against environmental maladies.

New dangers were not only ecological. By 1980, suburban populations had surpassed those of cities and rural areas.[8] This ascendance occurred as the United States experienced a spike in violence and criminal behavior driven by dire economic conditions and made more visible by law-and-order politicking and the continued pursuit of the wars on drugs and crime. These politicians and policy makers posited an America rife with lawbreaking and, in response, implemented punitive criminal justice reforms. This aggressive action to restore safety on American streets resonated in a time of urban crisis and led to the escalation of "tough on crime" policies.[9] Those politics and policies stoked the fear of crime that continually reproduced the notion that average citizens were in danger. In this period when many Americans feared being victims of violent crime, suburbanites, too, came to experience criminal endangerment and see themselves as imperiled. In particular, the "bucolic burglary wave" and the specter of home invasion, as Linda Saslow noted, dotted the daily news as the suburban home came to be seen less as a sanctuary than as a target for intruders who, news media and popular culture suggested, were lurking in every neighborhood.

Similarly, spaces outside the home, such as the shopping mall—formerly imagined as a secure and inclusive civic venue—became locations of conflict, danger, and fear because teen "arcade addicts" and "mallrats" who now congregated there were seen as dominating and controlling those spaces.[10] Still other groups of young people, such as hardcore punks and more loosely organized assemblages of disaffected teens, gathered in recreation centers and liminal communal areas like parks and undeveloped land. While there, according to police, parents, and popular culture, they drank, used drugs, fought, and demonstrated other "antisocial" behavior, lending credence to fears of the decline of the American family and the call to restore the mythic "family values" of 1950s suburban society.[11]

Enabled by both the discourses of law and order and family values, suburban parents, news media, and popular culture discovered a supposed kidnapping epidemic in the aftermath of the abduction and murder in 1981 of six-year-old Adam Walsh, who was taken from a Hollywood, Florida, mall in the middle of the day. The highly rated 1983 television movie *Adam*, based on the crime, further suggested to a prime-time national television audience that invisible criminal threats were lying in wait for unwitting suburban children. Even though no kidnapping epidemic existed, countless news articles and dozens of educational games and videos warned that children who had once roamed freely on the streets of places like Levittown and imagined their world to be as placid as a sitcom suburb should now fear for their lives whenever they walked out the front door. Together, these new understandings of suburbia, fueled by real incidents and their reproduction in the media, both altered the long-standing expectation of that space as safe, particularly for children and teens, and buttressed the overriding, and often exaggerated, sense of criminal danger.

As suburban "public" space came to be understood as increasingly perilous and even as homeowners worked to secure their houses against invaders, parents and public officials encouraged a return of children and teenagers to the more controlled space of the home. Yet, like burglars, cultural invaders jeopardized the sanctity of domestic space. Even though it fueled suburban growth, this endangerment came from the consumer culture that was central to suburban life and postwar US economic growth. To be sure, suburban moral panic was nothing new. In the 1950s, parents and culture critics fretted about "dangerous" products such as comic books and rock-and-roll records, widely available and marketed to children and teens.[12] By the 1980s, the problem of dangerous media had proliferated. Cultural outlets increased in number, and content reflected the liberalization of popular culture. Rock albums, music videos, television shows, movies, and video and board games were more explicit, more widespread, and more easily accessible because of unrated cable television programming, video cassette recorders (VCRs), home video rentals, and other home entertainment technology that were the spoils of middle-class suburban living. More and more of these products came in through the front door, over the air, and via an inconspicuous coaxial wire feeding young consumers with content that was increasingly framed as immoral, even fatal, in the discourses of the culture wars.

The pervasiveness of family values politics and the battles of the culture wars made it easier for concerned parents to see explicit depictions of sex and violence as an existential danger.[13] For conservative activists, politicians, and religious leaders in the late 1970s, cultural threats, from prime-time television to hardcore pornography, symbolized a moral erosion born of liberal political causes that put the idealized vision of breadwinner suburbia under siege.[14] They argued that these trends signaled the catastrophic moral failure of postwar American society as middle-class suburban households, once seen as paragons of American virtue, were being corrupted by amoral culture industries and liberals espousing "moral permissiveness."[15] By locating media and popular culture as an important site for the dissemination of detrimental images and ideas, these politicians and activists showed parents how to see this influx of images, stories, and products as dangerous and directly tied to the diminution of parental power, the worsening of teen social ills, and, ultimately, the dissolution of the nuclear family.[16]

Concerned parents on the battlefield of the culture wars in the 1980s and '90s readily adopted this framework. They saw popular culture products as "Trojan horses" rolling up to suburban homes. Packaged as innocent entertainment, these products smuggled into the home dangerously persuasive ideas about alcohol, drugs, sex, and the occult that had deadly consequences. Employing this conservative cultural logic, concerned parents argued that the malign influences of "porn rock," satanic heavy metal music, occult-themed role-playing games such as *Dungeons & Dragons*, violent video games, and goth culture led to the visible increases in the rates of suicide, murder, teen pregnancy and in instances of occult worship and substance abuse in the suburbs.

As suburbanites saw the threats around them as dangerous and pervasive, the ascendance and institutionalization of conservative politics and culture in the last quarter of the twentieth century facilitated their power in responding to a crisis of privilege. The activism and agitation of earlier "suburban warriors" grew the conservative movement from the grassroots to national prominence and mainstream acceptance.[17] Due to their work, the 1970s saw the New Right, inclusive of Christian and social conservatives, and their standard bearer Ronald Reagan, successfully espouse for the nation a belief in "protection and nourishment of privatism" through opposition to government intervention in everyday life.[18] Through a message and governing philosophy that emphasized small government, local power, expansive property rights, and the primacy of the nuclear family, Ronald Reagan fused cultural and fiscal conservatives into a winning electoral coalition that proved culturally and politically powerful through the end of the twentieth century, thanks in large part to the suburbanites who enacted that agenda in their neighborhoods and backyards.[19]

The successful mainstreaming of the New Right and the Reagan Revolution, then, was also another product of earlier suburban development whose national impact was visible by the late 1970s. However, unlike the products of postwar suburbanization that led to danger, this outcome led to power. The ascendant conservative worldview of that era combined a feeling of personal aggrievement with a sense of spatial and cultural empowerment focused on families, homes, and neighborhoods that fit perfectly with suburbanites' emerging sense of endangerment as they looked to respond to new, local dangers in the 1980s and '90s.

Rather than simply be imperiled, suburbanites responded by leveraging their endangerment through a process I call productive victimization. In actions posed as necessary to defend home, family, and neighborhood against new threats, suburbanites actually increased their control of local spaces and the people in them and further entrenched the white suburban family as the paradigm of American values.

To turn their endangerment into power, suburbanites relied on the hazards described above being experienced as demonstrably real, local, and continuously threatening (even if unlikely). In this way, the materiality of people poisoned by toxic waste or the grim sadness of kidnappings in the suburbs provided the raw material for legitimate fear that justified suburban action. News media and popular culture turned this raw material into images and narratives that reproduced and often exaggerated the dangers while figuring them as pervasive and requiring action. Together the materiality of hazards and their cultural reproductions enabled a sense of ongoing endangerment, a crisis of the privilege to ignore or evade such hazards, that legitimated reasonable claims of hazard on the part of suburbanites who otherwise appeared safe.

Once reasonably endangered, suburbanites were justified in defending themselves against these threats. However, their responses to new local dangers went beyond mere defense. Through actions posed as pragmatic and protectionist, suburbanites extended their control of homes and neighborhoods and further asserted the primacy of the suburban household in debates about American family values; in this way, productive victimization facilitated the privatization of many functions of the state and the leveraging of state power to achieve private ends.

Environmental threats allowed suburbanites to shape the physical landscape. While the ecological view of the natural world remained culturally prevalent, the Reagan and Bush administrations rolled back many environmental regulations in the 1980s while touting individual and marketplace solutions to these problems.[20] Opportunistically, suburbanites combined these worldviews for their own private, local purposes by identifying mortal ecological dangers but only acting to protect themselves and their neighborhoods.[21] Homeowners asserted "Not in my backyard!" (Nimby!) to stop seemingly dangerous projects such as nuclear power plants and garbage dumps in order to protect *their* homes and families, not to mount an environmentalist crusade. In identifying the hazards of a new project, they leveraged privileged relationships with the state and corporations to enact their desires to "protect" local space. When successful, Nimbys often displaced ecologically dangerous projects into the backyards of less powerful communities. However, that action, though premised on ecological endangerment, was also often about protecting against cultural dangers presented as environmental that could undermine the character of suburban living. In responding to the possible siting of a rehabilitation clinic or apartment complex in their neighborhood, suburbanites simply asserted that their fear of cultural contamination trumped civic needs. Through Nimbyism, then, suburbanites made their environmental endangerment useful. They powerfully acted locally and expressed private concerns while still self-interestedly enlisting corporations and the state to control local space and protect homeowners from environmental threats in ways that often endangered other communities.

Similarly, suburban home and business owners undertook their own safety measures to regulate space and combat crime, actions that valorized property rights and the expansive power necessary to defend them. They installed alarm and closed-circuit television surveillance systems, patrolled neighborhoods, built gated neighborhood entrances, and employed private security forces to supplement or even displace local police, making what had been a municipal function an instrument of suburban advantage. In this same era, increasingly conservative courts and legislatures empowered suburban homeowners to aggressively police local space themselves through Stand Your Ground laws and expansive interpretations of the Castle Doctrine. This privatization of police and security functions meant that suburban property owners exerted more authority over private and public space. Through that increased authority, they regulated those spaces and the people within them explicitly to protect home, family, and property.

These practices, premised on the notion of pervasive criminal endangerment discussed above, facilitated and were facilitated by the tough-on-crime culture and politics of the day. Largely white suburban populations policed their own streets and secured their homes, often with the assistance of law enforcement and using new surveillance technologies. In stark contrast, the state subjected urban citizens of color to surveillance and harassment that fueled the mass incarceration epidemic and the new Jim Crow.[22] By continuously highlighting their imperilment and acting in their own defense, suburbanites seemingly gave evidence of the rising tide of crime used to justify both their ever enlarging power to police space and the increasingly harsh criminal justice policies that disproportionately impacted populations of color.[23]

As part of the same world of productive victimization, suburban parents responded to spikes in teen suicides, drug abuse, and other social ills largely by working to empower people like them—white, middle-class suburbanites. Rather than pushing for legislation or broad-based social change, they leveraged culture warriors' critiques to further emphasize the power and importance of pragmatic, local remedies carried out by families, not government, for addressing the family in crisis. Through advisory pamphlets, parenting manuals, and instructional videos, groups like the Parents Music Resource Council and individual concerned parents emphasized the essential role of parents in protecting their children against dangerous popular culture and its presumed harmful.

This focus marginalized scientific or medical explanations for teen social ills and public policy solutions that would address all children and teens in danger. By offering practical, seemingly nonideological ways for parents to confront social problems, the groups promoted the inherently political idea of the nuclear family as a cultural ideal, an ideal premised on the notion that suburban children and teens were innocent victims in need of defense and capable of redemption.[24] In contrast, urban populations of color and their familial arrangements were consistently demonized and marginalized and were, therefore, subject to the continued interventions of the state.[25] For example, the responses to suburban cultural products like heavy metal or even role-playing games were about protecting vulnerable consumers from moral corruption by those ostensibly innocuous products. When it came to black culture, particularly rap music and hip-hop, culture critics and politicians made no distinction between producer and consumer, addressing them all as essentially degenerate, criminal, or both.[26]

In taking these actions to make victimization productive, suburbanites framed their actions as commonsense, necessary, and nonideological because they were defending against legitimate existential threats, not advancing an agenda. In their telling, they were not wide-eyed activists with a plan to change the world but concerned parents and endangered homeowners left with no choice but to act to quell emergent threats. This mode allowed suburbanites to address hazards as local problems and pursue private interests while eliding ideological debates that might detract from their ability to exert local power. Despite this framing, and whether intentional or not, suburbanites' actions were ideological. Their actions often exacerbated race and class divisions wrought by the politics that empowered them. Further, suburbanites reflected and advanced postwar cultural and political shifts toward localism, privatism, and family values through their expansive responses to environmental, criminal, and moral threats.[27] Their actions symbolized the viability and success of the New Right's governing philosophy and cultural outlook. In addition, as Lily Geismer argues, suburbanites' emphasis on local interests and privatism reoriented the Democratic party around those ideals and away from the priorities of its blue-collar base as the party's politics tacked right to court suburban voters.[28] Ultimately, suburbanites proved essential to the rightward shift in American culture and politics, no matter the party in power. They were opportunistically driven and locally focused voters, consumers, and constituents who supported cultural causes and political parties as long as they were parochially productive.[29] As a result, suburbanites enacted a new formula for power. The discovery, identification, or manufacture of seemingly legitimate threats justified extensions of privilege and authority as national politics increasingly focused on suburban issues and on empowering suburbanites.

The measures suburbanites took, then, did not simply combat threats but facilitated their shaping of the landscape and cultural life to satisfy their priorities in ways that might not have been possible without the emergence of new, local, and seemingly pervasive threats to their expected privileges. And, by enacting these local, private solutions to emergent threats, they exemplified conservative visions of the proper functioning of family values, self-determination, and property rights. Suburban actions also furthered the neoliberal project that continues to undermine the efficacy of the state, weaken nonsuburban communities, and marginalize viable explanations for and solutions to visible social problems.

Ironically, federal and state governments had created the world of postwar suburban privilege, and, with the emergence of new, local hazards, suburbanites expected their collaboration in protecting and even expanding it.[30] Rather than simply being the problem, as Ronald Reagan emphatically declared in his 1981 inaugural address, the state functioned as both facilitator and foil of expansive suburban power through productive victimization. On one hand, material endangerment from burglars, kidnappers, or toxic waste allowed suburbanites to call upon government at all levels to act in their defense or support their private efforts at protecting themselves. On the other, the state functioned as a foil that could easily and credibly be blamed for failing to protect them in an era when Americans and their representatives increasingly questioned the value and effectiveness of government action in defending citizens or prioritizing their interests. From Reagan's characterization of the role of the state to Bill Clinton's declaration of the end of the era of big government, antigovernment politics was commonplace. It was thus not only plausible but likely that suburbanites would see the state as a cause of their newfound endangerment and that saying so would be politically viable. In framing government as a scapegoat, then, they could continue to pursue local prerogatives with its help while still reproducing the very notion that they must protect themselves because government couldn't or wouldn't defend against these pervasive criminal, environmental, and moral threats.

Yet suburban dwellers still needed the state to help make their victimization productive. Opposition to an environmentally hazardous project like a nuclear power plant usually required the state to intervene on suburbanites' behalf if asserting "Not in my backyard!" was to actually prevent construction. Similarly, if suburban action was to be viable in regulating local space, it needed the state's legal and logistical approval (or acquiescence). Neighborhood watches and private security forces, though sometimes a nuisance, acted in concert with local law enforcement, while lawmakers and the courts strengthened homeowner rights in defending their homes and families through judicial validation of the Castle Doctrine and the passage of Stand Your Ground laws.[31] Even when confronted with moral threats from popular culture, suburbanites benefited from the state's (non)intervention. Through hearings on violent video games that did not result in legislation or the V-chip for controlling television watching in the home, the resulting rhetoric empowered suburban parents to address these problems as family matters and, quite simply, left them alone to do so. In these ways, the state facilitated and enforced suburban privilege even as "government" was pilloried as onerous and threatening to middle-class families.

In addition to the changes discussed thus far, racial and ethnic diversity increased during this period, as historians have shown.[32] While an important and ongoing shift, it did not fundamentally destabilize the understandings of suburbs or the priorities of suburbanites that centered on white people. The nearly homogeneous suburban populations of the immediate postwar era made later diversity relatively easy to achieve and apprehend. Indeed, the changing suburbs of the 1980s and '90s were still largely populated by whites and defined by racial and ethnic segregation. Thus, even as African American, Asian, and Latinx populations have moved into places commonly understood as suburban, such as Prince Georges County, Maryland, most of these communities in the twenty-first century remain unintegrated according to recent studies. Further those studies show that white people are the most segregated population overall and even more segregated in suburban areas.[33] Thus, even as diversity increased, it was usually not attended by integration.

Nonetheless, some of the power and privilege of suburban living became available to homeowners simply by their moving in. Homeowners of color who overcame the historical and economic barriers to buying a home made legitimate claims to power even though what they experienced was not assimilation or recoding of racial identity. Still, the historical record is quite clear that racial identity and racism were essential to establishing postwar suburban identity as white and to whites' articulation of their power. In some places, as diversity increased, white residents moved into sprawling development, returned to gentrifying cities, or lived in places featuring small communities of color. This often meant that black suburbanites, in particular, did not usually enjoy the same privileges as their white counterparts.[34] As historian Andrew Wiese argues, black suburbanites "remained spatially differentiated," living in largely segregated neighborhoods in the 1980s and '90s with little evidence that "African Americans' racial or class identities were on the wane in suburbia."[35] Hence, this increasingly multiracial world was not one of equality of power or prominence. Despite increased diversity and a demographic trajectory suggesting later integration, the suburbs in the period discussed in this book remained largely white and segregated and therefore focused on the culture and priorities of those residents.

In sum, this book makes three central claims. First, the suburban crisis was one of imperiled privilege where homeowners expected to live free of everyday confrontations with hazard. Instead, the mid-1970s marked a new era of endangerment in which they faced new, local environmental, criminal, and moral threats born of earlier suburban development and made increasingly visible through the media. Second, in response to these threats, suburbanites leveraged their presumed imperilment through the process of productive victimization not only to defend themselves but to expand spatial power and cultural authority. Third, despite framing their actions as pragmatic and nonideological, suburbanites' measures facilitated and were facilitated by the era's dominant conservative culture and politics. Together, they normalized the notion of government as inept and corrosive to American values while valorizing local, private power as more effective and efficient when exercised by homeowners seeking to enjoy the expected privileges of suburban living. In all of these efforts, from consciousness raising about emergent threats to actions in response to them, suburbanites made victimization essential to their expansion of cultural and spatial influence—a process that had devastating effects on those who lacked the power and privilege of suburban living.

In making this argument, I approach the suburb as a historically constructed category of meaning articulated in and through space. This study, then, is not a search for the "real" or "true" suburb of the past or an analysis of a conspiracy to protect suburban privilege. It is an investigation of the shifting meanings of suburbs and the implications of those understandings for their residents and the nation in the late twentieth century. To account properly for this history, each chapter details a different area of hazard and response. The real events, media and popular culture representations, and practices by suburbanites woven into each chapter show the complex ways in which threats emerged, were reproduced in culture, and led to suburbanites' expressions of power. In some cases, news media and popular culture publicized a threat, creating a framework to understand subsequent, similar real events. In others, the impact of an actual accident, crime, or disturbance was amplified by portrayals in cultural outlets. Ultimately, each chapter analyzes the relationships between culture, events, and practice within public discourses to show how they made and reproduced a new common sense about suburban life. No longer middle-class enclaves marked by assumed safety and security and fundamentally defined by rigid racial barriers, suburbs came to be understood and experienced as dangerous places riven with fear and insecurity, a pale imitation of their parents' sitcom suburbs. It wasn't simply that suburbanites made the perennial discovery that perfection in their neighborhood is a façade. Rather, when they removed the façade and demystified the cultural tropes, they discovered that suburbs were worse than fake: they were neighborhoods of fear.

This book traces the contemporary manifestations of suburban politics and power to their roots in the emergence of productive victimization beginning in the 1970s.[36] In spite of falling crime rates through the end of the twentieth century, suburbanites today continue to build nearly impenetrable neighborhoods and to expand homeowner rights, reflecting the culture of crime analyzed here. The Nimby ethic also remains powerful in shaping local land use. Governments and corporations planning suburban construction projects must anticipate that local residents will exercise their veto and preemptively approach them lest there be a protest. Further, the broad sense of toxic hazard that emerged in the 1970s buttresses the cultural awareness of health, wellness, safety, and survival that now manifests itself through affective salves and miracle "cures," culminating in the hyperawareness of allergies and lobbying against compulsory vaccination; meanwhile urban residents lack clean water and are perilously exposed to toxic chemicals.[37] The suburban culture warriors, too, have provided an effective method for responding to moral crises into the twenty-first century. Like the earlier responses to porn rock, satanic rituals, and suicide, cultural causes and cures trumped systemic explanations and solutions. Continuing epidemics of school shootings and opioid addiction, in particular, are still considered through the framework of moral failure and parental involvement, marginalizing voices for gun control, universal health care, and increased spending on social programs.[38]

The first two chapters analyze the ways suburbanites recognized and dealt with different kinds of environmental danger. Chapter 1, "Age of the Nimby," examines how the emergence of legitimate environmental threats from industry enabled suburbanites to shape their local environments through Nimby protests. Other environmental threats proved still more insidious. Chapter 2, "Neighborhood of Fear," analyzes suburbanites' perception of their world as inescapably suffused with chemicals, toxins, allergens, and irritants in the very products they used every day, such as frozen foods, hairspray, perfumes, and cars. Although suburbanites could not expel these toxins as they could hazardous public projects, they did legitimate these as new diseases and mitigate them by deploying resources most Americans did not have. Together, these collections of environmental hazards highlighted the pervasive sense of lurking toxic danger in a new era of risk, while the responses to them demonstrated how potential victimization empowered suburbanites while deepening divisions of race and class.

In chapters 3 and 4, I examine how new threats to homes and public space facilitated privatized spatial regulation, enlisting and sometimes supplanting the power of the state. Chapter 3, "'Fear Stalks the Streets,'" examines suburbanites' compulsion to protect themselves from the criminal threats of home invasion and kidnapping. To protect against seemingly omnipresent criminals, they installed home security systems, began neighborhood watch programs, and employed private security forces that increased their sense of safety while serving as daily reminders of endangerment. Chapter 4, "Punks, Mallrats, and Out-of-Control Teenagers," details the threats disruptive teenagers posed to people and spaces outside the home and responses to those threats. At the recreation center, the shopping mall, and the video game arcade, teenagers emerged as both dangerous and endangered, leading parents, police, and business owners to more strictly regulate these spaces in ways that called into question what actually constituted suburban *public* space.

Chapter 5, "Parental Advisory—Explicit Content," argues that real tragedies and the actions of concerned parents and culture critics produced the idea of the home as endangered. News narratives of suicide pacts and ritualistic murders pointed to satanic worship as the cause, an influence smuggled in by popular culture products brought straight into homes over the air, on a wire, and through the front door. Empowered by organizations like the Parents Music Resource

Council and Bothered About *Dungeons & Dragons*, as well as the broader conservative cultural politics of the age, parents did not seek a centralized solution to the "problem" of dangerous popular culture. Instead, they protected a "traditional" vision of the family through individual actions which made clear that protecting one's household from the deleterious effects of popular culture was a manifestation of suburban privilege, not an expectation of American citizenship.[39]

Chapter One

Age of the Nimby

*Environmental Hazard and Spatial Power
on the Suburban Landscape*

In his 1991 book, *Siting Hazardous Waste Facilities: The Nimby Syndrome*, political scientist Kent E. Portney found that, "public opposition to facility siting has now reached the point where it has been given status as a full-scale public malady—the NIMBY, or Not-in-my-backyard, Syndrome."[1] He was not alone in making this observation. The United States was in the midst of what the *New York Times* called the age of Nimby.[2] Activists, journalists, and other critics decried the growing number of homeowners opposed to siting public projects in their suburban neighborhoods.[3] This "syndrome" was a strain of suburban disease, a form of "affluenza," according to detractors, where the assertion of property rights in the face of even remote environmental hazard trumped the public good in preventing construction of a power plant, trash incinerator, or other project proposed as an essential public service.[4]

In 1988, journalist Bella English described this suburban exercise of power as endorsing the need for a civic project without accepting any risk or responsibility—a strictly parochial view of citizenship. "Invariably, the line goes like this," English wrote in the *Boston Globe*: "'We are not opposed to the (homeless, mentally ill, retarded, AIDS patients). We believe they should be cared for, but not here. It is too (urban, rural, populated, unpopulated). Those people would be better off (in your neighborhood, anyplace else, Mars).'"[5] According to political strategist and Nimby critic David Gergen, the effective use of Nimby meant that "stupidity reigns" in the practice of suburban land use, as local fears stopped or displaced projects designed to benefit a broad constituency.[6] But if "not in my backyard" protests were antidemocratic and a manifestation of sheer stupidity in preventing needed projects, why were they so prevalent and powerful in shaping the suburban landscape in the 1980s and '90s? The answer lies in suburbanites positioning themselves as indispensable constituents and consumers whose legitimate claims of environmental danger in the "industrial garden" could not be ignored by government or corporations.[7]

The success of the environmental protection movement and the New Right in postwar America made it possible for Nimbyism to be a powerful and practical response to emerging environmental hazards. Though in most senses contradictory, these two movements proved compatible for suburbanites who positioned themselves as nonideologues defending against local, ecological threats. The environmentalist movement established nature as endangered and needing active protection to preserve human health. For postwar homeowners, "nature" included the inheritance of presumably clean suburban natural surroundings even as construction abounded—further highlighting the contradictions of the machine in the garden.[8] Concurrently, the New Right, a coalition of conservative groups, successfully pushed for the devolution of power from the national to the local level and from the government to the individual, in particular the individual property owner.[9] By effectively positing environmental threats and local action as the best defense against them, these movements empowered suburban homeowners to legitimately and forcefully cry, "Not in my backyard!"

These movements also enabled Nimbys by laying the ideological foundation on which they could fashion themselves as locally focused pragmatists defending their homes and not fanatics pursuing broader, nonprovincial goals. Journalist Walter Truett Anderson captured this stance in 1989: "NIMBY people are not interested in ideology, spirituality or rolling back the clock. They just want to keep their local communities from being destroyed by development and/or pollution."[10] As avowedly ideologically agnostic, Nimbys staked out a "reasonable," nearly unassailable logic of defense against suburban environmental hazard that media and popular culture suggested was nearly everywhere. Yet, despite their antidogmatic posturing in service of local objectives, suburban Nimbyism significantly aided and was aided by the ideologically driven localism and privatism of the Reagan revolution, which adversely affected those who often relied on the state to protect them. By eschewing labels and declaring "Not in my backyard!" to defend themselves, suburbanites actually maintained the spatial power and privileges of suburban living while often displacing these projects into other, less politically powerful communities.[11] As a Cienega, Arizona, city councilor presciently noted in 1988, "There is a danger in the 'not in my backyard' philosophy. It clearly discriminates against people with fewer financial resources."[12]

The process and impact of Nimbyism are well illustrated in the case of nuclear power. By 1979, the broad view that these plants were needed in the midst of energy crises and environmental activism against dirtier forms of energy production turned apocalyptic, particularly for the suburban communities adjacent to many of them. In March 1979, the accident at the suburban power plant Three Mile Island (TMI) made nuclear power a visible, material threat, not an energy panacea. Media and popular culture echoed and extended that feeling of danger by producing threatening visions that vividly linked the plants with imminent catastrophe on the suburban landscape. News media narratives detailed the problems at TMI leading up to and following the accident, and indicted the industry as incompetent, unprepared, and lacking credibility. In popular culture, the 1979 film *The China Syndrome* provided a powerful shorthand for understanding nuclear disaster wherein mismanagement and poor regulation, both in the service of corporate greed, lead to a nuclear meltdown that theoretically goes all the way to China. This was an important frame for making sense of the accident at TMI, which occurred just two weeks after the film hit screens. The movie primed the public to see the nuclear power industry as corrupt and dangerous—a vision reinforced by the real accident and its media portrayals. The accident worked with these images and narratives to generate suburbanites' claims of legitimate endangerment from the nuclear power plants sprouting up on their local landscapes, even as those plants helped meet their increasing demand for electricity.[13]

In this new world of suburban environmental danger, Nimbys on Long Island leveraged the potential victimization embodied by the nuclear power plant as a disaster-waiting-to-happen in order to stop construction of generators at the proposed site of Shoreham on the island's North Shore. In the years after the events of spring 1979, thousands of local residents joined a small number of antinuclear activists near the site to oppose the new plant, eventually succeeding in 1989. To highlight their imperilment, they repeatedly invoked the images of nuclear meltdown and regulatory malfeasance widely available in the aftermath of Three Mile Island and *The China Syndrome*. In doing so, suburban Long Islanders clearly marked themselves as the likely victims of the Long Island Lighting Corporation's plan, backed by the local, state, and federal governments, to put a nuclear time bomb in their neighborhood. However, while Long Island Nimbys fashioned themselves as victims mistreated by government and corporations, they still needed institutional power to materially enforce their claims. By leveraging their perceived endangerment and power as constituents and consumers, suburbanites forced the closure of the Shoreham plant before it could ever produce a watt of energy. Yet, stopping short of pursuing the broader antinuclear power agenda, these Long Island residents returned victorious to the restored safety of their homes satisfied with the result of their now-productive victimization.

The defeat of this suburban nuclear power plant was symbolic of the broader power of suburban homeowners. In the age of the Nimby, emboldened suburbanites across the country took aggressive stances against a number of other threats broadly posed as environmental. Through the 1990s, they opposed just about any project that might endanger their local environment or undermine the privileges of suburban living, viewing such defiance as reasonable and any resulting obstruction as necessary. From health clinics to helicopter pads to trash dumps, Nimbys resisted the siting of projects in their neighborhoods and very often succeeded. When built, many of these projects, particularly the most toxic, ended up in communities unable to oppose them and safeguard themselves in the ways that suburbanites did.[14]

Nimbyism was essentially an expression of privilege and spatial power clothed in the seemingly legitimate fears of environmental imperilment widely visible on the physical and media landscapes. And it proved powerful because of the ascendant postwar politics of both liberals concerned with environmental dangers and conservatives looking to devolve power to local government and the individual, even when it came to "protecting" the environment.[15]

Environmental Consciousness and Suburban Expectations in the 1970s

Postwar suburbanites promoted and sought to preserve a nineteenth-century vision of the natural environment. In that earlier era, homeowners both dominated and were in harmony with their natural surroundings, allowing them to control nature's wilder elements while still enjoying clean air and unspoiled waterways. Once it was established, boosters and planners sold this lifestyle as an antidote to the glaring environmental dangers of the nation's burgeoning metropolises.[16] Planners such as Frederick Law Olmstead designed suburbs to be like urban parks, not only a respite but also an amelioration of the social ills associated with teeming masses of immigrants and rampant disease found in late-nineteenth-century urban centers.[17] However, unlike parks designed for the public, suburbs provided a cure for urban ills designed specifically to be owned and accessed by the privileged classes, as middle- and upper-class white people had the wealth and social standing necessary to leave the city for a country home and all that it entailed.[18] This idea of a sequestered refuge from environmental threats shaped the understanding and expectations of postwar homeowners. Following the Great Depression and World War II, and in the midst of a housing crisis, these emigrants from the urban core came to find a peaceful, clean, and antiurban habitat that linked environmental purity and power over their natural environs with the privileges of suburban living.

Prior to the 1970s, as massive and often haphazard suburban development occurred, suburbanites seeking to preserve their environmental ideal were essential to the emergence of a nationwide environmentalist movement.[19] Their claims of endangerment from chemicals and pesticides were early articulations of broader ecological values and often gave substance to subsequent environmentalist arguments and helped the movement gain traction into the late 1960s. In that era, suburban homeowners filed lawsuits, banded together in the marketplace, and lobbied government to protect a natural environment they understood to be pristine. In doing so, they fought to maintain the nineteenth century environmental ideal of the bucolic suburb through traditional organizing and legal tactics that largely supported the goals and values of the environmental movement.

By the mid-1970s, that broader movement succeeded in making dangers to the natural environment appear pervasive and ecological disaster plausible. Environmentalists raised public consciousness about a wide spectrum of hazards and their connections to human well-being, as reflected in environmentalist milestones from Rachel Carson's *Silent Spring* published in 1962 and the first Earth Day in 1970, to the Keep America Beautiful organization's public service announcement featuring a "Native American" man tearing up at the sight of litter. This cultural shift was accompanied by passage of a battery of federal environmental protections, including the Clean Water Act (1963), Clean Air Act (1972), and Endangered Species Act (1973), that were continually updated and improved, as well as the later creation of the Superfund program to clean up abandoned waste sites.[20] These political and cultural achievements prompted the *New York Times* to dub the 1970s the "environmental decade," an era in which widespread public concern arose that the natural environment was in danger and needed protection.[21] Yet, for most of the 1970s, through the energy crises and economic "stagflation"—the once-unthinkable combination of rampant inflation and stagnant economic growth—suburbanites saw the costs of development largely in economic rather environmental terms, leaving racial integration and taxes, not environmental issues, as the central sources of suburban conflict in the late 1960s and early '70s.[22]

As more and more homeowners moved into the suburbs in the 1970s, they believed they were accessing a residential alternative that was healthier and safer than the modernist concrete and steel landscapes of postwar cities, riven with their own array of environmental hazards. From pollution and smog to crime and disease, the city did not represent a viable alternative for those who could leave and were being incentivized to do so by government and industry.[23] Even the urban parks, designed as a respite from hectic, dirty, and dangerous city life, fell into disrepair during the economic downturn of the 1970s, making the suburban environment even more attractive by comparison.[24] As environmental historian Andrew Hurley has written of Gary, Indiana's suburbs, "The appeal of suburbia lay in the fact that it brought together all those qualities that middle-class families found lacking in the inner-city."[25]

Whereas some environmental dangers lay dormant through the early postwar years until "discovered" on the suburban landscape, others suddenly became understood as threatening only in the 1970s. These new threats, such as toxic waste and nuclear power plants, were of a different magnitude than the 1960s concerns over soapy water or failed septic tanks in that they portended and sometimes led to catastrophic results. In doing so, they undermined the suburbs' Arcadian legacy and suburbanites' expectations of environmental safety, and called forth an active, local defense that reflected and reproduced the ascendant politics of privatism.

The Nuclear Issue Becomes Suburban

Before 1979, nuclear power was a suburban issue to the extent that it provided cheaper energy to homeowners who were using more and more electricity in an era of energy crises.[26] The danger of a catastrophic accident at a nuclear plant seemed remote, while the economic benefits directly impacted a suburban household's bottom line.[27] Indeed, public opinion polls before 1979 showed a majority of Americans supported nuclear power, and six state referendums in the 1970s endorsed its use.[28] To meet that demand, energy companies built or planned to build hundreds of plants in the 1960s and '70s. In that original wave of construction, companies sited plants in suburban places; for example, the Dresden power plant was built outside Chicago, and the Oyster Creek reactor in Lacey, New Jersey. In other cases, plants originally sited in "remote" locations ended up being adjacent to suburban towns because of the sprawling expansion of housing developments that took place during the same period of nuclear power plant construction.[29] Whether built originally in suburban areas or encroached upon by sprawl, nuclear power plants were becoming part of the politics of suburban land use—a politics that significantly shifted in the spring of 1979.

Two intertwined events of spring 1979 created an overwhelming public sense of nuclear power as risky and dangerous: the release of the film *The China Syndrome* on March 16 and the accident at the Three Mile Island nuclear power plant in central Pennsylvania on March 28. Accidents had taken place at domestic nuclear power plants before 1979, chief among them a partial core meltdown at the Enrico Fermi plant in 1966 and Karen Silkwood's contamination from exposure to plutonium in 1974. The *New York Times* reported the Fermi accident could "set back the breeder program by more than 20 years."[30] Yet, in an era of nuclear power expansion and governmental and popular support for the industry, the public was unwilling or unable to think about nuclear power in catastrophic terms. The nuclear-friendly cultural climate soon shifted to widespread antinuclear power sentiment after the combination of the popular culture portrayal in *The China Syndrome* and the wall-to-wall news coverage of the accident at TMI.[31] As a result, the American cultural imagination could no longer hold a place for a "minor" accident at a nuclear power plant. However, it was not just that nuclear power shifted from being understood as an energy panacea in a time of need to a disaster waiting to happen. The events of spring 1979 showed nuclear power plants to be always already disastrous and primarily located in suburban communities, spurring action in places that at one time welcomed new plants and thereby ushering in the age of the Nimby. As a May 20, 1979, *New York Times* headline declared, "The Nuclear Issue Becomes Suburban."[32]

Disaster Movie Come True

The China Syndrome, a thriller about an accident at a California nuclear power plant, was released on March 16, 1979, twelve days before the accident at Three Mile Island. In depicting power plant owners and regulators as exaggeratedly corrupt, it created the notion of "nuclear plant as bogeyman in a doomsday thriller."[33] Profits, not safety, were of paramount importance for the nuclear power industry and media corporations as portrayed in the film. The plant owners falsify safety documents to build the Ventana plant, where the accident occurs, and to secure government approval for another, called Point Conception. The film strongly argues that the federal regulatory process was fatally flawed as corporate cost-cutting measures and safety lapses were missed or ignored. In addition to its depiction of a corrupt nuclear power industry, the film also introduced the concept of the "China syndrome" into the vernacular as shorthand for nuclear disaster. As explained by a nuclear physicist in the film, the "China syndrome" occurs when a nuclear reactor overheats and melts through its housing into the ground below, theoretically boring all the way to China.

While the accident may have made the filmmakers seem "right" about nuclear power, the movie more importantly provided a frame for understanding the accident in Pennsylvania as something other than routine, minor, or aberrant for a 1970s public already skeptical of institutions like the government or corporations to work in their interest. *The China Syndrome*'s vision of nuclear power centered on a severe crisis of credibility throughout the industry from builders and managers to owners and regulators. This crisis in public trust was symbolized and consolidated by a familiar moniker denoting a succinct narrative of nuclear meltdown that helped make sense of the events at TMI as the result of mismanagement, poor regulation, and greed.[34] As the accident happened, news media, for example, framed it as a "disaster movie come true" and nearly a real life version of *The China Syndrome*.[35] The film proved so powerful a way for understanding nuclear power that a Metropolitan-Edison spokesperson invoked the film on the first day of the accident, saying, "We are not in a China Syndrome type situation," even as *Time* described the incident as an "inescapable parody of *The China Syndrome*."[36] Despite this assurance, *Newsweek* noted, "The greatest risk of all was a catastrophic 'meltdown' of the sort fictionalized in a popular new film called 'The China Syndrome.'"[37] This cinematic vision of nuclear power was, another *Newsweek* article asserted, "a piece of popular entertainment that immediately foreshadows a major news event and then helps explain it [the accident at TMI]."[38] In this new formulation introduced by the film, made material by the accident at TMI, and further disseminated by news coverage of the Pennsylvania plant disaster and the film itself, the looming cooling tower came to embody danger for the suburban residents who lived in its shadow. In turn, that visible, material threat enabled protests against nuclear power and a wider "Not in my backyard!" resistance to other "dangerous" public projects throughout the 1980s.

The film begins by establishing the suburban locale of nuclear power as the camera soars over rolling hills connected by power lines to reveal Ventana Nuclear Power Plant. A television crew led by reporter Kimberly Wells (Jane Fonda) arrives there to do a story explaining the "magical process" by which matter is turned into energy, and how nuclear generation will make America less reliant on foreign oil, a benefit affirming the economic valence of nuclear power for most of her audience. Yet the film still centrally suggests that the public's opinion of nuclear power should shift from safe and cost-effective to catastrophically dangerous.

As the crew tours the plant, they look down on the control room as an alarm sounds. Cameraman Richard Adams (Michael Douglas) surreptitiously records the intense action taking place in the plant's nerve center. Amid the confusing array of gauges, buttons, valves, and indicator lights, plant manager Jack Godell (Jack Lemmon) and crew attempt to diagnose the problem. A second and third alarm sound and are shut off as Godell and his assistants make increasingly panicked attempts to slow the steady rise of pressure in the reactor. "We're almost at steam level!" someone hisses, suggesting something disastrous is imminent. The operators press buttons and flip switches chaotically, but nothing seems to be working, underlining the notion of a nuclear power plant as unmanageably complex. Godell takes another look at the gauge that shows high pressure in the reactor. He taps it lightly, and it begins to descend. Panic ensues as the men realize that they have been dumping water out of the reactor and are about to uncover the core, to deadly effect. Once Godell has identified the problem, he directs the men with the proper fix, and after two minutes of silence, the indicators return to normal. Despite the scare, Godell asserts that the system worked—a sentiment echoed by a Metropolitan-Edison spokesperson in reassuring the public of Three Mile Island's fail-safes. Despite these assurances, and informed by the broader cynicism about politicians and corporations, both the public in Pennsylvania and the reporters in the film received this idea skeptically.[39]

In depicting the nuclear power industry as corrupt or incompetent at nearly every level and even some technical failures such as broken gauges as unavoidable, *The China Syndrome* forcefully contended that disasters at nuclear power plants were not questions of *if* but *when*. The crew, though not legally allowed to film the control room, has captured the frantic scene, and Kimberly Wells returns to the station with "the top story." Network executives, fearful of their liability for broadcasting contraband video, shelve the piece. When Wells and her crew pursue the story anyway, they find failure at every level of the industry. The safety contractor forged documents, allowing the construction of faulty reactors. Shortcuts taken by plant executives prevented full investigations into the possibly flawed plant because they would cost too much in both money and reputation. Plant manager Godell also learns that federal regulators suppressed public airing of these failings and the likely deleterious effects of the cover-up. As a whole, the film presents nuclear power as dangerous because of mismanagement, corporate and federal undermining of safety guidelines, and a deliberate lack of transparency about the risks of nuclear power.

This portrayal of a wide-ranging conspiracy fell into line with other film narratives that appeared in the 1970s about the misuse of corporate and government power.[40] Emblematic of a decade of cynicism about institutions, and part of a 1970s genre defined by portrayals of collusion, secrecy, and paranoia, *The China Syndrome* emphasized that neither the power industry nor television news were immune from treachery and complicity that endangered the public. In doing so, the film presented the previously marginalized fears of nuclear disaster voiced by environmentalists, liberal activists, and Luddites as mainstream and part of a broader skepticism of American institutions. As a *Time* magazine writer theorized, *The China Syndrome*'s "basic premise will no longer seem so farfetched to those moviegoers until now unattuned to the nation's debate over nuclear power."[41] With its audiences already prepared for institutional failure, the film raised the new suburban fear of meltdown while creating an accessible and simple way to talk and think about nuclear disaster that became crucial as, two weeks later, the public struggled to understand a real nuclear disaster unfolding in the suburbs of Harrisburg, Pennsylvania.

Credibility Meltdown

Narratives of the accident at Three Mile Island reinforced those of failure and neglect in *The China Syndrome* and provided the essential understanding of how and why public projects should be seen as risky, particularly when slated for construction in your backyard. From the federal government's investigation, to newspaper and television news reports, to oral history interviews conducted in the aftermath of the accident, these varied accounts of the accident confirmed the crisis of credibility for the nuclear power industry that had already affected so many other institutions in 1970s America and that would buttress the emerging Nimby movement and its attendant politics of privatism and localism.[42]

In the early morning of March 28, 1979, twelve days after the release of *The China Syndrome*, an alarm sounded in the control room for reactor two of the Three Mile Island nuclear power plant in Middletown, Pennsylvania, approximately ten miles outside Harrisburg, the state capital. Setting off a scene staggeringly reminiscent of the chaos of the control room in *The China Syndrome*, the alarm signaled that cooling water had stopped running to the reactor core and pressure inside the reactor was building.[43] Engineers opened an emergency valve to decrease the pressure but, once sufficient reduction was achieved, were unable to shut it. The open valve allowed cooling water to be released and the core to continue to overheat. None of the indicators in the control room told the managers on duty that the valve remained open, so no one knew about the dangerous loss of coolant. Thinking the core was being properly cooled, plant operators slowed the flow of water. By intervening, they eventually exposed the core and partially melted it, thereby escalating a fixable problem into a potentially calamitous reactor meltdown.[44]

In the days following the accident, state and federal officials worked with Metropolitan Edison (Met Ed), the owner and operator of the Three Mile Island plant, to stabilize the reactor and limit the release of radioactive gas. This was no easy task as experts differed as to the correct methods for avoiding a larger disaster. This confusion among the scientists on the nature of the problems (including the size of a possibly flammable hydrogen bubble in the reactor) caused disagreement among government officials responsible for disseminating accurate information and instructions to inhabitants of surrounding areas. What should they say? Pennsylvania governor Richard Thornburgh had to balance the risk of meltdown and radiation exposure with the risk of pandemonium if a full evacuation was ordered unnecessarily; he chose to recommend the evacuation of pregnant women and children under five, prompting many others to become fearful and leave as well. On Sunday, April 1, three days after the initial accident, it was determined that the hydrogen bubble inside the damaged reactor could not burn or explode. With the help of Nuclear Regulatory Commission physicists, Met Ed and the Pennsylvania government managed to avoid a total meltdown of the core and catastrophic damage to surrounding areas and populations. However, the failures and missteps on the parts of Met Ed and the state and federal government in regulating nuclear power and handling the emergency had far-reaching effects. Their actions weakened the nuclear power industry for years to come, called into question the siting and regulation of similar projects, and enabled Nimby protests.

The confusion about what was happening and could happen was manifest in the daily media coverage of the accident at TMI. Local and national news organizations published contradictory reports that reflected the failure of scientists, public relations personnel employed by the power company, and the government to agree on an accurate assessment of the situation and a strategy for properly informing the public.[45] Declaring a "credibility meltdown," headlines reduced the narrative of the accident to one simple idea repeated daily in the news coverage: confusion.[46] An Associated Press report in Harrisburg's *Patriot News* published the day after the accident, chronicled the various bits of conflicting information about a radiation release, the topic of greatest concern to the public. "The answers about radiation after Wednesday's accident . . . were slow to come and confusing. They were still confusing on Thursday."[47] After recounting the multiple bungled television news conferences on the first day of the accident, the story gave an hour-by-hour account wherein the characterization of the accident by various officials moved from minor to significant to severe to minor once again.[48] This article and other news coverage conveyed the profound sense of bewilderment that fueled an escalating sense of terror. The public living near the plant were left in limbo with no definite sense of what danger the odorless, colorless threat posed or what to do if a meltdown occurred. This uncertainty included the mayors of Goldsboro and Middletown, towns surrounding the plant site, who were not immediately notified about the accident or were given specific instructions about what to do.[49] For the American public, the fact that the accident had occurred and no one seemed to know what to do when faced with it became the accident's lasting legacy as government officials, academics, and journalists gathered and disseminated more information about what had gone wrong.

The President's Commission on the Accident at Three Mile Island, a blue-ribbon panel chaired by Dartmouth College president John Kemeny, issued a comprehensive analysis exposing the failures at TMI in particular and of the nuclear power industry in general. The panel's report also reinforced what had been apparent in the media coverage of the accident—the plants did actually endanger local communities across the country. The report found there were human failures at every stage—construction, management, oversight, and emergency administration. "As the evidence accumulated," the president's commission asserted, "it became clear that the fundamental problems are people-related problems and not equipment problems."[50] Emphasizing this point, the committee continued: "We mean more generally that our investigation has revealed problems with the 'system' that manufactures, operates, and regulates nuclear power plants."[51] In an era when Americans already viewed the federal government and corporations with growing suspicion, the report did nothing to dissuade them that both entities had failed again to protect average people.[52] A Middletown resident signaled the shifting cultural ground when asked about the accident by ABC News correspondent John Martin. As he picked up his child early from school because of the accident, he said in a defeated tone, "It's worse than what they're telling us. Typical lies. They oughta close all those nuclear power plants down."[53] His resigned, cynical attitude toward

Figure 1.1. Three Mile Island nuclear reactors during the first day of the accident, March 30, 1979. This photograph captures the new sense of terror that was caused by the image of the cooling tower. AP Photo / Barry Thumma

the power company in that moment reflected and reproduced an increasingly common view of government in the era of American "malaise." In that cultural climate and spurred by the TMI accident, homeowners could justifiably be scared of nuclear power plants, built by corrupt corporations and regulated by an ineffective government.

The President's Commission also reinforced the widespread dissatisfaction with the straight story presented in the mainstream press.[54] Rather than a deliberate "cover-up" a la Watergate, the commission found that representatives of the plant and the government had disseminated incorrect information believing that it was correct, but had done so in a manner that was not reassuring to the public. Press briefers were often not sufficiently knowledgeable, but, more crucially, both Met Ed and the Nuclear Regulatory Commission experts also gave out significant misinformation to the government and the public.[55] This led to the commission's damning assessment of the communications at TMI: "We therefore conclude that, while the extent of the coverage was justified, a combination of confusion and weakness in the sources of information and lack of understanding on the part of the media resulted in the public being poorly served."[56] In the wake of Watergate the lack of a cover-up was reassuring, but incompetence in its place had much the same effect, as the credibility meltdown further undermined trust in those institutions tasked with protecting the public. As a resident yelled at a Met Ed spokesman during a press briefing at the plant, it came down to one simple question for homeowners, "What are you going to be doing to protect my family?" As the 1970s came to a close, it appeared to suburbanites that the answer was "nothing," so they must do something for themselves.[57]

Interviews conducted by Dickinson College students in the aftermath of the accident confirmed the crisis of institutional credibility locally and nationally, a crisis that facilitated and fueled Nimbyism. One college employee who worked in the area of Three Mile Island at the time of the accident was asked whether it had caused her to doubt the government's policies. She responded, "It didn't help. It really didn't help. But it's something I've been thinking for quite a while."[58] Editorial letter writers echoed this sentiment as well. Gilbert D. Thompson wrote one of a series of letters by disgruntled citizens published in the *Washington Post* in the aftermath of TMI. "There is one clear lesson to be learned from the nuclear power plant disaster," he declared: "that we can't trust the nuclear power industry or their apologists at the Nuclear Regulatory Commission."[59] These skeptics clearly saw the failures at TMI as part of a broader pattern of wrongdoing and incompetence that fueled a larger attack on government, which in turn facilitated and was facilitated by homeowners' claims of danger posed by these projects.

These sentiments reflected the complementary but seemingly incongruous politics of suburban Nimbys: they needed the government and corporations to ensure their safety but did not trust them to carry out that responsibility on their own. Writing for the *Nation* a year after the accident, McKinley C. Olson observed that residents near Three Mile Island continued to distrust their government and the owners of the plant despite an inclination before the incident to believe in them.[60] He wrote that the citizens of Middletown "have an inordinate respect for authority. Most of them were willing to put their blind trust in nuclear power simply because the government and the business told them that nuclear power was safe, cheap, efficient, and reliable. Today they know better. That faith has been shattered. They have been frightened."[61] In articles published in the *Washington Post* between April 8 and 11, 1979, multiple authors rehearsed and extended both the sense of shattered faith in nuclear power plants and the shifting mood of the nation at large. The authors summed up the state of affairs after the accident: "For the time being, however—and perhaps for a long time to come—the very concept of 'normal life' would be a relative term for people un-lucky enough to live near the nation's first serious nuclear mishap."[62] As these and other articles demonstrated, in the wake of TMI, the public lost confidence in the ability of industry and government to manage something that was sud-denly understood as dangerous. They symbolized the shifting notions of nor-malcy for suburbanites who still expected cheap power and a safe natural envi-ronment but who now lived with a sense of impending terror and an unexpected crisis of lost privilege.

Given that distrust, catastrophe seemed more likely to accompany or even be endemic to nuclear power than it had as late as 1977. According to a *New York Times* poll from July of that year, 69 percent of Americans approved of building more nuclear power plants, and 55 percent approved of having a plant con-structed in their community—the highest recorded support for nuclear power in American history.[63] After the events of spring 1979, however, public views shifted: "Now, the nation knows all too well about the China syndrome, reactor meltdowns and life's chilling ability to imitate art even in the nuclear age," and nuclear power companies were "facing their biggest credibility crisis in their 30 year history."[64] Citizens across the country asked: How can we feel safe about living near a nuclear power plant if we don't trust the people who regulate and run it? In the wake of the accident at TMI, governor of California Jerry Brown put it another way, "Fear is going to change the fabric of our political process."[65] And, it did.

In the events of spring 1979, reality and fiction collided to alter Americans' understanding of nuclear power from safe to inherently dangerous—"a nuclear nightmare."[66] That fear caused thousands of people to join No Nukes protests in 1979 and led suburbanites who had stayed on the sidelines before to join or sup-port activists, gadflies, and true believers whom they had previously ignored.[67] Yet, by defending against the possibility of environmental disaster and the loss of privilege, Nimbys focused on shaping their local landscapes and did not take up the broader antinuclear cause, making clear how, for whom, and to what ends localism and privatism worked in Reagan's America.

Nimbys and Nuclear Power on Long Island

Pursuing a plan announced in 1965, the Long Island Lighting Company (LILCO) began construction on the Shoreham plant on the North Shore of Long Island in 1973. While other nuclear power plants were proposed around the country and built without incident, Shoreham suffered numerous delays and setbacks in the years between its announcement and the events of 1979. Despite the sense of nuclear power as safe, the federal government over that period increasingly toughened the regulatory process in response to lobbying by environmental activists. With a lengthier and more invasive licensing procedure designed to ensure protection of people and the environment, the process began stretching over years rather months.[68] Those delays directly affected the bottom lines of power companies as costs increased and the opportunity to recoup those costs was postponed even longer, while the information gathered for approval provided ammunition for critics of nuclear power.

Along with this more stringent process, a small, committed, and tenacious coalition of local groups opposed to nuclear power, known as the Sound and Hudson against Atom Development (SHAD) Alliance, along with gadfly attorney Irving Like, fought against the Shoreham plant, among several targets of their protest actions.[69] Armed with mounds of data on the environmental dangers of nuclear power plants gleaned from mandatory environmental impact statements, the SHAD Alliance slowed Shoreham's licensing through expert testimony and detailed questioning at public hearings.[70] At the same time, it used direct action protests such as picketing, rallies, and even blocking access to the construction site.[71] Nuclear power advocates countered by sowing division, attempting to turn LILCO clients against these nuclear power critics by pointing out that the price of electricity was rising due to the delays caused by activists. The power company essentially said that antinuclear activists did not represent suburban Long Island values, which in that moment was true.[72] Most Long Island suburbanites stayed on the sidelines of the Shoreham debate, hoping that a new reactor would lower their bills as the economy sputtered.[73]

In this and other ways, the pre-1979 protesters and activists were different from the suburbanites who became Nimbys. These objectors were true believers in the antinuclear cause and other liberal social justice movements, as evidenced by their publicity materials and meeting minutes. They repeated a commitment to stopping nuclear power because it was a threat to all humanity, not simply a local issue for them as Long Islanders. In a 1978 introductory leaflet, "What is SHAD?" the group wrote, "Members of the SHAD Alliance recognize the threat to the Earth and all its inhabitants that is posed by nuclear power," making clear that since reactors were dangerous, the group must focus on stopping nuclear power everywhere.[74] SHAD's antinuclear agenda, unlike suburban Nimbys, was part of an explicit and broad ideological commitment and plan for political action. SHAD supported the "Manhattan Project," for example, and planned a

"Take It to Wall Street" campaign in fall 1979 to protest banks that were underwriting nuclear power and other unacceptable practices, such as redlining in real estate and apartheid in South Africa.[75] SHAD also sought to persuade workers at the Shoreham plant to make exposure to radioactive materials a labor issue.[76] In short, the alliance's scope went beyond Long Island and the Shoreham plant. SHAD activists traveled to Washington, DC, and Seabrook, New Hampshire, to protest nuclear power and drew a number of causes together to critique global capitalism. All of these efforts demonstrated an ideologically driven, multifront attack that included fighting the spread of nuclear power and eradicating it for the sake of environmental protection as a goal in and of itself.

This activism and ideological commitment stood in stark contrast to Nimbys' focus on nuclear power as a local threat endangering suburban health and privilege. These new antinuclear dissenters were not "hardy critics" who fought nuclear power or protected the environment on principle.[77] Following the accident at Three Mile Island and the release of *The China Syndrome*, the prospect of living in the shadows of these towers of terror motivated previously uninterested Long Island residents to declare, in one way or another, "Not in my backyard!" Attendance at direct action protests, usually consisting of hardcore activists, grew wildly from forty people on August 20, 1978, to fifteen thousand on June 3, 1979, after the accident at TMI.[78] Nimby opposition made bigger and more powerful a movement against Shoreham that had subsisted as a small, ideologically motivated crusade.[79] As Nimbys came to see cooling towers as reminders of dread, particularly the "mysterious and unseen radiation that will maim generations to come, or may somehow explode," those on Long Island became invested in opposing not nuclear power but the Shoreham plant.[80]

Writing in the Long Island section of the *New York Times* editorial page in January 1982, Island resident Francis Brady vented frustration with the ongoing conflict over the Shoreham nuclear power plant, which was supposed to serve the suburban communities of Suffolk County. "If my speculations are not responsible or funny," Brady wrote, "neither is the construction of a nuclear power plant on the shore of a dead-end island inhabited by some three million people. Partisans in the nuclear debate, take note: I (and perhaps others) don't care who is right. Just argue about it somewhere else, will you please?"[81] Brady's statement showed not only dismay over the shortsighted construction of a plant on a narrow island with limited escape routes, but also a fundamental suburban impulse in the age of the Nimby. Opposition to the plant was expression of local fear and not ideological opposition to nuclear power.

Lewis J. Yevoli, Democratic state assemblyman from Long Island, highlighted local concerns about the planning and construction of Shoreham, if not necessarily other plants: "I don't think closing Shoreham can be a blanket indictment of all nuclear-power plants throughout the country, but it will serve as an example that, when you plan these things, you'd better make sure you've covered all your bases in terms of evacuation, community sentiment and such."[82] Another critic, Kathleen Boylan, a Mineola, New York, resident and wife of a LILCO executive, voiced concerns even though the company building the plant employed her husband. She declared she would boycott LILCO and demand a halt in the Shoreham plant's construction no matter what it cost her family economically. So invested in their homes and families, residents like Boylan showed a willingness to sacrifice economically (a sacrifice they could more easily make) in order to reshape local land use and protect their neighborhoods. After 1979, suburbanites like Brady, Yevoli, and Boylan did not care about the merits of nuclear power as a technology, its associated cost, or the public need for a cheaper domestic power source. They cared only that a nuclear reactor was being constructed in their community that could at best force them to move and, at worst, maim or kill their families.

The events of March and April 1979 echoed through the news media and Long Island residents' discussions of Shoreham, demonstrating their impact on suburbanites' understanding of nuclear power. Under the headline "Nuclear Power at Shoreham: Who Makes the Decisions?" the *New York Times* juxtaposed a photo of the newly constructed control room at the Shoreham plant with a corresponding image from *The China Syndrome* showing Jack Lemmon's character in the Ventana control room.[83] Published just a week after the accident at TMI, the article and accompanying image framed the nuclear power debate in terms of the film's narrative. By drawing a clear parallel between the new plant and the faulty one in the film, the article figured Shoreham as essentially dysfunctional, the product of a flawed process. The accident at TMI also continued to loom large. Three years after TMI, Suzanne Greco of Wading River, Long Island, still used it to frame her opposition to Shoreham: "We cannot afford an accident similar to Three Mile Island on Long Island. . . . I warn my children about talking to strangers and cavities and that plant."[84] In expressing her fears of the Shoreham plant, Greco fused the fear of nuclear power with the overriding culture of dread and anxiety permeating suburban life in the neighborhood of fear.

Other local residents shared these same fears on the op-ed pages of the *Times*. On May 20, 1979, Edward Werth of Freeport, Long Island, wrote, "I cannot believe the continuing naiveté of the public and elected officials when it comes to the ability of companies like Lilco and a bureaucratic sham like the Nuclear Regulatory Commission (which does more promoting than regulating of nuclear power) to pull the wool over our eyes about the dangers connected with nuclear power."[85] Werth wove together the various strands of thought that motivated Nimbys to write letters, attend meetings, and support political candidates, activities centered on their one issue—stopping nuclear power in their backyard. He decried the ignorance of others as to the clear danger made evident just a few weeks earlier in Pennsylvania and on movie screens. Further, he articulated a continuing critique of government and corporations as conspiring to exploit the average citizen for their own benefit. At the end of his letter, Werth brought the reader to the seemingly logical conclusion for an American suburbanite in that moment: the only way to avoid a full-scale nuclear accident on Long Island, he argued, was not to have a plant there at all.

Demonstrating their local focus and political pragmatism rather than ideological or party fealty, Long Islanders supported political candidates across party lines as long as they opposed Shoreham. In 1982, Suffolk county executive Peter Cohalan, hoping to court potential voters, articulated what he thought to be the conventional wisdom about a plant that would lower electricity rates: "I don't think the county is in any way qualified to say whether that plant is safe or not. . . . I think it's an issue that has been completely swung out of proportion."[86] A year later, however, the contest between economic and environmental values was no contest at all. Long Island's suburban voters made closing the plant at Shoreham *the* electoral issue of the 1980s. After declaring his hope that the new plant would lower rates, Cohalan based his 1983 reelection bid on his opposition to opening Shoreham, an explicit acknowledgement of his constituency's laser-like focus on stopping the plant.[87]

To demonstrate his change of heart to voters during the campaign, Cohalan debated LILCO chairman Charles R. Pierce about Shoreham's future.[88] LILCO and Pierce had tried to rally utility customers around economic concerns by arguing that out-of-touch gadflies were costing consumers money with every delay.[89] Cohalan retorted: "We feel that those who tell us that we should put the plant on line because of the economics are asking the government officials of Suffolk County to spin the wheel of fortune and take a gamble on the plant never having an accident, purely because of the economic necessity involved."[90] That exchange encapsulated the shifting perception of nuclear power on the part of suburban residents as Nimbys and not antinuclear crusaders.[91] Local residents considered their natural environment, especially Long Island Sound, despite years of postwar development, as part of the privilege of living there. The price of energy could never be low enough to assuage the fear of nuclear meltdown and destruction of what made suburban life on Long Island worth living. Cohalan summed up his position, "The question we're addressing here from the standpoint of Suffolk County is public safety and public safety only."[92] In reversing his earlier position, Cohalan appealed directly to the Nimbys, causing an uproar in the news media and at campaign stops about their one abiding concern—stopping Shoreham.

As a position based on local issues and fear of losing personal property, Nimbyism demanded to be reckoned with by elected representatives not so much as protesters or activists than as "concerned citizens" whose demands were reasonable and whose power was at the voting booth. Both Peter Cohalan and Governor Mario Cuomo became anti-Shoreham to appease this large block of suburban voters. Those politicians who did not fall in line with this position on Shoreham saw their power base evaporate. US representative John Wydler's defense of nuclear power and Shoreham in the pages of the *New York Times* brought rebukes from his constituents. They wrote in direct response to him that nuclear power is not cheap or safe and his understanding of the issues demonstrated "an appalling ignorance of the energy and environmental issues we face."[93] Since he was retiring that year, Wydler could take an unpopular stand and not have to face the wrath of the voters.[94] Louis T. Howard, on the other hand, lost his post as presiding officer of the state legislature because of his pro-Shoreham stance.[95] US representative William Carney chose not to run for a fifth term under heavy pressure from his party because he continued to support opening Shoreham.[96] As anti-Shoreham candidates from both parties won in every contest of the 1980s, they demonstrated both the dominance of nuclear power politics and the Shoreham plant issue in Long Island elections, and the visibility and power of Nimbys.[97]

Despite a last-minute bid by the George H. W. Bush administration to save the plant, LILCO sold the Shoreham plant to the state of New York for one dollar in 1989. The state, then, made it the first nuclear power plant to be fully decommissioned and the first to be shut down without ever running at full power.[98] Shoreham's closure marked a triumph for local environmental activists who had effectively intervened throughout the 1970s to delay the building and opening of the plant. More important, Nimbys on Long Island demonstrated the power of potential environmental victimization. By articulating a pervasive public dissatisfaction with the prospect of a nuclear power plant, Nimbys and environmentalists were strange but victorious allies.[99] While other nuclear power plants did go on-line during the 1980s, Nimbys transformed a small, niche movement into an effective mainstream effort and, in so doing, changed both the literal and political landscapes of suburban Long Island before returning safely home.[100]

Nimbys and the Politics of Backyard Protection

Although the impulse, if not the term, for segregating dangerous or undesirable projects away from one's property has been present throughout modern American history, the "Not in my backyard!" expression and its accompanying political concerns were specific to the suburban homeowner starting in the 1970s. The established privileges of postwar suburban living and their particular cultural and political values facilitated this version of local, politically pragmatic protest and demonstration of spatial power.[101] No fan of Nimbyism, Perry L. Norton, professor emeritus of urban planning, explained in 1987 how the parochial focus and lack of ideological coherence of late-twentieth-century Nimbys facilitated their power: "It does not no good to label one another Commie liberal or ignorant bigot. The needs we have portrayed are metropolitan in scope."[102] In an increasingly polarized political world, posing a Nimby protest as a pragmatic and reasonable response to real threats, rather than as an explicit articulation of an established ideology, demonstrated its power to persuade both other homeowners and the politicians seeking to represent them. This "common sense" stance was enabled by environmentalists who argued that ecological threats were both legitimate and ubiquitous, and by the New Right, which emphasized local, private solutions as most effective. In that cultural and political climate, homeowners claimed legitimate danger and the need for local action against it without embracing either movement beyond its efficacy for maintaining suburban privilege.

When faced with a threat such as the siting of a nuclear power plant at Shoreham, Long Island, suburbanites exploited the environmental hazards that would likely result from a nuclear meltdown in order to serve their own local interests whether or not it supported the broader environmentalist agenda.[103] Their "metropolitan scope," as Norton characterized it, ushered Nimbys into the public sphere as reasonable homeowners, not activists. Rather than "fiery-eyed environmentalists," Nimbys "force close scrutiny of what is proposed, and as the residents of Love Canal, Bhopal and Three Mile Island know all too well, the experts are not always right or the sponsors sufficiently responsible."[104] The dangers posed by nuclear power plants undermined the essential understanding of the suburban environment as clean and healthy and forced a new urgency for residents to "hang on to what they have" by making good on the Reagan era's clarion call for local control.

Concurrent with the rise of a sustained environmental movement, a "gathering storm" of conservative political thought and grassroots organizing emerged and went mainstream in postwar America, becoming known as the New Right.[105] The New Right's antigovernment, antitax, and pro–property rights agenda valorized the sanctity of the suburban home by emphasizing privileged localism and privatism that movement leaders touted as the rightful benefits of home ownership.[106] Conditioned by this politics to see themselves and their local environment as a sacrosanct material benefit of home ownership, suburbanites, when confronted with a nuclear reactor in their town, saw it as not a just a threat to their wellbeing but an attack on their privilege.[107] And yet, because of this privilege, suburbanites were not simply the victims of failing bureaucracies or greedy corporations that ignored the rights of homeowners.[108] They had the power to protect themselves and their surroundings even if that power was based partly on their perceived victimization. The focus on local life and institutions emerged as the preferred route to the self-determination and expression of property rights rather than reliance on extralocal governmental forces, which seemed so often to fail. For suburban homeowners, this view of individual liberty and property rights made Nimbyism possible and powerful. It allowed them to ignore the broader benefits of public projects and pursue their hyperlocal interests with the express goal of protecting *their* home and family as a civic duty, for "if we each defend our backyards, we will cumulatively protect our communities, Westchester County, the state, and even the nation."[109]

Although Nimbys fashioned themselves as nonideological actors invested solely in the protection of their backyards against greedy corporations and incompetent regulators, they still needed local and state government as foil and facilitator in order to shape their local landscapes. The "mounting community resistance" that gained significant steam in the aftermath of the events of spring 1979 relied on the perception of the state as incompetent while simultaneously counting on its responsiveness to keep dangerous projects out of suburban backyards. It was not simply that local or state government should listen to its constituency but that the municipalities regulate the landscape according to the prerogatives of this vocal constituency. Working with and for suburbanites to address environmental threats endangered other communities and further institutionalized suburban interests as part and parcel of municipal authority.

In casting the state as a foil, Nimbys figured it as part of the incompetent regulation of inherently dangerous nuclear technology that justified their fears and protests. In reference to the licensing process for the Shoreham plant, the chair of the Wading River Board of Fire Commissioners lamented how little the government had done to protect citizens: "Now, in effect, we are looking after ourselves."[110] Nimbys could easily point to the failures of the NRC and government in general to protect them at Three Mile Island and in licensing a plant in their own backyard. Ultimately, as panelists at a 1989 University of Massachusetts seminar on siting controversial facilities noted, "the problem is distrust in the people or institutions who dispense decisions without local input."[111] The legacy of regulatory failures and deceit by the federal government in the 1970s combined with the antigovernment sentiment of the ascendant New Right politics to portray the government as unable or unwilling to help unless forced to do so.

If the cry of "Not in my backyard!" was to do more than express fear or displeasure, however, Nimbys needed decision makers who wielded instrumental parochial power to bring their desires to fruition. In 1988, the *New York Times'* William Glaberson described the Nimby relationship to institutional power: "They twist the arms of politicians and they learn how to influence regulators. They fight fiercely and then, win or lose, they vanish."[112] The invisible aspect of privilege apparent in Glaberson's formulation was access to local governments and the assumed relevance of suburban issues. Suburban residents did not need to fight for visibility or acceptance but rather to simply highlight their concerns and the twisted logic of privatism as civic duty.

As an outcome of decades of suburbanization, the political consolidation and insulation of suburban privilege in the postwar era made suburbanites essential as constituents and consumers, an importance that yielded them great influence. By the 1980s, Nimby's made good on that influence by casting their desires as commonsense responses to new, existential threats rather than making a systemic critique of entrenched political power. Exploiting their centrality to the consumer's republic and avoiding explicit ideological attachment, they were successful, as seen on Long Island. By crying "Not in my backyard!" loudly and persistently, suburban Long Islanders forced LILCO to close Shoreham without producing a single watt of energy. They then "vanished," returning to the presumed safety of their homes and neighborhoods, only to reemerge in response to other threatening projects planned for their neighborhoods.

Nimbys Are Everywhere

As real disasters established environmental threats and popular culture and the news media reproduced them, Nimbys all over the United States laid what seemed to be a rightful (political) claim to feeling endangered by a public project such as a landfill, jail, or power plant. In 1988, the *New York Times* put it more succinctly, "Nimbys are noisy. Nimbys are powerful. Nimbys are everywhere."[113] Given the seemingly unassailable logic of home defense in the face of real and immediate threats, Nimbys rejected other projects broadly understood as socially necessary but environmentally undesirable, at least in their backyards. Byrl N. Boyce, the director of the Real Estate Center at the University of Connecticut, characterized this perspective: "People think things like prisons are a good thing, but the attitude is 'Don't put it next to me.'"[114] Nimbys rarely expressed an ongoing extralocal ideological opposition to a garbage dump, jail, or an AIDS clinic.[115] Part of their politics of persuasion was embracing the *need* for that project, just located somewhere else. In essence, they had limited, local objectives that centered on preserving the most appealing aspects of suburban life and tried to avoid any visible ideological stakes while nonetheless promoting privatism and homeowner rights. As one editorial described Nimbys' approach, "They yell, they scream, they oppose, and then they go back to whatever they were doing before."[116] These were intensely parochial movements expressing the essential privilege of suburban living: to pick and choose one's opportunities for involvement in civic life and articulate that choice through the prism of private interest.[117]

In the Nimby age of selective citizenship, nuclear power reappeared in the debates over land use because of the controversies surrounding the siting of the power plants' waste repositories.[118] Nimbys frustrated the Nuclear Regulatory Commission in the 1980s by advocating for safe disposal of nuclear waste—in someone else's backyard. "All of these people have essentially the same message, 'Not in my back yard,'" said an exasperated NRC official.[119] In 1987, the vice president of the Edison Electrical Institute said, "There are no foreseeable technical roadblocks" to siting waste repositories, but there was another, nontechnical problem—Nimbys.[120]

This nontechnical problem sprang up all over the United States in the 1980s and 1990s. Nimby protests, from Massachusetts and New Jersey to Florida and California, expanded the notion of what constituted an environmental threat to suburban privilege. From the clear implications of a nuclear meltdown, such protests moved to highlighting the social and cultural dangers of numerous kinds of public projects. In Gloucester and Quincy, Massachusetts, suburban residents blocked the siting of a home for the mentally ill in their neighborhoods because "this is simply not the proper place for such a home. We are in the vicinity of three schools here."[121] In this case, the remote chance of a resident of the home simply encountering a child was unacceptable because it undermined the notion of suburban living as safe and "normal." Similarly, in 1987, a trash barge left New York City but could not come into port because suburbanite protesters throughout the mid-Atlantic region prevented the waste from being deposited in their communities. No town wanted to be known for its garbage dump, let alone be subject to its rancorous odor. Residents Against Dumping of Noxious Soils in New Jersey (RADON) and Residents Against Garbage Expansion (RAGE) on Staten Island, among other groups, led New Jersey governor Tom Kean to describe in frustration "an irrational attitude that cares not for the health of the planet as a whole, but only for the part of the planet that is located in our backyards."[122] Buying not just a home but a way of life meant that suburban homeowners could and should stop dangerous projects near their small patches of the planet despite the desires of corporations or government or the needs of the public at large. Nimby critic Henry D. Royal, associate director of the Division of Nuclear Medicine at Washington University Medical Center in St. Louis, summarized the power and logic of Nimbyism in a 1989 op-ed: "With nuclear waste, they (politicians) are powerfully aided by the 'Not In My Back Yard' (NIMBY) mentality. No one wants prisons, homes for the needy, garbage dumps or nuclear waste facilities in their backyard."[123] Although Royal believed that Nimbyism symbolized an illogical, antiscience view, he knew it was powerful and persuasive for suburbanites as it fused cultural concerns with legitimate fears of toxic contamination into a single protest.

Still, suburban residents did not exclaim "Not in my backyard!" without a reason. As with nuclear power, they often mobilized around real doubts about contamination and environmental danger that continued to emerge. Sterling, New York, residents did so twice in five years. They first stopped the siting of a toxic-waste landfill in 1983 and then successfully opposed a dump for radioactive waste because it posed a danger to drinking water.[124] Suburban protesters in other places, like Hillsborough, Florida, and Bellevue, Washington, blocked the building of new power stations and power lines in their communities despite the need to update the infrastructure in those regions.[125] In these instances, suburban Nimbys based their apprehensions about power lines and electromagnetic fields on an emerging literature written by doctors, activists, and conspiracy theorists suggesting that living near power plants and lines could lead to illness and death.[126] Nimby protests such as these power line cases and the protests against nuclear power demonstrated that private interests often dovetailed with legitimate environmental and health concerns. Indeed, if the protests were to be taken seriously, the sense of legitimate, lethal hazard must be apparent. Yet, despite such authentic fears, local interest still trumped civic duty. The displacement of the dangers that often resulted from the local, rather than global, opposition to these technologies posed a problem for other communities. As the environmental justice movement continually pointed out, Nimbyism was an exercise of power that made clear the fault lines of privilege between suburbanites and their urban counterparts.[127]

Other Nimbys linked more broadly defined environmental dangers with economic concerns. Some communities in the southeastern United States were able to destroy or move trailer parks in a southern expression of slum clearance cum Nimbyism. The Kings Mountain, North Carolina, city council closed three trailer parks, and Pearl, Mississippi, aldermen banned additional lots for mobile homes.[128] Such expressions of local power marked a broader use of Nimby. These suburban residents and governments called trailer parks eyesores and homes to "trailer trash" who would undermine their way of life. Through Nimbyism these suburbanites sought to preserve the property values of permanent homeowners and prevent cultural change that undermined a fundamental reason to live in the suburbs. On the wealthier end of the class spectrum, residents of upper-class suburb Basking Ridge, New Jersey, opposed location of a helicopter pad for AT&T executives in their neighborhood. The main critic of the helipad articulated classic Nimbyism as a commonsense, middle-of-the-road approach. "We're not against A.T.&T., and we're not fiery-eyed environmentalists, but if there isn't some kind of control on noise and traffic patterns of helicopters, a condition with very serious environmental impact will result."[129] That result, of course, was the sounds of helicopters flying overhead, landing, and taking off, annoyances that would make both living in the neighborhood and selling a home more difficult.

As these Nimby interventions showed, suburbanites believed they were entitled to protect a wide range of interests, because their happiness and environmental safety trumped the perceived public good to be achieved by a municipal or corporate project. With Love Canal, Three Mile Island, and hundreds of other, as-yet-unknown toxic time bombs ticking around the country, suburbanites felt justified in moving to protect their communities by proclaiming "Not in my backyard!" and invoking the underlying logic of necessary home defense. They were not merely parroting environmental critiques but revising them to include any number of local grievances broadly understood as environmental. They did so, not to support environmentalism per se, but to achieve the suburban dream of political autonomy and spatial separation in the face of widespread threat. In each of those circumstances, Nimbys exercised privilege and power unavailable to many other communities. Foremost among those privileges, suburbanites expected to live in a world safe from environmental hazard. As favored consumers and constituents, they also presumed that local government and corporations would bend to their will when threats did emerge. By crying "Not in my backyard!" they leveraged those privileges to shape the landscape, protect their interests, and often imperil others.

Starting in the 1970s, real events, news narratives, and popular culture texts associated suburban America with environmental disasters while producing fears of more such cataclysms on the horizon. In the age of the Nimby, environmental dangers appeared less as aberrations on the suburban landscape than as the expected outcome of government and corporate failure to protect average citizens and as symbols of lost suburban environmental privilege. Justified by the imperative of home defense and the legitimate belief in environmental danger, Nimbys leveraged that sense of danger to persuade the government and corporate bureaucracies they criticized to ultimately do their bidding. Through that productive victimization, Nimby protest power shaped the suburban landscape and the predominant associations of the natural environment of suburban America.

This shifting notion of suburban life is clearly seen in the seemingly pragmatic responses to the siting and construction of nuclear power plants after the events of spring 1979. Suburban protestors were successful in Long Island and elsewhere because the rightward shift in American politics and culture that encouraged skepticism, particularly of government, made it possible to leverage liberal critiques, like those of environmentalism, for private advantage. In that cultural climate, the dangers of nuclear power were neither an isolated incident nor the fantasy of liberal activists. Richard Cohen, in the *Washington Post*, articulated this thinking in explaining how he went from distrusting demonstrators against nuclear power to believing they were right. Echoing the general distrust of American institutions in the 1970s, he asked, "How could energy companies build something unsafe? Why would they?" Turning to the supposed safety of nuclear power, he wrote: "It was something we wanted to believe. It was as mean and big a lie as that. It was this system and that system and even if there was a meltdown you could never have the sort of thing they talked about in 'The China Syndrome.' The stuff would never go all the way to China. Ha, ha they said. Don't be ridiculous, they said, who do we think we are, they said. Liar, I say. That's who they are."[130] In the world born of the deceptions and dangers of Vietnam, Watergate, Love Canal, and Three Mile Island, suburbanites made use of an environmentalist mindset and a conservative political perspective to protect and extend local suburban privilege, as seen at Shoreham and across the country, in the age of the Nimby.

Nimby victories over the nuclear power industry lasted beyond the viability of Nimbyism itself. Residents stopped many plants from being built in suburban locales while also helping to brand the industry as reckless, poorly regulated, and inherently dangerous. This view of nuclear power became so entrenched that *The Simpsons* frequently used it over the animated sitcom's thirty-plus seasons as a comic trope to depict the fictional Springfield's nuclear power plant.[131] The 1990 episode "Two Cars in Every Garage and Three Eyes on Every Fish" portrayed the Springfield power plant owner Montgomery Burns callously allowing contamination of the water supply so he could earn more profit. With a lovable three-eyed fish named Blinky and the newspaper headline "Mutation Caught at Ol' Fishing Hole—Is Power Plant Responsible?" *The Simpsons* episode further reflected contemporary doubt about the ability and willingness of government, industry, and environmentalists to keep people safe.[132] In later episodes, Mr. Burns is shown to be totally corrupt and the plant to be irredeemably mismanaged. Into the 1990s, an economic boom that included cheap oil and gas rendered debates about alternative energy, including nuclear power, largely moot. The general lull in building new plants continued through 2014, with a few previously approved reactors beginning construction in 2012.[133] International events also intervened periodically to remind the public of the dangers of nuclear power. On April 26, 1986, in Chernobyl, Ukraine, and on March 11, 2011, in Fukushima, Japan, catastrophic nuclear power disasters reinforced the notion that while nuclear power provides certain advantages over traditional sources of energy, a nuclear reactor was still inherently capable of massive destruction.[134]

Yet, by the mid-1990s, Nimbys had lost the political middle ground on which their power depended, as critics questioned the broader implications of their vision of home and neighborhood defense. Those on the right decried Nimby opposition to office parks in ever-growing rings of suburban towns as the narrow, self-interested, and antigrowth view of the few who sought to live in "elitist preserves" rather than facilitate land use policies that promoted economic development.[135] On the left, activists who were increasingly invested in environmental justice rejected the inequality resulting from the relocation of undesirable projects to less politically powerful communities.[136] Eco-justice advocates pointed out the implications of homeowners' Nimby logic. Like other "colorblind" policies and tactics of postwar suburbanites, Nimbyism had a profound impact on race and class. By shaping the suburban landscape through the displacement of public projects to rural and urban places despite residents' objections, suburbanites turned a blind eye to the effects of their practices on politically and socially marginalized groups.[137]

Still, thanks to the success of Nimbyism, suburbanites became central to the process corporations and government followed in siting public projects. Hoping to avoid a spectacle that may turn public opinion against a project or even a whole industry, they dealt directly with local residents before building. In some cases, communities received some kind of monetary compensation (e.g., lower taxes, reduced power rates) in exchange for allowing a project to be built in their town, reflecting a renewed emphasis on economic values and willingness to compromise in lieu of protest.[138] The federal government also sought to avoid local agitation by frequently reviewing and improving environmental laws and procedures so as to protect communities; the Superfund program to clean up abandoned waste sites is one example.[139] "Not in my backyard!" had become an epithet in American culture denoting an irresponsible middle-class suburban attitude by the end of the 1990s, but the suburban privilege and spatial power it represented endured.[140] Indeed, while Nimbyism became marginalized, suburbanites became stakeholders privileged enough to no longer even need to protest.

The examples analyzed in this chapter demonstrate that Nimbys nearly always protected privilege by dressing it up as commonsense, necessary behavior. As the *New York Times* reported in 1990, "Neighbors, these days, are much less likely to submit to municipal authority with docile good citizenship." A *Syracuse Post-Standard* editorial argued that "no one wants nuclear waste, even the low-level stuff, anywhere nearby; no one wants an incinerator, or worse yet, a landfill down the road; no one wants nearby farmers to work sludge into the soil."[141] This avowed ideological disassociation, then, was actually ideological investment in place and privilege rather than in national or identity politics. As a New York City Council member said of Nimbyism, "There is no doubt that citizens rising up in fear and rage to fight what some corporation or government agency has planned for their neighborhood has added to the cost of these projects, often delayed them and sometimes killed them outright. That is the purpose of Nimbys."

But what is the alternative?"[142] For Nimbys faced with toxins and cooling towers, there was no other tactic that kept their privileged status as middle-class home-owners safe from these local threats.

Yet insidious everyday threats from industrial sites that made postwar suburbs possible and from the consumer products that made suburban life comfortable marked that life as environmentally hazardous. Unlike nuclear power plants, how-ever, these other dangers were invisible chemicals and toxins that Nimby protest could not protect against. The following chapter analyzes how, under siege from invisible threats without a clear cause or solution, popular culture texts, individu-als, and "experts" imagined affective solutions and psychologically prophylactic practices to help suburbanites cope with the contamination inherent in modern suburban living.

Chapter Two

Neighborhood of Fear

Toxic Suburbia, Affective Practice, and the Invisible Prison

In 1980, President Jimmy Carter called Love Canal a tragedy. Since the 1950s, toxic waste had silently poisoned the town's water supply, causing chromosome damage, birth defects, miscarriages, and multiple kinds of cancers.[1] As home to the tragic fallout of industrial suburbia, Love Canal became the symbol of corporate malfeasance, failed government oversight, and suburban environmental danger. As argued in the previous chapter, dangers like these caused a continuing sense of environmental threat among suburban residents and facilitated the productive victimization of the Nimby ethic. The disaster at Love Canal also initiated a view of the suburban environment as home not just to visible public hazards like a nuclear power plant but also to lurking, silent killers in the soil and water left behind during the deindustrialization of postwar suburbia. It served as an example of the real and potent danger of toxins threatening the very survival of middle-class, suburban families that had taken for granted their bucolic surroundings and seen the home as a refuge in an unsafe world.[2] In a *Time* article entitled "The Neighborhood of Fear," one Love Canal resident expressed the new fear that suburban life itself might be killing the family it was created to protect: "We've lived in fear for a long time. Now we'll wonder what we've passed on to the children."[3]

By making manifest the consequences of cheap but haphazard corporate and industrial waste practices as well as the failure by government to prevent them, Love Canal helped imbue civically oriented projects with the taint of environmental disaster while casting new doubt on assumed spaces of safety like homes, parks, and schools. The federal government soon confirmed these fears as the news media consistently reported them.[4] In 1978, *Newsweek* declared: "There is no doubt that chemical time bombs are ticking away in the environment—and that locating all of them, let alone disarming them, will prove all but impossible."[5] According to *Time* in 1980, "Love Canal is only the tip of a tremendous toxic iceberg. A 1978 Environmental Protection Agency study identified 32,254 toxic waste dumps around the U.S., some 800 of which posed 'significant imminent hazards' to public health."[6] Although Love Canal spurred the creation of Superfund and local antidumping laws, its legacy highlights the dangers that heavy industry posed to space heretofore presumed safe and clean. Lying dormant for decades and emerging without warning, these toxic hazards appeared alongside those from seemingly dangerous public projects. Together, they marked the era of toxic suburbia.

At the same time that suburbanites became aware of toxic industrial dangers, a spate of popular culture representations broadcast narratives of other hazards, in the form of new allergies, disorders, and maladies that seemed to directly affect middle-class suburbanites. These portrayals showed suburbanites exposed to toxins that usually could not be seen, smelled, or touched until their damage was apparent, suggesting a new vector of environmental danger that might not be preventable and might have to be accepted as the price of other suburban privileges. Two popular examples of such narratives were the 1981 film *The Incredible Shrinking Woman* and Don DeLillo's 1985 novel *White Noise*. Though very different in artistic aspiration, the movie and the book both portray a suburban realm populated by products designed to make everyday life easier and more fulfilling but that also have dire physical and psychological effects.

For Lily Tomlin's character in *The Incredible Shrinking Woman*, the repercussions are obvious. The cleaners and sprays she uses to ease her household workload, and the makeup, perfume, hairspray, and other beauty products she uses to be attractive to her breadwinning husband, cause her to shrink and make her unable to fulfill her domestic roles. Instead, she becomes a curiosity for daytime television audiences while on a quest to cure her condition and return her household to normalcy—a nostalgic vision of the home and its inhabitants that contrasted with the dramatic changes in sex, gender, and work in that era that exposed the myth of the "traditional" household.[7]

Although DeLillo's characters in *White Noise* are less sure about what everyday products and environmental hazards specifically do to their bodies, they also consistently articulate an existential fear of lethal contamination that cannot be prevented. Ultimately, such fears shatter the notion of the suburb as safe, and the characters take a drug to quell their ongoing fear of toxic death and restore the privilege of not seeing danger or feeling endangered. In the era of hundreds of Superfund sites and a steady drumbeat from the news media about "Toxic America," texts such as *White Noise* amplified public consciousness of chemical dangers. Their portrayals reinforced the sense that nostalgic visions of the home as sanctuary were untenable without psychological intervention and that suburban privilege was fragile, even if it was endangered by suburban practices themselves.

Similarly, environmental illness (EI) and multiple chemical sensitivity (MCS) appeared as "diseases" of affluence in the 1980s, emerging directly from the circumstances of modern consumer culture, inextricably enmeshed in suburban living. Like Lily Tomlin in *The Incredible Shrinking Woman*, sufferers were mostly women who located the cause of their distress in the many things intended to make life easier, domestic work more efficient, and the space of the home more comfortable: sprays, cleaners, beauty products, fabric protectors such as Scotchgard, air conditioning, and so on. Rather than enhance comfort, security, and domestic tranquility, sufferers contended, these products contained chemicals and toxins that bombarded, overwhelmed, and damaged their bodies. Such complaints demonstrated another way in which "traditional" domestic roles were damaging to suburban women, and suggested the continuing instability of such arrangements, now further undermined by toxic exposure.[8]

To find relief, sufferers consulted their physicians. Faced with the real pain of patients and the contemporary depiction of their lives as inescapably polluted, some doctors attempted to treat patients with these symptoms, while others dismissed their maladies as psychosomatic. Ultimately, though, the medical establishment did not recognize EI or MCS as diagnosable diseases given the difficulty of establishing a direct causal relationship in a world of multiple, possibly dangerous environmental stimuli.[9] As Jerry Hook of the Michigan State University Center for Environmental Toxicology explained already in 1980: "We know that ingesting these things is probably not good for you. At the same time, we should not go shooting our mouths off and scaring everyone."[10] Researchers and doctors could say little with certainty about the connection between diseases and exposure to toxins in everyday life. This scientific conundrum and the common dismissal of women's suffering by many mainstream medical practitioners often drove patients to alternative treatments. In the midst of an evolving culture of self-diagnosis, rehabilitative self-care, and "medicalization," they managed their own health, hoping for a cure but often accepting the assurance of palliative treatments.[11] One common approach was visiting a scientifically trained clinical ecologist, who, while not a physician, attempted to programmatically pinpoint the particular toxins that were causing pain. Others relied on less empirically inclined pseudo-scientific healers who prescribed natural remedies and daily prophylactic practices—affective solutions that might make a patient *feel* better by doing them but would not actually remedy their disorder, presaging the era of mainstream consumer wellness culture that is as much about feeling well as it is about physical health.[12]

Whether recognized as a diagnosable disorder by the medical establishment or a manifestation of a psychological condition, MCS and other manifestations of modern toxic culture demonstrated both the power and the failure of productive victimization in addressing less visibly material threats, particularly for women. Unlike Nimby protests that could stop or relocate a dangerous project, the threats from everyday products were ubiquitous, invisible, and unstoppable unless one simply dropped out of modern society and gave up the hard-won privilege of suburban living. The medical profession's categorization of MCS or EI as a form of affluenza suggested that these maladies were manifestations of privilege.[13] Journalist Lisa Jones Townsel quoted a family doctor as saying, "If you're poor, you simply can't afford to have Multiple Chemical Sensitivity syndrome." He added, "Typically, they're well off enough that they can afford to drop out, if they're allergic to their entire environment."[14] Despite their otherwise comfortable lives, many privileged people with access to health care and various palliatives lived in the invisible prison described by MCS victim Evelyn Todd as "symbolic of life with MCS—inside a drab room but with attractive, enticing possibilities outside because there are bars."[15]

This was the situation that Carol Johnson (played by Julianne Moore) faced in Todd Haynes's critically acclaimed 1995 film, *Safe*. Carol is a suburban housewife struggling with environmental illness, shown in the film to be a suburban disease of modern origin. Carol's condition cannot be cured or remediated through collective action to eliminate the toxins that surround and destroy her body. She tries to survive everyday life as the very things that make her domestic duties easier and give her self-esteem erode her health. Deodorant sprays, dry-cleaning chemicals, car exhaust, and hair salon treatments bombard her body, causing bloody noses, lack of appetite, and overall lethargy. Carol eventually comes to believe she has a malady in which "certain people's natural tolerance to everyday substances is breaking down due to chemical exposure." This revelation causes her to reconsider her comfortable upper-middle-class lifestyle and eventually to consult lay experts who recommend a desert oasis where she can live nearly toxin-free. Like many real sufferers, Carol is a woman victimized by the very home constructed to be a refuge. For her, what causes pain and distress is not domestic abuse or the "second shift" of domestic labor but her home, a venue for ongoing toxic exposure that she must use her class and race privilege to escape—an option not available to many others exposed to noxious chemicals in their homes.

The news stories, popular culture representations, and medical and lay literature on MCS and EI normalized the idea of multiple environmental threats as expected parts of suburban living, the toll paid to gain other kinds of cultural and spatial power. Beyond reproducing the notion of silent, deadly suburban hazards, these texts presented methods of amelioration that provided hope of survival in a toxic suburban world. Although these hidden toxins were largely beyond the reach of material power, suburbanites discovered and cultivated the affective solutions they found in popular culture narratives and the experiences of victims of contamination and toxicity available in print and on television and film. These narratives showed suburban characters developing tactics to evade, belittle, or make peace with invisible toxic threats, tactics in service of "being" suburban through the embrace of a consumer culture of comfort and convenience. The "incredible shrinking woman," Pat Kramer, actually grows back to normal size because of exposure to cleaners, while in *White Noise*, DeLillo creates a nihilistic world where everyone has a vague malady of indeterminate origin mitigated only by the continuous rehearsal of response to a catastrophic disaster—essentially getting used to being endangered. Alternatively, the main character of *Safe*, Carol Johnson, uses her privilege to escape to the quarantined environs of the Wrenwood Center.

The emergence of MCS and EI stood as an eerie parallel to the immediate postwar period, when the "traditionally" gendered suburban home was supposed to contain social change and produce healthy citizens largely through the labor of wives and mothers, even as it was often a space of physical danger and emotional distress for them.[16] By the 1980s, the home was also endangering the women tasked with managing it through the products and devices invented to ease their household workload, much as earlier domestic technologies had ironically made that work harder.[17] Although MCS and EI did not afflict only women, it was mostly suburban women who emerged as victims of these conditions, and as heroes, in narratives of survival. Just as Lois Gibbs started her activism as a mom who advocated for change in response to Love Canal, victims of toxic America like Susan Abod and Bonnye L. Mathews, as well as their fictional counterparts Pat Kramer and Carol Johnson, gave voice to the gendered peril of suburban chemical exposure.

These characters and real-world sufferers of MCS and EI understood "that modernity could no longer automatically be associated with health; in fact, many felt the opposite was true."[18] Given that reality, suburbanites managed these threats through personal behavior and consumer choices, sometimes eschewing institutional or mainstream medical solutions to toxic threats, while at other times finding themselves rejected by doctors and psychologists. Ultimately, these tactics, like Nimbyism, highlighted and reinforced the inequalities of environmental hazard in twentieth-century America, where suburban privilege meant access to help, be it in the form of doctors, healers, or new products to mitigate toxic exposure.

Nightmare in Niagara

By the 1970s, Love Canal, New York, was a typical working-class suburban community of homeowners and families. Mother-turned–environmental activist Lois Gibbs said of living in Love Canal in that era, "With lots of trees and children playing outside, I thought it would be a peaceful, safe place to raise my family."[19] Yet, beginning in 1976, residents of this development near Niagara Falls experienced an usually high rate of illnesses, some of them very unusual.[20] Leukemia, birth defects, miscarriages, and mental impairment plagued the town. Responding to pressure from residents, New York State health commissioner Robert Whalen initiated an investigation that found "an extremely serious threat and danger to the health and safety of those living near [the town]."[21] As the investigation continued, the cause of the crisis was found: the town was constructed on an industrial dumpsite once owned by the Hooker Chemical Corporation. The company had haphazardly buried its toxic waste and paved over it. Hooker subsequently sold the land for one dollar to the town, which then constructed a school on the site. For the following twenty years, the waste leeched dozens of chemicals into the water supply, including the school's drinking water.[22] *Time* described the unfolding disaster as a series of "harrowing tales of noxious odors leaking into homes, of sinister-colored sludge seeping into basements, of children playing in potholes of pollutants and, worst of all, of abnormally high rates of miscarriages and birth defects, of nerve, respiratory, liver and kidney disorders and of assorted cancers among people of Love Canal."[23] Ultimately, Lois Gibbs and the Love Canal Homeowners Association, the news media, and cultural representations of the tragedy made "Love Canal" synonymous with residential toxic waste and initiated a broader investigation into the thousands of chemical waste sites across the United States.

Between the discovery of the waste in 1978 and President Jimmy Carter's signing of the Superfund bill into law in 1980, visceral imagery and heartbreaking stories of loss in the news coverage of Love Canal quickly raised suburbanites' consciousness as to the dangers from chemical toxins in their local environment. On August 21, 1978, *Newsweek* described the disturbing scene of daily life in Love Canal: "Everything seemed fine until the mid-1970s, when heavy rains began flushing out the chemicals. Suddenly a stench was everywhere. Trees turned black. Children would throw rocks against the pavement and watch them ignite and flash bright colors. Dogs sniffing in the landfill developed nose lesions that never healed. And when children ran across the site, the oozing slime burned holes in their sneakers."[24] Ominously, unlike the danger posed by a new public project whose possible hazards seemed clear, whatever lay buried beneath Love Canal was nearly undetectable. Love Canal resident Walter Mikula noted, "You try to forget what's in the ground, in the air, in your home. But you can't. You can't put it out of your mind for a minute."[25] Lying dormant and leaking slowly into the ground and water, "today's toxins act more insidiously. They are invisible and often scarcely detectable."[26] The school, homes, and the canal itself all showed dangerous levels of more than eighty chemicals that could lead to abnormally high rates of disease. Exposure to buried toxic waste turned a quaint suburban community into a postapocalyptic hellscape, undermining a key tenet of suburban privilege: to live without fear of environmental danger.

Aired in 1982, the CBS made-for-TV movie *Lois Gibbs and the Love Canal* portrayed everyday threats posed by toxic waste and the actions taken by a committed, local citizenry to protect themselves.[27] Advertised as a film about the "American Dream, undone by modern technology," it focused on the Gibbs family as they discover the cause of son Michael's many maladies.[28] His mother, Lois, reluctantly becomes an activist working to organize her neighbors to protest the do-nothing attitude of school and town administrators. In the film, she says that she is not a radical. Rather, "all I want is to be safe and healthy. All I want is for my kids to be safe and healthy. I don't want to be dumb anymore." In trying to protect herself and her family by tirelessly lobbying the federal government to get involved, she motivates her neighbors—who wonder, "Where am I supposed

Figure 2.1. A house on 99th Street in Love Canal, New York, on August 4, 1978, built over a toxic waste dump. The sign heralds the emergence of toxic suburbia. AP Photo/TK

to sleep when my own house is killing me? Where am I supposed to go?" The film fused multiple and overlapping news media narratives into a single, two-hour movie that dramatized both the actual damage done to local residents and the sense not only of real fear of being exposed to dangerous, invisible chemicals but of losing power over one's local community.[29]

Yet, Love Canal was only the tip of a toxic iceberg that became a growing problem of suburban development.[30] As an Environmental Protection Agency administrator noted in 1980, "We just don't know how many potential Love

Canals there are."[31] That same year, Julius Richmond, the US surgeon general, predicted that "throughout the 1980s the nation will confront a series of environmental emergencies" posed by toxic chemicals that "are adding to the disease burden in a significant, although as yet not precisely defined, way."[32] The two federal officials proved correct as thousands of sites were identified and further environmental and human devastation emerged. Also in 1980, journalist Ed Magnuson identified three communities confronting serious problems resulting from toxic time bombs: Elizabeth, New Jersey; Seymour, Indiana; and Montague, Michigan. A toxic fire raged in Elizabeth following a chemical explosion, and Montague residents suffered a fate similar to that in Love Canal as 20 billion gallons of groundwater was contaminated with waste, also from the Hooker Company. In "Hazards of a Toxic Wasteland," reporter Natalie Angler chronicled industrial dangers around the world though her article focused on the United States.[33] Environmental threats need not entail a huge accident, she explained; secondary disasters that evolve slowly could also contaminate air and drinking water, often without notice until people became sick. One cause of such hazards was that nearly 90 percent of waste in 1984 was dumped into the most conveniently located "rivers, inadequate landfills, abandoned mine shafts, old missile silos, swamps, and fields." As Angler explained, "The full effects of these gradual seepages may not be felt for ten to fifteen years, the time it takes for some cancers to be recognized."[34] Dumping sites like these, once located in urban outskirts and often believed to safely store toxic waste, became suburban problems as populations grew and development sprawled, leading to "liquid wastes flooding yards, living rooms and the elementary school grounds."[35]

Although the Superfund legislation was designed to fund the cleanup of these sites, its passage and implementation magnified fear of toxins. The fault lay in part with the failure of the Environmental Protection Agency (EPA) to use the funds to quickly begin cleaning up designated toxic sites. One resident of Love Canal argued that the "EPA was as a dependable as a wet noodle" while he waited for the cleanup of his community so he could return home.[36] By early 1983, three years after the fund's creation, the EPA had cleaned up only 5 of the 418 sites it saw as most dangerous, designated "ticking time bombs."[37] In cases like Love Canal, residents packed up and abandoned their town or neighborhood rather than risking their health by returning, or relying on the government to clean up the chemical mess.[38] The advent of Superfund also meant that the location and severity of toxic exposure was public information, vetted government data that further spurred homeowners' environmental fears. In 1979, as the EPA came to grips with the crisis, it was not sure just how many sites there were or how dangerous they might be.[39] By 1982, however, the agency had detailed lists of sites, toxins, and a rating of their dangers all made accessible to the public. Still, even though the EPA reported in 1989 that Superfund sites were not nearly as dangerous as believed, the sheer number of the sites affirmed that toxic-chemical danger was apparent in thousands of communities and might be invisibly lurking in many others, giving credence to fears of invisible exposure and contamination.[40]

Death Made in a Laboratory

Like the tragedy at Love Canal and narratives about it in the news and popular culture, other toxic discourses in literature and film vividly portrayed the dangers that man-made chemicals posed to what was believed to be a pristine suburban environment.[41] Don DeLillo's provocative work of high-minded literature *White Noise* is an award-winning novel, and *The Incredible Shrinking Woman* starring Lily Tomlin is a mainstream popcorn movie. Despite differences in purpose and audience, both the novel and the movie tackled toxic aspects of modern suburban life and signified the cultural power and familiarity of these threats in post–Love Canal America. Their very existence and popularity made clear that setting stories of toxic exposure in middle-class suburbs was not unusual or unexpected. Further, in telling their stories, they both demonstrated the boundaries and conundrums of suburban privilege in this new age of environmental endangerment. Though constantly exposed to dangerous chemicals in everyday consumer products, their characters do not leave their comfortable environs nor combat these threats in the Nimby manner analyzed in the previous chapter. Instead, they make peace with their chemical exposure while trying not to relinquish other suburban privileges.

White Noise is the story of "Hitler Studies" professor Jack Gladney, his fourth wife, Babette, and their children in the suburban town of Glassboro. They live "at the end of a quiet street in what was once a wooded area with deep ravines," suggesting a familiar and seemingly bucolic setting slowly encroached upon by postwar suburban development.[42] In that setting, the book chronicles the events leading up to, during, and following an "airborne toxic event," the result of an accident involving a train carrying Nyodene D, a noxious chemical with unknown effects on humans. Throughout the novel, the characters contemplate the hazards of contact with Nyodene D, and these thoughts raise questions about other, more mundane chemicals like those in sugar-free gum and all-weather plastic lawn chairs. In this way, the characters consider their tenuous existence in a seemingly safe suburb as they sense and see danger nearly everywhere as the continuous white noise of their otherwise comfortable lives.[43] Through the depiction of hazards hidden in quotidian products like toothpaste and hairspray and of a toxic industrial accident, DeLillo portrayed a suburban environment under siege.[44]

The source of enduring fear was not only actual contamination from toxic chemicals but the possibility, the *near* certainty, of such contamination, the likelihood that everyday objects were a threat to health, a thousand lurking environmental threats becoming the noxious white noise in the background of suburban life vaguely seen or heard but assuredly experienced and felt. Jack and Babette constantly talk about how death is all around them, yet they can never pinpoint just what will cause it or when they will actually die:

"What if death is nothing but sound?"

"Electrical noise."

"You hear it forever. Sound all around. How awful."

"Uniform, white."

"Sometimes it sweeps over me," she said. "Sometimes it insinuates itself into my mind, little by little. I try to talk to it. 'Not now, Death.'"[45]

While acknowledging the futility of seeking out the source of their endangerment, Jack and Babette try to become comfortable with the pervasive hazards in their lives. Babette is attempting to quit smoking by chewing sugarless gum. When she learns that the sugar substitute in the gum causes cancer in lab rats, Babette realizes that without the gum she will either not be able to quit smoking or gain more weight, but that continuing to chew the gum may kill her.[46] Similarly, Jack's son matter-of-factly informs him that "when plastic furniture burns, you get cyanide poisoning," and also that there is going to be plane crash footage on the news.[47] From spectacular to mundane hazards, each character senses and articulates an ongoing sense of dread and futility in the face of inevitable toxic exposure.

In response to the white noise of death surrounding them, DeLillo's characters are presented with limited choices that stave off immediate demise but ultimately create more anxiety. One of those options is a drug called Dylar made by a pharmaceutical company capitalizing on this persistent sense of dread. Rather than cleansing the body or the environment of dangerous chemicals, it works psychotropically to remove the fear of death and essentially return its users to a prior mode of existence, before catastrophes like Love Canal and Three Mile Island and the pervasive sense of environmental danger that came with them. In the context of the neighborhood of fear, then, DeLillo imagines an affective salve for its victims by creating a way to access the peaceful state of mind of the postwar suburbs. Dylar is deemed too dangerous and is not made commercially available, yet it can be procured, for a price. To the extent that class privilege provides access to this affective solution unreachable for others, Dylar is reminiscent of palliatives for afflictions like environmental illness. DeLillo's deployment of Dylar as a curative to everyday toxic exposure serves to further the idea that the suburban home and family were in constant danger and were left to leverage what suburban privilege remained in order to cope. He shows how diet soda additives or a chemical spill in the middle of town compromise the same expectation to be free of environmental worry. In doing so, he positions Dylar as a kind of ingestible nostalgia tablet that tricks users into believing they are safe. Just as nostalgia sugarcoats the past, Dylar masks the real threats endangering someone who takes it.

DeLillo imagines coping with the ever-present sense of danger and death in another way, as well: through something called Simuvac, short for "simulated evacuation." A Simuvac official explains that "the more we rehearse disaster, the safer we'll feel from the real thing."[48] This constant rehearsal reinforces the sense of imminent local disaster, making catastrophe seem a likely, even perfunctory part of suburban living. In 1980s North America, suburban towns and municipal authorities initiated drills like Simuvac to prepare for disaster and, to some degree, make peace with its inevitability. In 1983, Rockville, Maryland, simulated an accident incredibly similar to the one in *White Noise*.[49] In their rehearsal, a train hit a school bus, releasing toxic acid from a railroad tank car. At the conclusion of the drill, it was clear to officials they were not sufficiently prepared and would need to practice more. Mimicking Cold War–era duck-and-cover and civil defense drills, *White Noise*'s Simuvac and its real-world counterparts highlighted the encroaching sense that suburbs required a sense of order and discipline so residents could at least *feel* safe, a confidence achievable through predictable drills that would increase residents' comfort with existential danger though they might do little to protect them.

Yet, in DeLillo's novel, despite their "expertise" and continuing simulation practice, Simuvac coordinators and town officials are basically incompetent. "Remarks existed in a state of permanent flotation," Jack says. "No one thing was either more or less plausible than any other thing."[50] Echoing the confusion and poor communications following the accident at Three Mile Island, Simuvac's decisions are tainted by a sense that no one really knows what to do but that something must be done to quell panic. DeLillo identifies both the failure of Simuvac and the airborne toxic event as man-made disasters. He writes of the black cloud of Nyodene D, "This was death made in a laboratory, defined and measurable, but we thought of it at the time in a simple primitive way, as some seasonal perversity of the earth like a flood or tornado, something not subject to our control. Our helplessness did not seem compatible with the idea of a man-made event." The toxins in the air are made by corporations, presumably for some consumer benefit, but ultimately endanger them. Similarly, the government's Simuvac rehearsal and its incompetent response to an actual accident escalate the danger. Together, this combination creates a toxic natural and cultural environment that can kill people directly through chemical exposure while also eroding their sense of safety. Ultimately, *White Noise* contributed to the growing sense that man-made disasters were becoming a naturalized, expected risk of middle-class suburban life for which there might be no defense except ignorance or acceptance.

At the heart of *White Noise* is a fundamental lack of trust in the federal government and corporations to protect citizens and safely transport volatile toxins or to produce consumer goods that pose no harm. This distrust and the evidence of failure to prevent toxic exposure were also central to a class of exploitation films that took poisonous America for granted as the country continued to grapple with transportation and storage of noxious waste.[51] Among them were those made by the independent studio Troma Entertainment. The studio produced two quintessential examples of this genre in *Class of Nuke 'Em High* and *The Toxic Avenger*, which were lurid, didactic treatments of the toxic suburb in the mid-1980s.[52] Set in Tromaville, known as the toxic waste capital of the world, both films are what Vincent Canby called "satiric comic-horror films of stomach-turning grossness and exhilarating tackiness" that detail what happens when radioactive nuclear waste contaminates the local population.[53] Viewers are treated to rotting and burned flesh, green sludge pulsating from school water fountains, and characters with human features grotesquely misshaped by exposure to industrial waste.

In *Nuke 'Em High*, Tromaville High School stands in the shadow of the town's nuclear plant as arrogant and greedy plant operators, not unlike those in *The China Syndrome*, allow waste to seep into the school's water supply. The polluted water transforms average student Warren into a muscle-bound freak, like the Incredible Hulk. In his new form, Warren battles a demon in the school's boiler room, saving his girlfriend, Chrissy, from the monster and the Cretins, honor students transformed by the waste into a vicious gang. *The Toxic Avenger* tells a similar story about Melvin, a pipsqueak from central casting, who tries to kill himself by jumping out a window. Instead, he lands in a truck full of nuclear waste carelessly left outside the school. The waste transforms him into a hideous mutant, the Toxic Avenger, who uses his superhuman strength to fight crime on the streets of Tromaville.

White Noise and these two films take as their primary setting an everyday American suburb where toxic waste, hazmat suits, and chemical exposure were seemingly appropriate parts of a suburban landscape under siege from dangerous pollutants. At the time these fictional works appeared, homeowners and local governments were battling the federal government over the transport and storage of nuclear and other kinds of waste. As a result of the expanding knowledge about toxic America, the US Energy Department encountered "a wall of opposition from state governments and citizens groups all saying basically the same thing: 'Not in my back yard,'" as the government looked to create the first high-level radioactive dump.[54] To state officials and residents, a nuclear waste dump provoked "twentieth century anxiety" about a "killing ground" where 90 percent of toxic waste was disposed of improperly in 1984.[55] By 1987, none of the lower forty-eight states were willing to host the waste site.[56] Two years later, the federal government selected Yucca Mountain, in a remote area of Nevada, as the site given the small nearby populations and lack of local opposition.[57] Illegal dumping formed an even more pernicious problem as economic considerations proved more powerful than environmental ones.[58] In a documentary aired, as it happened, on the second day of the TMI accident in 1979, ABC News found more than two hundred contaminated water wells in New Jersey that were the result of illegal dumping practices across the state.[59] By the 1990s, citizens not only believed they would be endangered but saw that, as cultural representations, news media reports, and government actions strongly suggested, "it can happen here."[60]

As with *White Noise*'s "death made in a laboratory" and the toxic foundation of Tromaville, *The Incredible Shrinking Woman* portrays the effects of the toxicity of everyday suburban life on the household itself. As Patricia "Pat" Kramer (Lily Tomlin) walks out of her local grocery store with her two unruly children in tow, she is accosted by a film crew. They are making a commercial for Cheese Tease, cheddar cheese in a spray can. They ask her to honestly assess the product while their camera is rolling. Like everyone else, she hates the synthetic cheese "product." Then, as they drive home, one of her kids accidentally unleashes an aerosol spray, nearly choking everyone in the car. Not long after her chemical exposure in the car, Pat and her advertising executive husband, Vance Kramer (Charles

Grodin), go to bed and begin to make love as the camera pans away from them and across the room, revealing some fifty aerosol cans—hair spray, air freshener, spray starch, and the like. Tomlin's voiceover follows this sequence, "There I was, safe in the belief that nothing unusual ever happens in Tasty Meadows," thus signaling the broader shift from understanding suburban living as safe and boring to a dangerous undertaking.

The next morning, Pat begins to shrink, eventually becoming the size of a Barbie doll. She and Vance immediately go to doctors who cannot figure out what is wrong. Like the sufferers of MCS and EI, Pat ends up visiting "experts" outside the mainstream medical establishment, including the Kleinman Institute for the Study of Unexplained Phenomena, whose motto is "Science is Truth Found Out." The audience learns that the institute's benefactors are corporate CEOs who plan to shrink the world while developing a monopoly on the only antidote, which they will make from an extract of Pat's blood. The Kleinman Institute's researchers tell Pat that her shrinkage is the result of a combination of "flu shot, tap water, the glue, the perfume, talcum powder, bubble bath, hair conditioner, setting lotion, mouth wash, hair spray, breath spray, feminine hygiene spray, deodorant, toothpaste, detergent, eye drops, nose drops, hair coloring, diet soda, birth control pills, and smog, set off by an imbalance already present in your system." That explanation reinforces the compromise at the heart of suburban living. To enjoy its conveniences, the family, particularly homemakers like Pat, are exposed to an increasing number of chemicals and toxins. Pat's diagnosis also suggests the ways in which EI and MCS make sense of the causes of suburban women's pain as coming from toxic overload, especially when mainstream medicine can't or won't help.[61]

In this iteration of the danger posed by chemicals, they render Pat unable to perform any of her daily duties for her family. In a disturbing sequence, Pat dons a sexy outfit and climbs into bed with her full-sized husband. Luckily for the audience, Vance moves and manages to eject Pat onto the floor, thereby sparing the audience the vision of a six-inch woman attempting to have sex with a regular-sized man. Once she becomes tiny, Pat is also unable to control her children or manage her household as she can no longer effectively cook or clean or keep her children from misbehaving. Whereas the chemicals at fault were promoted as assisting overburdened suburban housewives who want to do domestic labor more efficiently and maintain their sex appeal for breadwinner husbands, the film argues they actually endanger the "traditional" family; or, as one Love Canal resident put it, "It's as if we're all mutants now."[62] Beyond promoting a continuing sense of toxic fear, the film sounded the alarm that suburban family culture was also under siege from a toxic environment.

Still, even though the movie's ubiquitous sprays and cleaners are dangerous tools that undermine family relationships and demean women's work in the home, exposure to them also returns Pat to regular size. Like the characters in *White Noise*, Pat does not leave her comfortable suburban home or eliminate chemicals from her life. Instead, she finds a way to make toxins work for her, and in this way, the film offers another articulation of technological utopianism, in which the home is imagined as rehabilitative in response to and then because of technological progress. As analyzed further in chapter 4, however, the crisis of the family and fears about proper parenting continued to be part of the neighborhood of fear as debates raged about the suburban home's moral environment in response to the toxic threats from popular culture.

Together, the news coverage of Love Canal and toxic America raised environmental consciousness as narratives of vulnerability reverberated in US culture. *White Noise*, the Troma films, and *The Incredible Shrinking Woman* made clear the existence and consequences of invisible toxic chemicals in what were otherwise considered safe suburban spaces. Like public projects such as nuclear power plants, these less visible threats called into question the expected privilege of suburban communities to live without fear of contamination from toxic chemicals. These narratives also suggested ways for coping with those dangers while retaining other benefits of suburban living. They posited affective solutions to the material issue of toxic exposure by providing a way to make peace with that danger through rehearsal, ignorance, or even embrace of the toxins, as when Pat Kramer uses the same chemicals that shrunk her to return to her nostalgic vision of domestic normalcy. The narratives created the context for the emergence of new afflictions later in the twentieth century—multiple chemical sensitivity and environmental illness—and middle-class methods for coping with their effects.

Home Unsafe Home

As a product of the rising awareness of "toxic America" and the "chemicals all around us," a general fear emerged of products, sprays, and even "sick buildings," a sense of dread organized and understood through the labels "multiple chemical sensitivity" and "environmental illness." Victims of these maladies, and the lay experts who studied them, promoted a sense of broad-based environmental hazard that could be explained only by chemical or toxic overload brought on by modern life. These articulations of new afflictions helped privileged people make sense of their illnesses at a time when mainstream medicine and the law found they suffered from no diagnosable disease. It was not that the headaches, fatigue, or joint pain did not exist for the sufferer, but rather that the medical establishment did not recognize these symptoms as a disease with clear causes, effects, and treatments. Instead, unlicensed experts and sufferers themselves dealt with painful symptoms by leveraging class and race privilege to access alternative treatments in ways that challenged the medical establishment while producing "scientific" frameworks through self-help manuals and other guides to EI and MCS.[63]

Nearly every account of MCS and EI found in news media accounts, self-help guides, and memoirs of sufferers detailed the ways in which innocuous, everyday things in the home were actually toxic, leading to what one sufferer called a new "housing crisis."[64] In a 1990 *New York Times* report on these sicknesses, journalist Robert Reinhold described one such sufferer: "Sitting on her floor, she seemed normal. But nearly everything in modern life can almost instantly disable the forty-one-year-old Oregonian. A whiff of kerosene fumes, formaldehyde on a new garment, perfume, roach spray, even a dose of electromagnetic waves from overhead power lines or an elevator, can cause a massive allergiclike reaction."[65] Earlier that year, columnist Jean Marbella of the *St. Louis Post-Dispatch* lamented all of the things that make a home dangerous: "Old cans of paint. Air fresheners. Paneling. Clothes fresh from the dry cleaners. Even hot showers. Ah, home unsafe home."[66] The *Philadelphia Inquirer* article "Inside Pollutants May Be Riskier than Outside Ones" explained: "When the environmental movement started more than two decades ago, most people associated toxic chemicals with soot-chugging smokestacks or sludge-filled dump sites. No one gave carpets a second thought. Well, things have changed. A growing body of evidence suggests that dozens of seemingly benign products found in and around the home, the living room rug included, are daily churning out their own stream of toxic fumes and chemicals."[67] Whether skeptical or supportive, mainstream news reports revealed that more and more people felt sick and found the causes to be common things that were supposed to provide comfort, convenience, and safety, particularly in the consumerist haven of the middle-class suburban home.

In addition to the news reporting on MCS and EI, the memoirs and personal stories of struggle gave evidence of the hidden dangers of the consumerism of suburban privilege. As sociologists of medicine Steve Kroll-Smith and H. Hugh Floyd observed in their study of MCS, "If built environments and the products typically found in them are sources of pleasure, comfort, and symbols of success for most of us, for the chemically reactive they are often perilous worlds of debilitating health risks."[68] MCS sufferer Bonnye L. Matthews illustrates this position of imperilment and privilege in the guide she authored, *Chemical Sensitivity*, intended to provide fellow sufferers tips from a real patient struggling with toxic overload and feeling left alone to fend for herself.[69] Matthews explains how sustained exposure to low levels of chemicals, including many of those seen in *White Noise* and *The Incredible Shrinking Woman*, destroyed her life.[70] She lost her job and was dismissed by doctors and insurance companies when she sought treatment.[71] Matthews's book is a self-help guide masquerading as a medical text, with long discussions of chemicals and medical terms and designations, intended to demonstrate her scientific rigor in approaching a "disease" dismissed by the medical establishment. More important, Matthews offers a number of ways to cope with rather than cure EI, suggesting a middle path between ignoring the symptoms or leaving society altogether.[72] She emphasizes a balanced approach because "there are times when the value of doing some particular thing outweighs the result of three to ten days of rough recuperation." Matthews's book, like others in this genre, articulated the privilege underlying MCS and EI. More often than not, sufferers chose to sustain exposure to toxins so as to enjoy the spoils of middle-class life, while leveraging their class status to spend money on a battery of alternative treatments. Her prescriptions for coping amounted to actions and behaviors that attempted to mitigate exposure while seeking help from healers, lawyers, support groups, and other individualized services that largely function affectively, services that reflected the broader contemporary shift toward marketplace solutions for social ills, including medical problems.[73]

The Invisible Prison

Evelyn Todd, a sufferer of multiple chemical sensitivity from the United Kingdom, claims that her 2015 handbook on living with the condition, *The Invisible Prison*, "is not a medical text," even though her excessive detail and explanations of her condition intimate that making this a medical text would not actually be useful for discussing this particular malady.[74] In this guide to coping with MCS, Todd gives advice about how to explain it to friends, families, and doctors, as well as various strategies for surviving in a toxic world.

In detailing her situation, Todd shows how exposure to new products and chemicals as part of her middle-class lifestyle ipso facto must be causing her symptoms. "It is quite obvious chemicals are all around us," she observes.[75] In talking about how to deal with MCS, she demonstrates her privilege by explaining costly solutions found outside the health care system, including cleaning one's home, creating containment zones, and purchasing "natural" remedies and even desert safe havens. Stories like hers demonstrated the power and pitfalls of middle-class suburban status: the causes of sickness come from the trappings of middle-class life, as do the tactics for coping with the sickness.

Like coping guides and memoirs of affliction, *Funny, You Don't Look Sick*, a 1995 documentary film shows the contradictions of suburban middle-class privilege for victims of MCS.[76] The film follows Susan Abod as she struggles with multiple chemical sensitivity. Speaking to an off-screen interviewer, Abod explains that since 1984 she has gotten sick—with fatigue, muscle pain, headaches—every six weeks. After feeling dismissed by her doctor, Abod took the advice of a friend with MCS (who traced the cause of her illness to oven fumes) and visited a clinical ecologist. Feeling validated about her suspicions that dangerous chemicals are attacking her, Abod spends nearly every day visiting doctors, herbalists, chiropractors, clinical ecologists, and other healers, trying things across the spectrum of traditional and alternative medicine. The film shows a written list detailing the things she has tried: "Acupuncture, homeopathy, cranial sacral, chiropractic, Alexander technique, bioenergetics, physical therapy, Chinese herbs, Exercise, resting/pushing through fatigue, Swedish bitters, kinesiology, anti-depressants, antigen shots, visualizations/affirmations, Enzyme Potentiation Desensitization shots." This list captures the victimization and privilege bound up in EI and MCS. Abod feels marginalized by doctors who do not see her condition as real or diagnosable—a common occurrence for women in the American medical system, and often the case with maladies that present similarly, such as chronic fatigue syndrome.[77] However, she and other middle-class women ignored or marginalized by their doctors had sufficient time and money to consult other people, who validated their pain and saw them as a patient and not as someone with a psychiatric disorder.

As part of her therapy, Susan Abod adapts her house to be environmentally safer. She has a detox room, where she changes clothes so as not to track dangerous toxins into her living space. Often, she immediately takes a shower after taking off her "contaminated" clothes (those worn outside the house) in order to minimize the spread of chemicals. She also has an "outgas" room, which serves to gradually decrease the amount of volatile chemicals found in new products. New shoes and clothes remain in this room until they are safe, and it is the permanent home of her refrigerator and its toxic emissions. Abod also uses a reading box for reading books and newspapers because, she contends, they carry so many chemical toxins. What is clear by the end of the film is that all of these efforts do not cure her condition or even prevent Abod from feeling sick. Indeed, it seems very little science undergirds her practices, as she constantly exposes herself to the chemicals that make her sick and, despite her efforts, cross-contaminates rooms like a cook who chops vegetables and raw chicken on the same cutting board. In perhaps the ultimate expression of her privilege, Abod is on both Medicaid and food stamps even as she pays for services from multiple healers and lives in her own home, thus eliding the stigma of federal assistance and accessing experts who see her as a legitimate patient who should be rehabilitated.

Still, despite these advantages, Susan Abod cannot move to a new home, not because of the cost but because of the lengthy number of accommodations she requires. Any new home needs to meet all the following conditions: "oil or electric heat, radiators or baseboards (no forced hot air heat), washer and electric dryer in ap[artmen]t, no smokers in building, no carpets, not near highway due to exhaust, no pets." Though physically disabled and therefore unable to work, Abod still operates with a number of expectations of privilege and safety and pursues them vigorously.

Whether or not Susan Abod's affliction constituted a diagnosable disease, she was able to suffer from it. She had the modern conveniences that supposedly poisoned her, the consciousness to detect the disease of MCS, and the ability to seek solutions outside traditional medicine offered by practitioners who addressed her, a middle-class suburban white woman, as a legitimate patient. These remedies were not available for many less privileged urban people of color exposed to verified toxins in, say, lead paint or drinking water.[78]

As evidenced by sufferers' experiences, doctors have largely dismissed MCS and EI as undiagnosable and thereby marked them as psychological or cultural phenomena, or both. For clinicians, it was nearly impossible to draw definitive lines of cause and effect between environmental toxins and weakness, fatigue, or headaches, and thus difficult to classify these conditions as diseases. They also called into question the treatment of chronic illness by those outside the medical establishment, fearing that some patients would miss much-needed treatment for diagnosable illnesses or see traditional medicine and unscientific treatments as equally valid.[79] In a 1994 report on MCS, the American Council on Science and Health wrote "that false claims related to 'multiple chemical sensitivity' and its associated pseudoscientific practices constitute a serious problem in our society."[80] Yet, in the 1980s and 1990s, despite long-standing skepticism of women's experiences of their own bodies, many doctors still viewed MCS and EI sufferers as legitimately in pain and requiring some kind of treatment. As psychiatrist and EI expert Harold Staudenmayer put it, the ethic of doing no harm requires doctors to treat these patients because they "are easy prey for charlatans, manipulators, and social parasites who offer diagnostic tests which have never been scientifically validated and phantom treatment couched in pseudo-scientific rhetoric."[81] This stance meant, then, that many doctors, in treating these disorders as psychosomatic or psychiatric, drove patients to seek alternative solutions most of which were available only to the privileged and that exploited both the sufferer's desire to feel well and their ability to pay for treatment.[82]

Are you allergic to the 20th century?

Embedded in the 1990s suburban landscape of gated communities and big-screen televisions, the movie *Safe* (1995) tells the story of housewife Carol Johnson's struggle with MCS. Over the film's first fifteen minutes, she moves effortlessly from home to strip mall to school and the gym while the music and camera give the audience a sense of unease as they wait for something to happen. What follows is not an event or action but a series of implications. We see Carol listen to a millennialist Christian radio DJ preach about the end times as the camera focuses on truck exhaust blowing directly at her car, leading her to cough and become woozy. As Carol starts to feel more and more ill, she also begins noticing the unavoidable prevalence of toxins in her world, such as those in her salon's hair treatment or her husband's deodorant. With her consciousness raised about chemical exposure, she spies a sign at the gym as she leaves her aerobics class:

Do you smell FUMES?
- Are you allergic to the 20th century?
- Do you have trouble breathing?
- Is your drinking water pure?
- Do you suffer from skin irritations?
- Are you always tired?

The ad seems to articulate her problems exactly, and, in contrast to the way her doctor visits end, she feels validated about her symptoms and their triggers in everyday life.

The Wrenwood Center representative who posted the sign tells Carol that her malady is real, not psychosomatic. According to the center's experts, she is suffering from environmental illness and needs to live in a "toxic free zone" in order to avoid crossing her "total load" for chemicals. The center, of course, houses just this kind of space. Cars are not even allowed to drop off new residents at the main office. At group meetings, patients repeat, "We are one with the power that created us. We are safe. And all is well in our world," reaffirming the connection between emotional status, mental outlook, and physical health seen in other contemporary texts about toxic exposure. The center's leader, Peter Dunning, argues that receding from the material world of suburban comfort will cleanse the body and restore the immune system; hence the necessity of living in the Wrenwood Center. For Peter and Carol, solutions are individual, not systemic, even if the causes are. She says, "It is up to the individual and it takes time." Her belief that "I made myself sick" leads her to retreat into a bunker at Wrenwood, further signaling the cultural and political shift toward an ethic of individualism, particularly for privileged suburbanites, that locates power to combat social ills in market solutions enacted by consumers.[83]

Safe represents the ascendant environmental fears of suburbanites in the 1990s. They had already seen environmental damage to the natural landscape and those who inhabited it, and had come to believe toxins lurked everywhere, even in the products used to make their lives easier and better. Like Carol Johnson, they were not able to make Nimby protests or deploy other forms of provincial power to materially eliminate a potential hazard. Instead, they relied on affective salves that provided a measure of emotional resolution—a sense of safety or an acquiescence to constant hazard through prophylactic practices. In this way, many suburbanites, unlike Carol but like the real sufferers of MCS and EI, chose to remain in their homes as part of a trade-off. They sought to mitigate open-ended exposure to dangerous chemicals and toxins because to avoid them would have meant rejecting the consumerism and convenience at the center of suburban life at the end of the twentieth century.

The emergence of toxic America with the discovery at Love Canal in the late 1970s was part of a new era of suburban environmental endangerment in which invisible toxins silently lurked beneath the surface of things, becoming visible only in the diseases and maladies of local residents exposed to these dangerous chemicals. After Love Canal, the news media and the EPA provided a near constant stream of identifications of new toxic sites in what ABC News called "The Killing Ground" in 1979. At the same time, popular culture narratives extended and expanded the sense of fear; at the same time, they provided modes of amelioration that helped possible victims and real sufferers cope with their toxic exposure while attempting to maintain suburban privilege and a nostalgic vision of domestic life.[84]

As in the reactions to threats from public projects, suburbanites leveraged race and class positions to fashion material and affective responses to chemical exposure. Sufferers of multiple chemical sensitivity and environmental illness posited themselves as victims requiring specialized, individual attention, as opposed to the treatment of toxic exposure in so-called "sacrifice zones" where entire communities could not escape toxic exposure.[85] In the cases of MCS and EI, the medical establishment's dismissal and marginalization of sufferers led them to seek out nonscientific, usually affective solutions to their illnesses available only to people of means. For one chemical refugee, Richard Pressinger, "Life is a beach," the *Washington Post* reported. "A clean, chemical-free beach. Pressinger, 33, retreats periodically to the shoreline sands of this Atlantic Coast community in a life-preserving effort to protect his health from airborne pesticides and synthetic chemicals."[86] In other cases, like that of Susan Abod, sufferers remained in their homes while seeking numerous kinds of alternative medicines and therapies to cope with their pain, an option that allowed them to maintain the other privileges of suburban status.

The emergence of the culture of affective defense against toxic endangerment was a particularly privileged reaction to hazard and expressed the cognitive dissonance of suburban environmentalism. The last quarter of the twentieth century saw an uninterrupted rise in consumption of material goods that often endangered users and polluted the natural environment, even as recycling became central to "being green" within consumer capitalism. Further, this cultural phenomenon helped normalize nonscientific afflictions as real and in need of treatment while encouraging individuals to seek their own answers using this same market-oriented mindset. Sufferer Bonnye L. Matthews demonstrates this in her handbook for dealing with environmental illnesses. She places medical journal articles alongside speculative, pseudo-scientific texts in order to probe the causes of MCS and detail the threats from all manner of allergens. Such manuals enabled the middle-class obsession with hidden hazards posed by food, water, vaccinations, and many other things in the twenty-first century.

In the late twentieth century, the sense of hidden, lurking, and ubiquitous danger was being woven into the fabric of suburban culture, and fears were not limited to environmental threats. At this same moment, local criminal hazards from burglars and kidnappers emerged as other seemingly invisible but potent threats to suburban privilege, leading suburbanites to see the home not as an invisible prison but as a literal one of their own design.

Chapter Three

"Fear Stalks the Streets"

Home Security, Kidnapping, and the Making of the Carceral Suburb

In the late 1970s, suburbia's reputation as a safe haven from crime began to erode. By October 1980, *U.S. News & World Report* journalist William L. Chaze signaled the visibility of this shift to a national audience. In his article "Fear Stalks the Streets," he wrote that "serious crime—on the rise again—is casting a pall over the lives of millions of Americans, not only in the nation's big cities but in the suburbs as well."[1] In this new formulation, a crisis of criminal endangerment in the suburbs nearly matched its familiar urban counterpart. Yet, as this chapter demonstrates, those conditions resulted in vastly different outcomes for inner cities and suburbs as suburbanites leveraged their seeming victimization to regulate local space and privatize police power, while urban dwellers were subject to the overwhelming power of the state.

Chaze was not alone in recognizing this change from safe to criminally endangered suburban space. In the pages of newspapers and magazines in the early 1980s, journalists and even homeowners themselves described a "bucolic burglary wave." These narratives made clear that the later waves of suburbanites had inherited not the peaceful suburban existence promised by their forebears but one pervaded by fear. Further, these experiences with and narratives of home invasion shattered notions of a secure suburban home by highlighting the sense of unease brought on not just by a rise in the number of break-ins but the personal sense of violation by strangers in private family space.[2] As *Consumer Reports* warned its readers in its August 1981 review of security systems, "You're away from home only a half-hour—a quick trip to the grocery store, say—but when you return, you find the house ransacked. You notice right away that the TV and stereo are gone. You search for the jewelry, the silverware, the camera. Gone. And, gone, too, is the feeling of safety that your home provided."[3]

Concurrently, the kidnapping of children by strangers emerged as a visible suburban threat via the well-publicized abduction and murder of Adam Walsh in 1981. News media breathlessly reported on Adam's disappearance from a

Figure 3.1. On April 7, 1978, the *Washington Post* raised the alarm about suburban home invasions in Judith Valente's article "A Bucolic Burglary Wave." From *The Washington Post.* © 1978 The Washington Post. All rights reserved. Used under license.

Hollywood, Florida, mall and the subsequent discovery of his remains in a creek one hundred miles away. The prominence of Adam's story was enhanced by a highly rated television movie, *Adam*, first aired on NBC in 1983 and rebroadcast in 1984 and 1985 with dozens of pictures of missing children shown at the movie's conclusion. *Adam*, beyond depicting a family torn apart by unexpected violence, led to a flood of news stories, television docudramas, educational videos, and novels about a kidnapping "epidemic," which only bolstered the sense of danger on suburban streets. Together, these suburban crimes and their iterations in the media added to the sense of endemic suburban criminal danger emanating not from an "urban" outsider coded as nonwhite but from an insidious, local threat that moved effortlessly through suburban space and that made itself known only through the crime itself.

This is not to say that race did not matter in the era's suburban crime culture. As seen in the senseless murder of Trayvon Martin by George Zimmerman in 2012, racial otherness did and still does represent threat to suburbanites. However, by the late 1970s, something changed in the active policing of racial boundaries carried out by white citizen's councils and individual homeowners in the immediate postwar period. While maintaining their suspicion of people of color, suburbanites could also imagine, fear, and be victimized by white criminals moving seamlessly through largely white spaces. Indeed, news media and popular culture presented crimes like kidnapping and burglary as committed by raceless actors moving undetected through these spaces. In this way, the actual crimes and their cultural reproductions often did not fit neatly the racist notions of the era as to who was a criminal or who committed crimes. In fact, their ability to fit in and move freely is what made suburban kidnappers and burglars so threatening. They could be insiders committing local crime who could not easily be identified or regulated. Racial outsiders of that period, then, were not the focus of suburban crime culture. Instead, they were caught up in the broader security practices of the era to devastating effect. One on hand, suburban protocols that sought to protect against insidious and apparently ubiquitous threats to streets, homes, and schools still assiduously identified and policed people of color. On the other, suburban ideas and practices premised on a rising tide of crime further sustained the wars on crime and drugs that largely focused on urban populations and had calamitous outcomes for those communities.

Popular culture both reflected and produced this change in the perceptions of suburban crime and the solutions to it. In the early 1980s, two popular pillars of the urban vigilante film genre, *Death Wish* and *Sudden Impact*, moved the settings of their latest iterations to the suburbs. As protagonists Paul Kersey and "Dirty Harry" Callahan search for serenity in the safe confines of quiet bedroom communities, they find crime there as pervasive and violent as in New York City or San Francisco, and traditional law enforcement methods just as incapable of fighting it. In depicting retribution for corruption, drug trafficking, murder, and rape, these films enacted vigilante fantasies of both preemptive power to stop crimes before they happen and righteous revenge through morally justified, extralegal responses to unrelenting menace. Not long after, John Walsh, the father of kidnapped and murdered child Adam Walsh, presented another vision of suburban vigilantism on Fox's *America's Most Wanted*. Though more grounded in the realities of law enforcement, the show also imagined a suburban landscape filled with dangerous criminals but with the homeowner as an "armchair vigilante." These illusions proved powerful in buttressing the notion that the individual suburbanite and not the state was the moral center of American life, capable of dispensing justice, and empowered to do so, on a newly embattled landscape.

To protect themselves, suburbanites made their perceived criminal victimization productive by creating new, private defensive measures to keep themselves safe when law enforcement could not or would not do so.[4] In increasing numbers, homeowners embraced neighborhood watch programs originally created to combat urban crime, installed alarm systems to secure families inside the home, and eventually, many moved into gated communities with private security forces.[5] In tandem with those initiatives, schools and parents implemented new security programs like Stranger Danger and bought educational board games such as *Safely Home* to prepare children for the dangers that strangers and family constantly presented in suburban spaces. Through these tactics adopted in response to the pervasive fear of crime, suburbanites reasserted and expanded their control of local spaces in ways that also buttressed the expansion of the carceral state by making material a continued fear of crime.

Suburban residents were empowered to control space through private means and advantageous relationships with the state that allowed and even facilitated suburban security practices. Homeowners safeguarded their houses, patrolled their streets, and regulated entry into their neighborhoods largely with the help of local law enforcement, while city police profiled, harassed, and brutalized city dwellers of color and generated historic rates of incarceration for those populations.[6] Yet the state served not only as a facilitator of homeowner action but also as a foil whose failures necessitated the privatization of security practices. Indeed, many municipal police forces, often with low numbers of officers, were caught between austerity politics and the increasing demands of local residents whose fear of crime was heightened despite declining crime statistics.[7] Meanwhile, urban residents had a fundamentally different relationship with massively funded and militarized city police departments.[8] Ultimately, this shift in both beliefs and practices lead to an increasingly privatized world of suburban security that provided a sense of safety while also reminding this otherwise privileged group of their daily imperilment.[9]

From alarm systems and Stranger Danger, suburbanites moved toward gated communities with private security forces (more than twenty thousand of them by 1998) and acted as the new suburban vigilantes, like the easy-chair crusaders among *America's Most Wanted*'s audience. Soon after, these cultural changes not only made way for the passage of the 1994 federal crime bill but also facilitated the creation of Stand Your Ground laws and expansions in the Castle Doctrine that made possible new vigilantes, such as George Zimmerman, empowered to kill while on neighborhood watch as a "color-blind" defender of property rights.[10]

Together, these co-constitutive changes in media, popular culture, and everyday practice transformed the central associations of the suburban landscape from the safe cul-de-sacs mythologized in 1950s and '60s sitcoms to an environment presumed to be under sustained attack from violent criminals. In this way, the cultural shifts created the carceral suburb, where homeowners functioned as both warden and inmate in a jail of their own design. This condition resulted from calling forth protections against crime that provided a *feeling* of safety and enabled local spatial dominion while simultaneously reminding suburbanites of pervasive criminal hazards limiting both their physical freedom and undermining the suburban liberation that the flight from urban crisis was supposed to have secured them.[11] Safety from crime was assumed to be an implicit benefit of suburban living in the postwar world. The city in crisis, marked by burglary, rape, robbery, racial discord, and general unrest, was not a particularly palatable option for whites who could move and were being enticed to do so by banks, developers, government, and real estate agents. As one Chicago resident said in 1983, "My suburban friends can no longer ask me, 'Aren't you afraid to live in the city?' Child-snatching, guns, robberies—these things give suburbanites an urban mentality."[12] Indeed, those who left for suburban housing developments like Levittown did so to create a new, more manageable world through racial segregation and local control and avoid the risks of danger and disorder in the city.

Yet, by the mid-1970s, suburbanites found that crime was not only more visible but local. This failure to inherit safe streets and secure homes, along with the ongoing fear that accompanied it, was the suburban crime crisis that emerged toward the end of the twentieth century. This crisis and suburbanites' responses to it allowed them to powerfully reshape their landscape and privatize police power. Their productive victimization was facilitated by the "tough on crime" culture in the era of mass incarceration, which encouraged seeing the world as endangered by crime that required an overwhelming response. In turn, the cultural reproduction of fear and suburban actions to address it gave evidence to lawmakers of the need for stricter laws, more police on the streets, and an expansion of the carceral state.

Our homes have become our castles under siege

In the late 1970s, suburbanites who had once left doors unlocked and windows open were feeling compelled by news reports and neighbors' tales of victimization to turn to security systems to protect themselves against home invasions because, as the *New York Times* reported in 1982, "the sanctity of suburban neighborhoods has long since been violated by crime."[13] These stories in the early 1980s depicted "brazen thieves" committing "a wave of home burglaries that has engulfed suburban areas nationwide," even though federal crime statistics from 1982 showed burglaries reaching a low since record keeping began in 1973.[14] This perceived wave encouraged suburbanites to see their environment as endangered and act to reverse a clear loss of what was best about suburban living. Suzanne Sprawel, a resident of a Connecticut suburb, summed up the changing view of suburban life in this moment: "You used to think that because you lived in a suburb you would be O.K. . . . Now you have to be alert no matter where you live."[15] News stories like these portrayed a real, persistent threat from home invasion that justified action by homeowners and, by the mid-1980s, seemed to require it.

According to homeowners and security experts, this new hazard could best be dealt with through private means like installing a home security system, because expecting prophylactic police protection was not reasonable.[16] As *U.S. News & World Report* observed, "People from coast to coast are acting on their own to obtain better security, no longer content to rely on law-enforcement officials alone for protection"; or, as alarm system owner Ginny Tyzzer said, "It's a great comfort knowing you won't be surprised coming home."[17] Similarly, a resident of a Greenwich, Connecticut, suburb confessed in 1980, "You can't live here anymore without a burglar alarm system. . . . It's a way of life. Just about everyone I know has been robbed."[18] In a 1981 *Chicago Tribune* article, "Here's How—Short of a Moat—to Protect Your Castle," author Patricia Yoxall echoed these concerns. She emphasized the primacy of a burglar alarm in protecting one's home: "Alarms are about your only defense unless you have someone sitting in the house all day."[19] Even sunny home improvement guru Bob Vila recommended homeowners look beyond strong locks and doors to home security systems to protect themselves against the alleged one-in-fourteen chance of a home invasion.[20]

These stories and many others like them demonstrated two powerful beliefs that suburbanites held about where they lived in the 1980s. First, actual incidents and the news media narratives of rising crime undermined suburbanites' views of their neighborhoods as the safe, quiet alternative to urban living where "you didn't need to worry about dark streets or menacing strangers."[21] Second, they explicitly advised suburban readers that they needed a security system as a crucial defensive measure to restore a sense of safety *and* control—guidance that both reflected and produced the sense that law enforcement could not be counted on. As retired detective James Motherway admitted in 1983, "Police don't have the manpower to respond quickly—if they can respond at all."[22] An Associated Press article put it more bluntly in 1980, "You may have no one but yourself to blame if your house is robbed."[23] In 1982, James K. Stewart, the Reagan-appointed director of the National Institute of Justice, summed up this moment of transition when, rather than rely on ineffective state action, individuals must protect themselves, as businesses already had, by exercising their power in the marketplace: "Individual citizens, too, have turned to substitutes for the kind of watchman services that public agencies can no longer offer. They have voted with their dollars to supplement publicly provided protection systems and to achieve a greater sense of safety. The unmet security needs perceived by many are increasingly being filled by private enterprise."[24]

This trend was in direct contrast to urban crime policies, particularly the surveillance and policing of public housing. The use of security technologies, ranging from controlled access to closed-circuit television surveillance, was implemented and controlled by the government, not by building residents. Even when residents instituted their own programs, they had to be approved by federal authorities before implementation. Instead of fostering a semblance of safety and control, such measures and devices reinforced the idea of public housing as chaotic, its residents as criminal and in need of constant policing by a supposedly effective security force.[25] Conversely, the emerging sense of the suburb as criminally endangered because of police failures there helped justify the privatization of suburban security that expanded suburbanite's local sovereignty. Through their perceived victimization, suburbanites continued to fuel the broader notion of rampant crime supporting punitive urban policing policies and reductions in urban aid for social programs.[26]

First-person narratives of suburban homeowners violated by home invasions recounted the personal horror of having the sanctity of one's households disturbed and articulated an ongoing belief that since police could not protect them, homeowners had to take personal action. As part of a series in the *New York Times* entitled "Once upon a Time in the Safety of the Suburbs," homeowner Linda Saslow wrote, "We followed the promise of security, and one by one our plans were thwarted; our dreams were shattered. And we have sadly been forced to compromise on our ideals, as slowly we began to contradict our original plans."[27] The suburbs that she remembered from her youth had turned into dangerous landscapes where "burglar alarms and panic buttons have been installed in more homes than ever before." The suburb was now a place where she and her husband "fear the consequences of allowing our children to play unsupervised in the neighborhood"—a marked contrast from the family-friendly suburban vision sold to the first generation of postwar suburbanites and their children.[28]

Just as burglaries were on the rise and people like Linda Saslow were looking for ways to protect their homes, the burglar alarm industry made systems a viable and affordable defensive option for middle-class suburbanites. In the 1970s, smaller and cheaper electronic parts allowed the industry to expand its services from a traditional focus on protecting banks and other large commercial enterprises to the home market, just as homeowners were feeling unsafe.[29] With little maintenance or expertise on the homeowner's part, the systems provided instant notification of a breach to the owner, a private security force, local police, or all three. Although these systems still relied on police to apprehend a burglar, by equipping homeowners with an alarm *they* could arm, security companies provided suburbanites with a greater *sense* of control over the borders of their homes. This was a privilege for those who could afford an alarm system and could still rely on local police as an on-call security force that would eventually show up to help them, rather than a presence to be feared in their neighborhood.

In the debate over the 1983 federal crime bill, some members of Congress echoed this concern about security as a luxury only for the privileged. They feared that without more funding for law enforcement, only the most affluent Americans would be protected because only they could afford to protect themselves. Indeed, a representative of the National Burglar and Fire Alarm Association had already noted in 1977 that the fastest-growing segment of his business was residential home alarm systems, which, at a cost between $350 and $1,500 were relatively expensive.[30]

Alarm systems' visibility in public discussion indicates that homeowners installed alarms at a significantly higher rate starting in the late 1970s.[31] An industry survey of 75 million homes with an alarm system showed a rise from just 1.9 percent in 1978 to 8.6 percent in 1983, when the aggregate US residential security business was worth $1.13 billion.[32] "I've been in business for 20 years and I've never been so busy," one alarm company owner commented in 1980.[33] Some municipalities saw alarm systems as essential to creating a modern suburb. New cable TV operators that wished to provide service to residents in the planned community of The Woodlands, Texas, for example, were required to provide home security monitoring.[34] Suburban police found themselves responding to a growing number of false alarms as a result of the dramatic increase in the number of homes with security systems. Rather than an intruder opening a door or climbing through a window, pets, kids, or forgetful spouses were the ones triggering the alarm nearly every time, suggesting crime statistics that showed a decrease in home invasions accurately portrayed the true threat of home invasion.[35] False alarms became so numerous—as many as eighty times a month in Weston, Connecticut, in 1983—that many jurisdictions moved to a fee system whereby homeowners paid local police when they responded to a false alarm.[36] Yet, by 1983, alarm systems had become as much a suburban fixture "as the lawn mower," as the *New York Times* quipped.[37] Just as mowers appeared necessary to maintaining the picturesque lawns thought essential to the American suburb, alarms were becoming necessary to maintain safe homes.

As home security systems seemingly became a suburban necessity, alarm companies played to ongoing fears of home invasions in selling their systems. From the late 1980s to the late 1990s, the security company ADT reproduced the sense of continuing danger of a burglary and the solution of an alarm system through its television advertising. Some of these ads echoed the feelings expressed by Linda Saslow in her essay on experiencing a home invasion. In one example, the viewer sees a first-person camera shot of a homeowner walking through their ransacked home as a narrator says: "No matter where you've been, there is nothing like the feeling of coming home. Unless you have been the victim of a burglary. It's traumatizing to lose sentimental objects, as well as your valuables. You feel violated, vulnerable. You've lost your piece of mind."[38] The commercial connects the fear of losing possessions with the broader loss of a feeling of safety, an assurance that can be restored only by buying an ADT home security system. Another commercial goes further by portraying a burglar entering the home when the owner is home alone, once again promoting the feeling of ongoing endangerment in the suburban home. The ad shows a black screen and various typewritten quotes such as "Did you hear that?" "Was that from outside?" "There it is again," as the viewer hears a window breaking, a door creak, and a long bang mixed with a menacing synthesizer-produced tone.[39]

In addition to showing the perspective of the homeowner dealing with home invasion, a different ad features actors playing burglars. Shot on grainy black-and-white film, the criminals explain all the ways they can break into a house without a security system. One of them advises, "If I had a family, I would want to protect them from guys like me."[40] In this advertisement, ADT argues that the fear of burglary is not a myth but a real and persistent threat because of men like the ones portrayed, criminals who will probe for every weakness in your home's defense. That ad built to another in 1993, showing a police officer returning home from work to a home protected by ADT. The threat was so severe that the narrator reminds the viewer that law enforcement personnel use it to protect their own "prized possessions," their wives and children.[41]

Even as crime rates plummeted in the 1990s, a 1999 ad reminded homeowners that they needed an ADT system. This commercial showed families holding signs touting the success of their ADT systems; for example, "Burglary free 9½ years." Those testimonials were posed as tenuous successes, however. As the danger from a burglar is continuous, the ad told viewers, they now need "security for life."[42] Although the ads mentioned that systems can help in the case of a fire or other emergencies, the campaign focused on stoking fear of a home invasion in order to sell ADT security systems. Using stark imagery and dramatic music, the ads were another reminder to homeowners that they were constantly being targeted by burglars. In that world of constant danger, an ADT system would give homeowners the feeling of security and control they longed for in the neighborhood of fear.

In addition to installing security systems, suburbanites also initiated neighborhood watch programs, appropriating an urban scheme and adapting it to their own needs.[43] These programs varied in levels of organization and community involvement, but their very premise revealed the culture of the carceral suburb. According to the basic design of the neighborhood watch program, citizens would serve as adjuncts to the local police department by working closely with

Know-how

Bottom line on securing the homefront

By Terry Osborne

According to FBI figures, a burglary occurs in the U.S. every 10 seconds. And recent Chicago Police Department statistics show that the home burglary rate rose 85 percent between 1981 and 1984. Any way you slice the numbers, the news is not good. As a result, the home security business has been very good.

And nothing ignites consumer awareness about home security more than a little paranoia. You've seen reformed burglars reminding you how vulnerable you are, only to promote a new security device. The technique hits home, because those of us who have had our homes burgled know those subsequent feelings of frustration and vulnerability.

But paranoia is not the answer. Let's take a calm look at the facts about burglary. Some of them are not pleasant, but once you accept them, you can make more rational home security choices.

First the good news. Securing your home is not only an intelligent idea, it is effective. Statistics show that most burglars follow the path of least resistance; so if your house resists enough, the burglar is likely to go elsewhere.

Now the bad news. If a burglar wants to get into your home badly enough, he or she will, regardless of whether your doors are wide open or made of solid steel and wired with an alarm. Given enough time and planning, a burglar can break in most anywhere.

The point is this: Everyone is vulnerable to burglary. However, you can lessen the risk of burglary by the degree to which you secure your home. The home with a full-scale, monitored alarm system is certainly safer than the same home with only single door locks.

But half the battle of home security is feeling comfortable with the amount of security you choose.

First, do your homework. Go to the local library. Books such as "Total Home Security," by Family Handyman magazine [Butterick, $6.95], or "Prevent Burglary," by Mick Davis [Prentice-Hall, $8.95], present chapters of security options and many helpful hints as well. Also, talk to friends who have beefed up their security.

Then assess your home and your priorities: How much security do you want, how much can you afford and how many of its drawbacks are you willing to live with? For example, if you don't want to worry about arming and disarming your alarm every time you go to the corner store, then you'd probably be happier with better locks and lighting. Be realistic and rational.

Here is a quick sampling of some of your options.

Before you think about hardware,

Continued on page 50

Illustration by Rick Tuma

Figure 3.2. The *Chicago Tribune*'s visualization of the carceral suburban home on March 7, 1986. Article by Terry Osborne; image courtesy of Rick Tuma

officers to observe neighborhoods, report crimes, and spot fugitives whose mugshots were shown on local "crime-stopper" television shows.[44] In this way, the programs articulated the new facilitator-foil relationship with police in which law enforcement couldn't possibly do the job alone but was still required for the watch to be effective. Beyond demonstrating the suburbs' changing affiliations with the state, these programs also revealed the dialectic of the carceral suburb. The essential tasks of the neighborhood watch, the patrolling of streets and marking of territory, functioned as affective practices that aroused and affirmed feelings of fear and safety. That suburban neighborhoods needed to be watched at all, let alone bear the material reminders of signs, stickers, and patrols, continually produced fear in residents. At the same time, the knowledge that residents were on guard and that police were on call inspired a sense of safety that bound together potential victimization with the power to regulate space.

In practice, the street patrol functioned as a mostly passive system of surveillance that sought to identify "outsiders" or other potential threats, from the strange man luring children into the mythical white van to the African American teen simply visiting a friend. A *Washington Post* article described the watch shift that a McLean, Virginia, couple performed in 1981: "They cruise along silent streets, glimpsing suburban life through open curtains. A cocktail party at one house, the kids glued to the television at another. A woman sitting behind a baby grand piano in the picture window across the way. And then there are the empty houses, the ones cloaked in inky blackness. The car slows to a creep. They peer into the shadows. They strain to see around the shrubbery. No one in sight. They move on."[45] The volunteers, it seems, stared into windows and snooped around yards as much for a sense of "active" crime prevention and a voyeuristic thrill as for actually catching a criminal or stopping any lawbreaking, particularly in the era before legislatures emboldened citizens to confront "threats" through Stand Your Ground laws. Richard M. Titus, writing in 1984 for a Department of Justice study on the community response to residential burglaries in the United States, noted that these programs in suburbs "give citizens some training and a lot of crime watch paraphernalia—stickers, signs, buttons, jackets—everything they need to watch crime except the popcorn and soda pop. They give people a feeling of false satisfaction that they are actually doing something constructive to reduce a problem that seems beyond everyone's control."[46] Instead of fighting crime, neighborhood patrolling was largely an affective practice that afforded participants the chance to revel in possibly seeing something beyond mundane suburban activities but, simultaneously, reminded residents they had the power to surveil and police and could avoid being regulated themselves.

The most common feature of neighborhood watch programs was the posting of signs and stickers to mark an area under "active" watch.[47] These markers encapsulated the culture of the carceral suburb, a territory under surveillance where signs reminded residents of the possibility of crime in their neighborhood but suggested that someone was watching who would help. Yet the posting of signs likely undermined actual efforts to stop lawbreaking, showing the limits of passive surveillance. As Titus observed in his study of neighborhood watch programs, "For a criminal, seeing the THIS IS A CRIME WATCH NEIGHBORHOOD sign is like giving him carte blanche to take whatever he wants without fear of being stopped. He knows he can go wherever he wants to, that no one will stop him, and that no one will dare to come out into the streets from behind their peepholes."[48] In its most effective incarnation, then, neighborhood watch was a program that mirrored the dominant mode of home security in that it worked as "a large alarm system" premised on the failure of law enforcement but needing the state to actually catch criminals.[49] These signs symbolized the values of the carceral suburb. Residents marked territory, regulated it, and, to some degree, acted in their own defense. Yet, in doing so, they likely did not prevent crime but produced a sense of their ongoing imperilment.

Narratives of suburban home invasion like these also surfaced in popular culture, most notably in a 1982 episode of the highly rated TV sitcom *Family Ties*, "Have Gun Will Unravel." Upon returning home from a movie, the Keatons find that burglars have ransacked their home and stolen valuables and mementos. As the episode progresses, we see members of the family move with trepidation through the home at night. When father Steven Keaton is startled by a broom falling to the floor, he tells the family, "We can't let fear take over our lives." Rather than install a security system, they decide to join their local neighborhood watch program, and after a local cop tells them that crime is rising and nothing really stops a persistent burglar, they buy a gun for protection. The first night with the gun, Alex (Michael J. Fox) noisily arrives home late at night, prompting his father to head downstairs to investigate. Startled by Alex's presence, Steven is thankful he left the gun upstairs; otherwise he might have shot his own son. They return the gun and choose to live with the fear of home invasion. This episode encapsulated suburban crime culture of the 1980s, in which privileged suburban families suddenly felt endangered by crime and called up to act in their own defense, only to find themselves trapped in their own homes and still in danger.

The need for neighborhood watch and the widespread installation of alarm systems symbolized the loss of what the suburb had once meant—the privilege of not thinking about safety. As Clark Mulford, who worked in the home alarm business, reasoned, "People hate to buy these systems. . . . It's admitting defeat. It's admitting that this is the way things are." And a *Washington Post* headline opined, "It's Time to Stop Letting the Criminals Imprison Us."[50] Homeowner Linda Saslow ended her "Speaking Personally" narrative of suburban crime with the hope that suburbs might yet return to the condition she had known in her youth: "Disillusioned and frustrated, we continue to hope for the day when once again we can enjoy suburban living for all the qualities that allured us, once upon a time."[51] She longed for a suburban world where she wouldn't have "to think, before turning a door knob or cranking a window, whether the alarm is on or off."[52] Although crimes like burglary and kidnapping surely happened in those earlier suburbs, an average homeowner was unlikely to know about or experience them firsthand. By the 1980s, however, crime was visible and sometimes real and, therefore, legitimately threatening. And, rather than denying the threat, suburban families took security measures that produced and even enhanced the sense of danger, creating the carceral suburb where families more heavily regulated their own homes and neighborhoods to feel safe.

Homeowner Susan Ladov lamented this daily reminder of her unwilling incarceration. In her essay for "Speaking Personally," she captured the essence of the carceral suburb—the continuing sense of fear and powerlessness that led to empowerment through private solutions to suburban crime, solutions that provided some security at the price of losing physical freedom and a sense of emancipation.[53] Following the burglary of her home in 1981, she wrote, "Each time I return home, . . . there is a moment when I imagine somebody retreating at the sound of the garage door opening. Walking into my bedroom, I remember my icy fear when two embroidered handkerchiefs lying on the floor told me that someone had been through my dresser drawers. I feel violated by strange hands that felt their way through piles of nightgowns and underwear." Ladov took that violation, and its implications of breached privacy and sexual assault, as visceral evidence that the suburbs were not as safe or secure as she remembered or hoped they still were. The ongoing trepidation about entering her own home lest a sexual predator lay in wait led Ladov and her husband to reluctantly install an alarm system. Their story reflected the tradeoff involved in having a security system in the new era of suburban life. Though ostensibly "safer," she felt "angry and saddened . . . when I recall the vanishing pleasure of wide-open windows" in the days before having to adopt her new, "secure" lifestyle.

As warden and inmate, many suburbanites enjoyed the privilege of security and experienced the restrictions of incarceration. However, that compromise, and the security crisis it represented, justified continued reinforcement of suburban security with walls, gates, and police forces, with private power being the ultimate manifestation of productive criminal victimization.[54] Still, it was not just home invasions that shifted the association of the suburb from safe haven to criminally endangered space. Kidnappings also contributed to the sense of fear and lack of belief in law enforcement that led to new expressions of suburban vulnerability, power, and privilege into the twenty-first century.

I thought crime happened somewhere in the inner city

On July 27, 1981, six-year-old Adam Walsh accompanied his mother, Revè, to the Hollywood Mall in Hollywood, Florida. While shopping for lamps at Sears, Revè left her son in the store with other boys playing video games. Moments later, she returned and could not find him. Adam's parents searched frantically for their son. Having not found him at the mall, they posted flyers, called other parents, and even appeared on local and national television to urge others to be on the lookout. Two weeks later, following the largest search for a child to that point in Florida history, police found Adam's remains in a canal in Vero Beach, Florida, a little over 130 miles from where he was abducted.[55]

Following Adam's death, John and Revè doggedly lobbied Congress to enact new kidnapping laws to empower the FBI and local authorities to move more quickly in the case of a missing child. Although the Walshes succeeded in this effort, Adam's story and its various elaborations in news media and popular culture profoundly changed how suburbanites understood and regulated their local spaces in the 1980s. His case, and the so-called kidnapping epidemic it represented, worked with narratives of home invasion to associate suburban space with criminal danger while spurring new educational and regulatory regimes to control that space with and beyond state assistance.

Before Adam, there had been few national news stories about a kidnapping committed in a public space by a stranger. One exception was the story of Etan Patz, a New York City child kidnapped on his way to school in 1978. His case garnered attention in the New York area when his parents created a private organization to find missing children, the Etan Patz Action Committee. The story, however, did not significantly disrupt Americans' ideas about the location and character of crime, as Etan Patz was abducted from a Brooklyn street during some of the city's darkest days in terms of crime. In addition, since he was never found, Etan's story did not have the narrative closure that might have helped his case transcend the New York City media market and fuel a greater fear about abductions.[56]

Three months before Adam Walsh's abduction and murder, dozens of abductions and murders of black children and teenagers, known collectively as the Atlanta child murders, came to light, but they also functioned differently in 1980s crime discourse. The series of twenty-nine murders beginning in 1979 initially prompted an overwhelming response from local, state, and federal law enforcement, including the intervention of Vice President George H. W. Bush.

Once suspect Wayne Williams was arrested and convicted in 1982 of murdering two men not on the list of abducted children, law enforcement stopped pursuing leads despite the fact that Williams was not prosecuted for any of the child murders. Nor did police forces begin to approach urban kidnapping as an epidemic, in part because the parents, relatives, and friends of the murdered children fared much differently than the Walshes and their allies did later. Mothers who rallied for justice came under scrutiny for allowing their children to be abducted, a reaction that built on the broad pathologizing of "dysfunctional" urban black families in postwar America.[57] In response to these crimes, black Atlantans, like suburbanites, also took to the streets to protect their families. With squads of men and teenagers roaming the streets with baseball bats, these communities sought to step in where the police had failed.[58] Unlike suburban neighborhood watch programs, these patrols were viewed skeptically by police. Not surprisingly, either, the affected communities did not welcome increased police presence in their neighborhoods, for what came was not protection but suspicion and often arrests. As in Adam's story, the Atlanta child murders did generate news coverage and a television movie. However, those media portrayals did not valorize the efforts of parents or lead to a broader cultural shift in notions of urban kidnapping, as *Adam* did for suburban communities.[59] Rather, these images and narratives reinforced the "ghettoization" of the inner city and policymakers' racist view that its residents had failed to successfully self-regulate, necessitating the intensified policing of urban spaces.

Adam's story, in contrast, struck a nerve and exposed parents' nascent fears of suburban crime, concerns already heightened by narratives of burglary and home invasion. Further, accounts that appeared about Adam Walsh built on the notion of the essential innocence of white suburban children embedded in American culture, an idea that amplified fear of stranger kidnappings.[60] According to reports, the boy had led a "very sheltered life" and had been "a well-behaved youth who never talked to strangers."[61] His tragic fate set the stakes for protecting children and established a frame for understanding stranger kidnappings as white and suburban in the 1980s. In calling for action on missing and abducted children in 1981, for example, the *New York Times* juxtaposed Adam's story to the announcement that over fifty thousand children were abducted each year and were, the story implied, likely to meet an end like Adam's.[62] Similarly, *Newsweek*, in a cover story titled "Stolen Children," held up Adam's story to claim that thousands of children were abducted every year in "a crime of predatory cruelty usually committed by pedophiles, pornographers, black-market baby peddlers or childless psychotics bidding desperately for parenthood."[63] Using the frame of Adam's abduction, news media raised the profile of child abductions by strangers to the level of an "epidemic."[64]

As it turned out, these accounts greatly exaggerated the number of stranger kidnappings per year. The oft-quoted numbers of fifty thousand to two million stranger abductions a year in the 1980s was closer to seventy-five per year according to federal statistics.[65] Though many children went missing, most were runaways who returned home within forty-eight hours. In nearly all the other cases, a parent or family member abducted the child as part of a custody dispute. Yet Adam's atypical story of being taken in a public place by a stranger became the symbol of the supposedly widespread threat of stranger abductions, a threat that forged the link between a kidnapping "epidemic" and suburban streets. Despite some backlash against the hysteria over child abductions, the overwhelming trend inaugurated by the Walsh story was a new mindfulness about children's vulnerability to this high-stakes threat and the state's failure to protect its children or even find those already missing. This awareness spurred many families to protect themselves.

The 1983 television movie *Adam*, aired nationally on NBC, connected the problem of stranger abductions to the need for preventive private action before police or the FBI would be called in to locate an already-missing child. Through the television dramatization of this story, "the nation was galvanized to stop child snatching and find other missing 'Adams.'"[66] Broadcast two years after the kidnapping, the film refreshed the public's memory of Adam's gruesome murder, and transformed that memory as well, as audiences did not just see grieving parents on television asking for help but a fair-haired child heading off to certain doom at the most quotidian of suburban locations, the mall. *Adam* effectively consolidated the story of the boy's abduction and murder, covering in less than two hours the sad saga: the kidnapping, the murder, the failures of law enforcement, and the aftermath, when his parents lobbied for stronger kidnapping laws and better law enforcement response to child abductions. Bringing the problem of missing children directly into American living rooms, *Adam* established that child abduction was a real, high-stakes threat, with stranger abductions supposedly in the tens of thousands each year, and it could happen in the safest of locales, even ones like the Walshes' sunny suburban town, if proper precautions were not taken.[67]

Adam accomplished all this by showing the Walshes as an average suburban family and their story as one that could happen to any household. The film opens with an exterior shot of the Walsh home on a sunny, tree-lined Florida street. Inside, the family is eating breakfast before John Walsh (played by Daniel J. Travanti) heads to work and Revè Walsh (JoBeth Williams) takes their son, Adam, with her to the mall. The shots of blue skies and a cheery family breakfast are quickly and ominously contrasted with the scene as Revè and Adam enter the mall. She leaves him with some other boys to play video games while she goes to the lamp store. When she returns after only a few minutes, Adam and the other boys are gone. The soundtrack kicks in with distorted, disorienting synthesizer tones, not unlike the score to the urban dystopian movie *Taxi Driver*, to emphasize her surprise and confusion at her son's disappearance. As reality sets in, Revè searches feverishly for Adam. He is paged by mall security while Revè and her mother-in-law comb the shopping center to no avail. Shortly thereafter, John arrives at the mall and joins the search. From this point forward, the filmmakers assumed the audience had some familiarity with Adam's demise. Rather than focusing on the mystery of Adam's whereabouts, the film centers on the Walshes' travails with law enforcement and the media in order to highlight suburban police departments' general ignorance about kidnappings, and to jolt the audience into action using the emotional fallout from the discovery of Adam's remains.

One of the film's central themes is the inability of the police to help the Walshes. Although *Adam* portrays law enforcement officers as well intentioned, it also shows them to be ill-equipped to deal with child abduction. The police officers in the film remain calm—too calm, it seems, given the enormity of the situation. They form search parties, call in help from other jurisdictions, and put out word to local television stations. Yet no one manages to read the notices sent between local police departments advising them to be on the lookout for stolen cars, let alone missing children. In a pivotal scene, John Walsh happens upon a long computer printout in a corner of the Hollywood Police Department. He and the audience realize that the word about Adam's abduction is not getting out effectively. That failure is compounded by the revelation that the FBI's hands are tied unless Adam has been transported across state lines or a ransom request has been made. John exclaims that the FBI has a database of missing cars but not missing kids.

With the terrible outcome of the kidnapping already known, the failures of the local police and the FBI in the film served as a visceral and damning reminder to viewers of the grave failures of law enforcement in dealing with child abduction, a threat that the educational segments run before and after the film posited as widespread.

These educational bookends to the program framed Adam's tragic story in terms of parental responsibility. They argued strongly that individual families had to protect against this epidemic with education and action. The film began with a public service message about kidnapping presented by *Facts of Life* star Nancy McKeon and her brother Phil, who appeared on the television show *Alice*. They recited startling facts about kidnappings in the United States and reminded the audience to stay tuned at the end of the movie for tips to help prevent their own son or daughter from becoming a statistic. When they returned, they gave viewers a set of "life-saving" instructions. The list included maintaining up-to-date photos and dental records, knowing the outfit your child wears every day, and following safe practices when parents were not around. With kidnappings on the rise, the McKeons reiterated, these bits of information, no matter how small, could save a child's life. These segments reflected a contemporary educational impulse that put the onus on parents and children to stop abductions— even going so far as to have the hosts suggest that if parents did not institute these new measures, their children would be in grave danger from kidnapping, molestation, and murder.

In the same vein, Home Box Office (HBO) produced and aired *How to Raise a Street Smart Child* in 1987.[68] That program, also available for purchase on VHS, went even further by portraying suburban kids actively being stalked and harassed by strangers in three different scenarios. The program opened with a blonde-haired child of five or six named Josh answering a phone. As the stranger talks to Josh, the camera pulls back from a close-up of the phone all the way across the street where, presumably, the stranger, asking about the boy's parents and offering ice cream, is surreptitiously watching him like a predator stalking his prey. This entire conversation is scored with a discordant, piano-and-synthesizer horror movie soundtrack that foreshadows the inevitable crime to come. Two vignettes follow in which a stranger approaches a boy fixing his bike on a suburban sidewalk, and another walks up to a young girl sitting on a diving board alone in her backyard. Host Daniel J. Travanti, who played John Walsh in *Adam*, then appears to explain that faces on milk cartons are not enough, because "the statistics are staggering." The threat of child abduction and molestation is too real and too pervasive for such passive action. "The time has come," he says, articulating the logic of productive victimization, "to replace fear with power." With murder and kidnapping as real threats, so the logic went, suburbanites must be proactive in protecting children and policing streets; otherwise they will be left searching for a missing son or daughter or burying a dead child.

This attitude is demonstrated by John Walsh in his memoir, *Tears of Rage*. "The cops meant well," Walsh argues, but were not up to the task.[69] He reiterated the failure of law enforcement in his testimony before Congress in 1984: "What have I learned in 2½ years? That every parent's nightmare is a reality in America. That most laws are medieval, or nonexistent, as they relate to child safety and protection. . . . This is 1984 not 1954. No matter how protective your environment is, or you think it is, tomorrow's victim could be your child or grandchild."[70] In essence, he argued times have changed, as homeowners violated by burglary also acknowledged. For this generation of homeowners, the expectations of postwar suburbia as safe and peaceful were illusions with tragic consequences. In confronting these dangers, they recognized no one will help you but yourself, a recognition leading to new practices to secure families, homes, and neighborhoods.

In a moment of profound anxiety about a supposed kidnapping epidemic in which the state had failed to protect children, nonprofit organizations worked with toy manufacturers and publishers to create new educational games and books designed to help children survive dangerous suburban streets. Like the educational segments of *Adam*, board games, flashcards, handbooks, and lovable cartoon characters taught children how to avoid criminal hazards, all the while reminding them that local schools, homes, and streets were unsafe.

Emblazoned with an image based on Adam Walsh's iconic Little League uniform photo, *The Child Awareness Game*, developed by the Adam Walsh Child Resource Center in 1986, was created "to educate adults and children about how to avoid dangers that exist for children in our society."[71] In the game, players move along the board through a number of dangerous scenarios in everyday suburban locations, getting rewards for safely evading a threatening situation. In the game's scenarios, the home itself is often the site of danger. One card reads, "You are staying overnight at a friend's house. The father comes into the bedroom to tuck you in, and he has no clothes on. Should you: Tell your parents nothing about what happened? [wrong] Tell your parents about what happened when you arrive home?"[72] Another card instructs a child home alone to lock all doors and never answer the phone.[73] According to this game and the educational game genre it represented, not even a sleepover at a friend's house or being in your own home was considered safe.

The games and books of this kind all involved similar scenarios and game play that mapped crime onto familiar spaces. By having players move across a game board of common suburban locations, they communicated to their audience that

Figure 3.3. The Child Awareness Game, endorsed in 1986 by the Adam Walsh Resource Center, helped kids navigate the newly dangerous spaces of the suburb. Author's collection

these places were potentially dangerous and young people needed special knowledge to have a chance to survive. Games like Pressman Toys' *Safely Home* (1985) helped children learn how to deal with an abduction or an encounter with a stranger. Players wended their way through a game board full of familiar, presumably secure locations, such as single-family, detached homes, schoolyards, sidewalks, and playgrounds. In *Strangers Dangers*, players "negotiate a route from school to home that is filled with potential hazards: sinister-looking strangers offering candy or a ride, vacant houses, railroad tracks. The winner is the first player to arrive home safely, no easy task."[74] Similarly, *No Thanks, Stranger* flashcards presented everyday scenarios rife with danger.[75] The cards depict strangers, who otherwise appear harmless, constantly trolling suburban streets for kids not prepared to defend themselves. These flashcards, along with safety handbooks like *Safe Kids*, attempted to cover every possible threat and included worksheets for keeping key information on hand, such as fingerprints.[76] These materials allowed children to "experience actual situations in an entertaining fictional setting."[77] However, they were part of a new regime that reinforced the constant sense of danger to children while inculcating the belief that children were responsible for their own safety on suburban streets.

By the late 1980s, the Adam Walsh case had already cast a long shadow on suburban life. Having brought to light a supposed epidemic of strangers abducting children in broad daylight and inaugurating a series of educational endeavors and defensive practices, Adam's story also created a new authority on crime and

Figure 3.4. The Child Awareness Game's board literally maps danger onto such familiar spaces as school, the baseball field, and the shopping center. Author's collection

victimization: his father, John Walsh. Walsh parlayed his public role as aggrieved parent and spokesman for victims' rights into a job hosting a new reality show dedicated to catching fugitives, *America's Most Wanted*. On the program, he delivered a weekly reminder of the real dangers to middle-class families and what they could do to stop them as they sought to relax in front of the television.

A Nightmare of Reality

In 1988, Fox Television, languishing in fourth place among the big-four television networks, debuted a show dedicated to catching fugitives and preventing

What if a stranger is following you?

Figure 3.5. The flash card game *No Thanks, Stranger* presented children with various threatening scenarios to help them escape unharmed when confronted with a stranger, whom the game posed as a likely predator. Author's collection

crime. Unlike many locally produced shows and news broadcast segments featuring "crimestoppers," *America's Most Wanted* was a slickly produced, nationally broadcast program determined to motivate viewers to help find the most dangerous criminals on the loose in their towns. This show—along with two others that premiered in 1987, Fox's *Cops* and NBC's *Unsolved Mysteries*—ushered in a new era of reality television programming that blurred the lines between news and entertainment and drew high ratings by making viewers a key part of the surveillance state.[78] *America's Most Wanted* was successful at doing both. The show was a hit, and viewer tips did lead to the capture of criminals.[79] Unlike *Cops*, which was largely a voyeuristic journey into working-class and impoverished neighborhoods, *America's Most Wanted* not only flogged its audience for information but also reminded them to be vigilant in the face of pervasive criminal dangers right outside their doors in middle-class neighborhoods.[80]

The casting of John Walsh as host gave the show credibility in urging its audience to be wary, inoculated the show against many critical reviews of its exploitive tendencies, and provided an important connection between the crimes depicted on the show and crime as part of suburban life.[81] In casting the program, Thomas Herwitz, a vice president at Fox Television, rejected the idea of hiring a professional to host the show, insisting the network hire a real person. It eventually settled on Walsh because he "bridges the gap, since his own life has been affected by crime."[82] As both the father of a murdered child and a well-respected advocate for missing and exploited children, producers chose Walsh because he could speak with authenticity and power on issues of victimization and crime.[83] An early review of the show in the *Portland Oregonian* identified the compelling mix that Walsh brought to the show. He was "the unabashed outraged citizen whose passion and zealotry bristle through. . . . He is the crusading aggrieved parent."[84] Thanks to his advocacy work, the show could present Walsh not as exploiting his victim status to become host of the show but as a genuinely concerned, tough crime fighter who "looks like J. Edgar Hoover's dream of a G-man."[85] Walsh was also a figure that the average viewer could relate to—a suburban dad whose life had been destroyed by senseless violence—and a larger-than-life crusader for justice whom audiences could admire, respect, and welcome into their homes weekly despite the fact that what he brought was news about violent criminals on the loose in America.[86]

During promotion of the show, especially during its inaugural season, critics and reviewers used Adam Walsh's murder to frame the mission of *America's Most Wanted* and thus forge the link between suburban crime and the job of viewers to protect themselves. Bob Niedt, in a review of the show for the *Syracuse Post-Standard*, characteristically referenced John Walsh's past: "John Walsh is alive and driven and hopeful there will never again be a son who is taken away from his father and family and friends in such a swift, brutal way."[87] In interviews, Walsh often invoked his family's story. In talking with Niedt, Walsh prefaced his thoughts on law enforcement by saying, "I'm speaking as the victim, the father of a murdered child." In a *New York Times Magazine* piece on the show, Walsh described the impetus for his transformation from suburban dad to television crime fighter. "At 35, I thought I had the American dream . . . [a] good job, a great family and a home in sunny Florida. Then, one morning my wife went to the store, and Adam was abducted. The killer was never found."[88] Even four years into the show's run, the news media still invoked Adam's story. In an article about the show's two hundredth capture, Donna Gable in *USA Today* identified Walsh as the show's unique ingredient: "They have something no one else has: John Walsh, the show's host. . . . Walsh's 6-year-old son, Adam, was kidnapped, molested and decapitated in 1981. The murder remains unsolved."[89] The show was thus inextricably linked with Walsh's personal story of his son's murder and the shattering of a seemingly perfect suburban life.[90] In whatever venue he appeared, including most prominently as *America's Most Wanted*'s host, Walsh brought his son's case and all of its associations with him. He was a reminder that crime happens even in the suburbs and, as an advocate and the host of *America's Most Wanted*, he reminded viewers to be vigilant in protecting themselves lest a similar tragedy befall them.

In format, the show functioned much like a telethon with John Walsh relaying information while urging his audience to call in with information rather than money. Usually, he would spur their action by featuring reenactments of crimes presented in a visceral low-budget style in which "the camerawork is hand-held; the music is urgent; there are a number of scenes in which guns are pointed or fired into the camera lens."[91] Through these minimovies, *America's Most Wanted* conveyed the moral certitude of the vigilante heroes in the film series *Dirty Harry* and *Death Wish*. The exhaustively reenacted crime left little doubt as to the alleged criminal's guilt while eliciting sympathy for victims by melodramatically portraying their plight and that of their families after their lives had been shattered by crime. These reenactments were crucial to achieving the show's purpose as they brought jarringly violent recreations of real crimes into American living rooms, thereby promoting the show's vision of crime as *the* vision of crime in America—graphic, immediate, and local. The producers presented the reenactments in this way to make the audience feel their participation was of critical importance to stopping criminals from committing even more heinous crimes, especially given the explicit suggestion that a criminal may soon be pointing a gun at them.

Compared to Walsh's campaign on behalf of missing children, *America's Most Wanted* was less critical of law enforcement officers but still skeptical of the criminal justice system. The show operated under a friendlier premise that no organization could keep up with crime or with wily criminals who killed without conscience. No matter the particular problem with law enforcement, the message was ultimately the same. The show urged the audience to act in circumscribed ways to protect themselves as a supplement to police action.[92] In an interview with television critic Tom Shales, Doug Linder, the producer of *America's Most Wanted*, said, "This show is sending a subtle message that the criminal justice system doesn't work."[93] Linder revealed that many of those who called the toll-free number hung up when they heard someone answer, because, he surmised, they expected the same result as when they might call 911: no one would actually be there to listen. Walsh and *America's Most Wanted* were careful not to undermine the system or explicitly endorse vigilantism even as they acknowledged the futility of relying solely on law enforcement. "I'm not a cop," Walsh said. "Nor am I some kind of vigilante. But there are 280,000 fugitives out there, and this is a chance to show that Americans can make a difference."[94] The message was not difficult to decode. If there were that many criminals running wild, the viewer must do something because traditional law enforcement was evidently unwilling or unable to stop criminals and prosecute offenders.

This explanation represented the balance the show was trying to strike, and the suburban politics in which it was engaged. Rather than airing an all-out critique of law enforcement each week, the show emphasized cooperation with authorities and made the "subtle" suggestion that the criminal justice system was failing, while asking its audience to do what they could from the safety of their La-Z-Boy recliners, because as Walsh emphasized at the end of each episode, "You can make a difference."[95] That was the mission of the show as John Walsh articulated it. "The American public needs to know that [violent criminals] are out there. This is not a screenwriter's nightmare. This is a nightmare of reality."[96]

Much like the genre of educational literature and games designed to teach children about danger in their neighborhood, a genre of self-help books for adults emerged that echoed the sense of fear and of self-reliance in fighting crime fostered by *America's Most Wanted*. In *Safe Homes, Safe Neighborhoods*, author Stephanie Mann (with M. C. Blakeman) made the case to suburban homeowners for "Why Crime Prevention Is Up to You and Your Neighbors," as the title of the book's opening section put it. In explaining why neighborhoods needed individual and community action, the authors noted, "In the past, when neighborhoods were more stable, . . . neighbors watching out for one another was a fact of life." However, that had changed. The authors cited statistics showing that most crime was local and police could not possibly protect everyone.[97] Similarly, *On Guard! How You Can Win against the Bad Guys* (1994) argued that crime is inevitable and homeowners must be vigilant protectors of their families.[98] This genre of self-help book continued the depiction of criminal threats as pervasive and local while doling out pages of advice on how homeowners must supplement or supplant law enforcement in order to stay safe and truly enjoy the privilege of suburban living.

Like this self-help literature and neighborhood watch patrols, *America's Most Wanted* epitomized the new suburban culture of crime prevention by asking the audience to peer out windows and phone in tips rather than taking more direct action. This appeal both produced and mobilized suburbanites' increasing sense of victimization and encouraged necessary private defensive measures. Still, though John Walsh and the producers of *America's Most Wanted* went to great lengths to spur audience action, they warned them not to turn to vigilantism lest the precarious relationship with law enforcement be upset. Although suburbanites understood crime as rampant and law enforcement as overwhelmed, they did not want to alienate the state agencies they needed to assist them. Alarm systems, neighborhood watch programs, gated entrances, private security, and, later, armed self-defense required the criminal justice system's support and acquiescence, which supposedly would not be possible if active vigilantism became a regular occurrence.

Go Ahead, Make My Day

By the premiere of *America's Most Wanted* in 1988, however, the vigilante film genre had already provided explicit, violent narratives that endorsed stopping crime through extralegal means and exacting justice outside an inept criminal justice system more interested in protecting the rights of criminals than victims. These films expressed white, middle-class aggrievement and imagined salvation through the vigilante's good works. Indeed, this genre portrayed the vigilante as what Vincent Canby has described "as nothing less than the redeemer" within a moral universe neatly constructed through a narrative that provided a fantasy of justice, an affective salve to the unstoppable problem of crime not unlike *America's Most Wanted* armchair vigilantes.[99] Yet those fantasies of private justice also worked with the broader suburban discourses of crime to undergird a more expansive doctrine of home and self-defense that legislatures ratified into laws and courts confirmed in rulings whereby suburbanites could and did legally kill.[100]

After the release of the original *Dirty Harry* (1971) and *Death Wish* (1974) films, the genre had run aground by the early 1980s with many poorly executed, low-budget imitations set in the assumed criminal wastelands of American cities in crisis.[101] However, in seeking to reimagine the genre and capitalize on the perception that suburban crime was also on the rise, the makers of the most popular series in the vigilante genre moved their stories of persistent crime and extrale-gal solutions out of the city and into the suburbs. In *Death Wish II*, released in 1982, architect-vigilante Paul Kersey moves to suburban Los Angeles to start over after the horrors recounted in the first film, while in 1983's *Sudden Impact*, "Dirty Harry" Callahan is put on administrative leave in a quiet community on the Cal-ifornia coast.

Death Wish II and *Sudden Impact* maintained the vigilante genre's critique of the criminal justice system while asserting that the suburban environment, too, had become dangerous and needed the action of the righteous vigilante to rescue it.[102] However, these movies' portrayals of vigilante justice were a fantasy that presented active defense in contrast to the largely defensive devices and prac-tices used by suburbanites to protect themselves until the early twenty-first century when laws further empowered homeowners to regulate local spaces. Populated by images of graphic violence and feelings of powerlessness, these films created a suburban world where the heroes act with moral clarity and with-out involving law enforcement or waiting for passive measures to ensnare a dan-gerous criminal already committing a crime. These popular depictions paved the way for lawmakers to pass so-called "make my day" laws. While invoking Dirty Harry's most famous line from *Sudden Impact*, states enacted Stand Your Ground laws that gave legal protections to people who use deadly force to protect them-selves anywhere they have a right to be. This legislation led to an astounding in-crease in "justifiable homicide" cases in states with the law on the books.[103]

Death Wish II opens with helicopter shots of the sprawling landscape of greater Los Angeles, a sunny alternative to the first *Death Wish*'s gritty setting of 1974 New York City. Paul Kersey, played by Charles Bronson, seeks a quieter life-style on a peaceful, tree-lined street, but he is not left alone to do so for long. While spending the day at an outdoor market with his new girlfriend, Geri Nich-ols, and daughter, Carol, who has been institutionalized following her assault in *Death Wish*, Kersey is mugged by a gang who steal his wallet. Then, the muggers use the information on his driver's license to find his house and break in. Kersey is knocked out cold while the gang rapes and murders his maid. The intruders abscond with Carol to their hideout inside an abandoned mansion, where they continually rape her. In an attempt to escape, Carol mistakenly jumps out of a window to her death. Despite the brutality of the initial mugging, Kersey tries to turn over a new leaf and calls the police. The film's message is clear, however, that he knows there is very little they can or will do. The vigilante plot is reener-gized by the intrusion of senseless, explicit, and brutal violence against Kersey's family into what had seemed the safe suburban spaces where he had sought to retreat from what he thought were urban hazards.

After meeting with the police, Kersey searches for the gang by living a double life. During the day, he remains a devoted boyfriend and successful architect while at night he stalks his prey on Los Angeles's skid row. The transition between the two landscapes is stark and enhances the moral clarity of the series established in the first *Death Wish*. His suburban home is always shown as sunny, clean, and quiet. On skid row, Kersey mingles with drug dealers, addicts, and street preachers while rooting out the gang. The movement back and forth between locales tracks a movement between respectability and criminality, and in some way provides the audience a mode of slumming as the thrill is doubled by Kersey's own voyeurism and vigilantism. Further, his taking a room in this location and living the double life suggest his ability as a respectable, middle-class person to transcend the criminal actions he takes and locations he frequents because of the righteousness of his mission. In the world of the vigilante film, he is not a criminal but a one-man justice system who can do bad things but not be essentially bad himself. He can safely return to the suburbs after he exacts his revenge. This notion is reaffirmed in the film when Kersey evades his own arrest and prosecution for killing the gang's members because the police fears that his "crimes" would be seen as noble by the public at large. At the end of the film, he returns to the suburb having helped remake it as safe (cinematic) space. Rather than an ongoing crisis, crime in *Death Wish II* can be stopped rather than accepted and coped with as it was by actual suburbanites.

Released a year after *Death Wish II* and featuring the iconic line "Go ahead, make my day," the Clint Eastwood–directed *Sudden Impact* takes detective "Dirty Harry" Callahan out of San Francisco. Having illegally seized some evidence that lets a criminal go free on a legal technicality, Harry is forced to go on a "vacation." In his new, bucolic, suburban home, Harry is soon drawn into a local case involving a serial killer. Just then, he meets his love interest for the film, artist Jennifer Spencer (Sondra Locke). On their first date, Jennifer says, "This is the age of lapsed responsibilities and defeated justice. Today an eye for an eye means only if you're caught and even then it means an indefinite postponement and, 'Let's settle out of court.' " Harry is intrigued if not overwhelmed by a beautiful woman essentially endorsing his worldview in which justice is clear, swift, and merciless.[104] Unbeknownst to Harry, Jennifer's views were formed years earlier by a violent incident. In previous scenes, the audience sees her and her sister gang raped on the beach, an incident that leaves the sister in a catatonic state much like that of Paul Kersey's daughter in *Death Wish*. Years later, returning to the scene of the crime, Jennifer finds all of the perpetrators going about their normal lives, reinforcing the notion of violent criminals living freely in a suburban setting. At that point, Spencer decides to exact the revenge the state could not. A rash of mysterious killings ensues that those same local police are unable to solve.

The film builds to a climax as Spencer attempts to finish off the last two members of the gang that raped her and her sister. She discovers that one of them is the police chief's son, who, it happens, has been left in a catatonic state after a car accident. The chief tells Jennifer he will essentially look the other way as to her killings so as to be rid of the "scum" responsible for her attack. As in the *Death Wish* series, vigilantism in *Sudden Impact* is sanctioned by police who seek expedient solutions to crime and necessary help in cleaning up the streets. However, Jennifer's vigilantism presents a dilemma for "Dirty Harry," as he endorses the elimination of criminals but also, if somewhat perversely, believes in the rule of law. Before he decides whether to turn Jennifer in, she delivers a searing critique of the justice system that encapsulates the politics of the vigilante genre and the emergent culture of crime in the 1980s: "What, are you going to read me my rights? Where was this concern for my rights when I was being beaten and mauled? . . . There is a thing called justice. Is it justice that they should all just walk away?" Already sympathetic to her cause, Harry is swayed by her argument and tells the local police that a gun found on one of the rapists was the one used in all the other killings.

Death Wish II and *Sudden Impact* helped alter the cognitive map of the suburbs to include the threat of crime while promoting a fantasy of individual agency whereby suburbanites caught criminals rather than just avoiding them while waiting for a failing system of law enforcement to enact justice. In showing the efficient removal of crime and criminals by empowered victims who unquestioningly deserve justice the system denies them, the films gave credence to the notion that crime was ubiquitous and justice could be simple if suburbanites protected themselves (or were legally permitted to do so, as seen with later expansions of the Castle Doctrine).

However, these vigilante solutions to crime were not ultimately practical, as *America's Most Wanted* warned. Although the television show portrayed a similar world of crime and justice, it demonstrated that vigilantism was largely imaginary since it asked its audience to supplement the work of law enforcement— catching criminals rather than stopping crime, even as John Walsh urged audience members not to be passive victims. "As I began to understand that tragedy," he once said about the loss of his son, "I decided not to be victimized by fear or revenge, but to share my realization that each of us can help—must help—stop crime. That's what *America's Most Wanted* is all about."[105] As armchair vigilantes, then, viewers could enjoy the visceral thrill of looking for a wanted criminal and vicariously enjoy his or her arrest by law enforcement, knowing they or someone just like them had played a part. *USA Today* characterized the show as thriving "on a collective preoccupation with random crime and voyeuristic crime-solving. Is your neighbor a runaway killer with a new identity—and an incriminating 'Mom' tattooed on his behind?"[106] Watching the show and looking for criminals, though largely reactive moves, let suburban viewers imagine they were actively participating in their own defense against crime, thus reinforcing the notion that active protection was necessary. In highlighting suburbanites' limited power in the face of crime and making use of their fantasies of aggressive defense, the show, the films, and the suburban culture of crime they represented made the expansive reinterpretation of the Castle Doctrine and new, Stand Your Ground laws appear logical and necessary in the twenty-first century expression of productive victimization.

If you have to retreat . . . you're a dead man

Facilitating suburbanites' privatization of policing power was the emergent and, ultimately, dominant, politics of law and order at the end of the twentieth century. That politics advanced a harsh, overwhelming response to crime as a correction to the prior era of law enforcement that many citizens and politicians believed had been too interested in protecting the rights of criminals over those of victims.[107] Under the new regime, arresting and jailing criminals was not meant to rehabilitate but to punish lawbreakers so harshly as to discourage further crime, reassert "order" as a means of social control, and restore a nostalgic cultural ideal of peaceful streets and self-governing citizens. Those broader political initiatives dovetailed with the budding cultural conservatism of suburbanites in the same era, a law-and-order politics focused on "limited government, moral leadership, and judicial firmness," as historian Michael W. Flamm has characterized it.[108] Each of those imperatives made possible the suburban expansion in privatized police functions, which came to seem more reasonable and necessary as more communities adopted the approach. Rather than rely on the state to protect them, which it had clearly failed to do in the earlier age of urban crisis and unrest, suburbanites felt not only empowered but required to protect themselves however possible.[109] In doing so, they continued to pose as aggrieved victims acting legitimately to beat back crime that was no longer relegated to the inner city; meanwhile, the state assailed people of color as inherently criminal and as subjects of legal discipline.

The legal movements to expand homeowner power and pursue the law-and-order politics that facilitated them were aided by the shifting tactics of the National Rifle Association (NRA) during this era. In the mid-1970s, the organization migrated from its roots in promoting marksmanship and gun safety to focusing on stopping gun control legislation by supporting pro-gun political candidates and extensive legislative lobbying.[110] The association's efforts also included an advertising campaign that sought to bring in new members who, it believed, would not otherwise be interested in guns or the NRA. The "I'm the NRA" campaign showed average citizens, including many women, as gun owners and was wildly successful in broadening the ranks of NRA membership, which, in turn, led to more money for lobbying against gun restriction laws.[111] Those members received the NRA's monthly magazine, *American Rifleman*, which further reinforced the sense of ongoing criminal endangerment and positioned gun ownership as crime prevention. In a regular section, gun owners told stories about preventing crime by using or brandishing a firearm. These efforts reinforced the idea of private regulation of crime and helped make homeowners' expanded powers to regulate space more deadly by making gun ownership more accessible.

Into the early twenty-first century, courts and legislatures endorsed homeowner policing of space by taking a hard line against criminals and a compassionate stance toward homeowners' "defensive" actions. Convicted defendants were subject to lengthy mandatory sentences and "three strikes and you're out" rules, which condemned many to a lifetime behind bars, while valiant homeowners defending property rights and the privileges of suburban life were exonerated and even hailed as heroes for using lethal force.[112] In particular, the Castle Doctrine, and its public-space extension through Stand Your Ground laws, embedded in the law the rights of homeowners to defend themselves at home and beyond with little risk of prosecution.[113] The Castle Doctrine provides for legal self-defense in one's own home or "castle" when confronted with an intruder. Stand Your Ground laws expanded the spaces in which a person may exercise lethal force in self-defense beyond the home in a place where the person has a "right to be," essentially making the protections of the Castle Doctrine portable.

These laws and their endorsement by the courts endowed homeowners, largely suburban, with the right to dispense justice in a wide array of spaces and to defend their actions as necessary self-defense.

Stand Your Ground laws marked a shift in the view of homeowner rights. Until late in the twentieth century, the Castle Doctrine included a duty to retreat or avoid the danger unless one is faced with what a reasonable person would consider a threat of imminent death or bodily harm; it did not include a right to stand one's ground regardless of the threat posed. The history of the doctrine in Florida, where George Zimmerman killed Trayvon Martin, is instructive in understanding the changes in the Castle Doctrine made possible by the shifting culture of suburban crime. For most of the twentieth century, Florida courts largely held a narrow view of when and where deadly force could legally be used by a homeowner and thus refrained from extending that right to an automobile or public space.[114] In a 2005 revision of state law, however, the legislature removed the duty to retreat when the person threatened is in a "place where he or she has a right to be," while extending the right of self-protection to any dwelling and any person in that dwelling.[115] Further, the law codified the common law principle that reasonable fear must exist for legally sanctioned lethal force. Although it did not permit all homicides in cases of self-defense (notably, shooting a police officer was not considered justifiable under the law), the shifting sense of suburban space as embattled and, hence, of a world where one should be legitimately fearful, was easily mobilized to justify these killings in the courts and news media. In essence, as legal scholar Wyatt Holliday argues, "the legislature was clearly and completely removing Florida from the minority of states requiring retreat before the use of deadly force" and, according to the Florida Supreme Court, risked making "innumerable castles" that could be legally defended.[116] By extending the right of nonretreat and substituting a person's sense of their right to be someplace as a rationale for self-defense, Florida codified the private power of homeowners in public spaces who had come to see their local surroundings as part of their private domain.

In the public debate over revising the state law, newspapers framed the Stand Your Ground law as the beginning of a new "Wild West," but often talking of the law in terms of a more modern reference: the vigilante film. In 2005, Jim Haug of the *Daytona Beach News-Journal*, "Tallahassee Dirty Harry may soon be in his rights to say, Go ahead, make my day and blast away at his attacker," while the *Palm Beach Post* titled an editorial, "Go Ahead; Pass this Bill" and warned, "When 'Make My Day' is in force, individuals will practice the racial profiling police forces have tried to eliminate. More innocent people will get shot."[117] Even in criticizing the law, these articles made the explicit link to the vigilante fantasies of justice and power dispensed by the homeowner, which was, to the many Floridians who supported the law, actually a compelling argument.

Indeed, supporters saw the change as necessary for the innocent to protect themselves in a world rife with criminal hazards. Republican senator Durell Peaden understood the bill as channeling the belief of most homeowners that they needed the legal safeguards of the bill so they could protect themselves without going to jail for it.[118] Despite his opposition, Senator Ron Klein, expressed the logic of suburban crime culture in the twenty-first century: "I'm not a big gun person but I recognize that there are a lot of people who think that criminals rule, that they've got the run of the land."[119] Similarly, Don Coppola of Charlotte County, Florida, explained, "The gun put me in command of the situation."[120] This sentiment pervaded comments by supporters of such laws. They saw the laws as legal sanction of the moral stance that when society abandons you, you must defend yourself, notwithstanding the history of the late twentieth and early twenty-first centuries that clearly demonstrated the myriad structural advantages enjoyed by suburban homeowners. David Kopel, director of the Independence Institute, a libertarian think tank, said, "These laws send a more general message to society that public spaces belong to the public—and the public will protect [public places] rather than trying to run into the bathroom of the nearest Starbucks and hope the police show up."[121] Kopel's remark demonstrated the pervasive fear, not just of crime but of the potential double victimization by a criminal and by the failure of law enforcement, a vulnerability that, in supporters' logic, required new private powers with which citizens could protect themselves.

The law-and-order regime had stunning effects on perceptions of crime, its perpetrators, and law enforcement policy and procedure. Florida was not alone in passing "make my day laws" in the first decade of the twenty-first century. According to the *New York Times*, by August 2006, fifteen states had expanded the right to use deadly force in self-defense, using the Florida law as a model.[122] They liberated suburbanites, largely white and middle class, to craft their own, privatized solutions to "threats" appearing on their doorsteps and in their neighborhoods.[123] These solutions—gates, volunteer patrols, private security forces, vigilante justice—would not have been possible without the conditions created by the politics of law and order and the new culture of suburban crime. That culture encouraged seeing the landscape as under siege. At the same time, passage of new, more permissive laws regarding lethal force used in self-defense empowered the lone, implicitly white, middle-class homeowner to defend the home in what the state itself acknowledged was a vacuum created by the implicit failure of law enforcement to prevent crime and protect the innocent. As the sponsor of Florida's Stand Your Ground law commented about his bill, "It's pretty much understood how we want to protect our homes and families"—namely, by exercising their unabridged rights to police space, regulate people, and dispense justice in their neighborhoods as the necessary response to out-of-control crime.

In the 1970s and '80s, overlapping narratives of crime and the defenses against it produced imagery, ideas, and practices that shifted the associations of the suburban landscape from safe to criminally imperiled. Portrayals of lawbreaking and violence—in cultural productions ranging from the television movie *Adam* to news and magazine stories of home invasions, educational board games and books, and vigilante television shows and films—confronted suburbanites with visions of local, endemic crime beyond the reach of law enforcement. In those spaces, safety became premised on personal vigilance and technological superiority that, while promising protection, undermined the essence of the postwar suburban project itself. However, the carceral suburb's emergence did not just destabilize the bucolic, utopian legacy of suburban life. It also created the cultural conditions for empowerment, whereby suburbanites consolidated and extended private police power through the turn of the twenty-first in response to the expanding sense of criminal hazard. The employment of walls, gates, fences, and private guards was a logical extension of the security ethos forged around the seemingly legitimate responses to criminal threats, even though by nearly every measure these threats declined during the emergence of this suburban culture of home security.[124]

Suburban Americans bought security systems, changed educational priorities, constructed gated communities, and employed private security forces not simply in response to encroaching "urban" dangers or as an explicit part of a broader political project to "get tough on crime." Although they were facilitated by and facilitated those political discourses, suburbanites acted to protect against local threats and made productive use of their perceived victimization for local ends. They enhanced and extended suburban exclusivity and local power in response to, and often without, the state—moving from securing the home to securing the neighborhood with barriers and guards at a time when local law enforcement appeared unable or unwilling to secure the cultural and material benefits of suburban living. This strategy allowed suburbanites to feel secure while ignoring the structural origins of and solutions to crime that might have had much farther-reaching effects on their lives if acknowledged and acted upon.[125] Instead, they remained focused on the local concerns of protecting and expanding the privileges of their safety and spatial power. All the while, their actions and the sense of ongoing criminal danger they symbolized bolstered the tough-on-crime political culture that created the "new Jim Crow," and the concomitant manifestation of the neoliberal carceral state as the "golden gulag."[126]

During this same era, the focus on spatial power and security would also appear in responses to teenagers in public spaces such as the shopping mall and arcade. Parents, police, and local municipalities moved to more closely regulate teenagers and the spaces they frequented, not only because of the era's increasing sense of criminal danger but also because teenagers themselves had become threats to orderly public space.

Chapter Four

Punks, Mallrats, and Out-of-Control Teenagers

Production and Regulation of Suburban Public Space

Adam Walsh's afternoon abduction from a shopping mall helped to recast public spaces as imperiled by lurking criminals. His murder, the supposed kidnapping epidemic of the 1980s, and other criminal threats were not the only catalysts shifting the understanding and regulation of suburban public spaces.[1] Teenagers and their activities figured prominently in the understanding of those spaces as part of the new era of suburban crisis. Their uses of public space, and news media and popular culture representations of them, undermined associations with safety and consumerism and spurred business owners, police, and parents to adopt new tactics of social and spatial regulation that exemplified suburban productive victimization.

By the end of the 1990s, suburbanites saw teens as threats to legitimate users of public space—namely, shoppers in the mall, kids playing games at the recreation center, families relaxing at the park—and to "good" kids (shopping and working) who could be turned "bad" outside the purview of parents and teachers. In response to this increasing sense of victimization of and by teenagers, authority figures exercised their power more forcefully. They imagined and policed public spaces in order to maximize their control over them and thereby remedy or at least ameliorate ascendant anxieties about the family and make the spaces safer for a particular kind of citizen-consumer.[2] This spatial solution to a cultural problem in turn diminished the "public" nature of suburban space while proposing the suburban home as the safe haven from dangerous public areas and their inhabitants.

One of the most prominent suburban teen spaces of the 1970s, the recreation (or rec) center, while still part of the landscape, had virtually disappeared as a teen sanctuary by the 1990s, with many directed instead toward young children and senior citizens. By then, popular culture depictions and news media narratives showed it to be a place menaced by teenagers rather than a secure space for socializing. In response, parents and municipal leaders turned away from the rec center as a place to control suburban teens, and teens moved toward the shopping center as their home away from home. The 1979 film *Over the Edge* provided a frame for understanding teen danger on the suburban landscape. Based on true events, the film presented a worst-case scenario of misbehavior in which out-of-control teens cause their recreation center to close by turning it into a breeding ground for their violent behavior and substance use.[3] Alongside this nearly apocalyptic vision of suburban teens, real disturbances across the country cemented the nefarious association between teenagers and the rec center. By the end of the 1980s, municipalities from Wisconsin to Florida had closed their centers or repurposed them as senior or community centers, signaling the power of the dangerous public teen image to initiate new regulations of public space in order to protect the public from teens and teens from one another.[4]

Similarly, real incidents of teen misbehavior and their elaboration in news media and popular culture associated the shopping mall and the video game arcade with teens and their transgressions. *Fast Times at Ridgemont High* (1982), based on Cameron Crowe's year as an undercover reporter at a suburban California high school confirmed what many suspected about the shopping center by showing teens using the mall as a venue for scalping concert tickets, finding sexual partners, and getting high.[5] Newspapers and magazines published countless stories of teen mall patrons, labeled *mallrats*, who made the shopping center their home away from home.[6] These narratives portrayed a "proliferation of teenagers at malls" that was leading to "prostitution, drug sales, gang rivalries and excessive drinking—all of which can erupt into deadly violence."[7] Even the video game arcade, once believed a place to attract and contain rowdy teens already frequenting shopping centers, became known as home to disruptive behavior despite rules specifically intended to prevent problems.[8] The emergence of the arcade as a dangerous space spawned outlandish popular culture representations like the teen exploitation film *Joysticks*, which further implicated arcade teens in "deviant" behavior.[9] In the same era, hardcore suburban punk rockers also associated the teenager with hostility, violence, and disorder in public space. Director Penelope Spheeris's films—*The Decline of Western Civilization* and *Suburbia*—as well as hardcore's lyrics, music, and public performances, elaborated those associations. Whether they were behaving well or poorly, teens in the recreation center, the shopping mall, and other liminal spaces embodied danger to the public and to other teens. For increasingly visible and powerful conservative leaders, teens signified a failure of the postwar suburban family to adhere to "traditional" values and produce proper citizens, as it had in the 1950s.

In response, parents, police, and mall owners reacted with stricter regulation of teenagers and their spaces, shutting down or severely curtailing the operating hours of places where they congregated. Shopping center owners modernized and professionalized their security forces. They employed greater numbers of better-trained guards who employed new technologies like closed-circuit television to crack down on the nuisances of shoplifting and highly visible loitering that discouraged shopping by other customers. Due to malign associations of video game arcades, towns from Mesquite, Texas, to Babylon, Long Island, passed ordinances to stringently regulate or even ban these spaces. Likewise, police limited hardcore punks' ability to congregate in public, simply by harassing and arresting them, often without cause. This eventually led to many punks leaving their local environs for big cities; there they could more easily cultivate a social scene where they were not so conspicuously out of place.

This new mode of viewing and policing public space as endangered because of the presence of teens was productive for suburbanites in a few specific ways. Under this new system, teens had little choice but to go back into the home, where they were supposedly protected from the dangers of public life and could pose no harm to the public. Bringing teens back into the evidently safe confines of the home allowed parents to reassert control over their children's lives and address fears of the decline of the "traditional" family, a fear characteristic of this age of "family values" politics (addressed more fully in the following chapter). Beyond the regulation of teens themselves, the notion of a dangerous suburban landscape supported the security culture analyzed in the previous chapter and its attendant practices. And, ultimately, the responses to out-of-control teens led to an increasing scrutiny of these spaces that substantially undermined their function as traditional public spaces and civic venues. Instead, through these new regulations, owners, their security forces, and police further made malls into spaces of privatized consumption for the benefit of consumers, shopping center owners, and municipalities while further undermining freedom of movement through other suburban spaces already enmeshed in an increasingly stringent culture of security.[10]

Watch Out for Children

The motion picture *Over the Edge* presents teen anarchy of the 1970s and '80s as a direct result of the failures of suburban planning. Former newspaper reporter Charles S. Haas cowrote the film based on the reporting of his *San Francisco Examiner* colleagues Bruce Koon and James A. Finefrock. In a 1973 front-page article "Mouse Packs: Kids on a Crime Spree," Koon and Finefrock told the stories of Foster City, California's problems perpetrated by preteenage gangs of "mousepacks": pipe bomb explosions, graffiti on shopping center walls, and sundry other criminal activities.[11] The article presented a lawless landscape in which teen and preteen violence was a frightening aberration for people expecting the docile, rule-following suburban children of *Leave It to Beaver* and *Father Knows Best*. In response, Foster City's municipal government sought to control these outbreaks of youth crime. For example, it mandated that junior high school students must be let out of school forty-five minutes before the high school students so that the older ones could not mug the younger students. Koon and Finefrock wondered whether the situation in Foster City might be "a fluke or a harbinger of things to come." This chapter argues that the "mousepacks" were indeed a harbinger. The long list of juvenile offenses in Foster City portended a new era of suburban danger posed by its own residents that would call forth new understandings and regulations of suburban spaces outside the home.

Over the Edge put the story of Foster City's "mousepacks" on the big screen. Set in the fictional planned community of New Granada, Colorado, a stand-in for the planned communities and new towns of the late 1960s and early '70s, the film offered a theory as to what led teenagers to misbehavior and violence.[12] It showed them as bored and angry because of a stultifying suburban lifestyle that caused them to act out violently against parents, teachers, and police. The film thus held what Roger Ebert called "a funeral service at the graveside of the suburban dream."[13] Through this portrayal, *Over the Edge* helped construct a vision of the out-of-control teen and a frame for understanding the recreation center and its patrons as essentially dangerous, a frame that justified new policies and practices for monitoring teens.

At the film's outset, a short preface is superimposed over a static shot of the bleak, lifeless landscape of New Granada. It attempts to put the misbehavior of

Figure 4.1. Over the Edge (1979). The film's tagline, "Watch Out for Children," suggested the emerging view of suburban teenagers as both dangerous and endangered. Licensed by Warner Bros. Entertainment and George Litto Enterprises, Inc. All rights reserved.

suburban teens in context: "In 1978 110,000 kids under 18 were arrested for crimes of vandalism in the United States. The story is based on true incidents occurring during the 1970s in a planned suburban community of townhomes and condominiums where city planners ignored the fact that a quarter of the population was 15 years old or younger." That preamble announces that this is a social problem film—a realistic portrayal of the failures of suburban development to address the needs of its teenage population in crisis. The teenagers in the film (played largely by nonprofessional actors) drink, do drugs, vandalize property, and assault and even kill one another. Ebert noted in his review that "the particulars of the plot aren't all that important; we're supposed to absorb a feeling of teen-age frustration and paranoia and we do."[14] Moving beyond the intimations of the *Examiner* source material, *Over the Edge* turned the utopian potential of a planned community into a hellscape populated by teens with nothing better to do than engage in dangerous, transgressive behavior that undermined the fabric of middle-class suburban privilege and made manifest the emerging suburban crisis of the late 1970s.

Yet, with the desolate landscape of New Granada as backdrop, where construction sites are silent and new housing sits empty, the film does suggest a space for its teen population—the recreation center. Apart from their school, this is the only space created specifically for them. In the film's opening sequences, the recreation center appears as an oasis in the middle of a desert landscape. Teenagers and younger kids play games and socialize from the end of school until the center closes at 6 P.M. However, because it provides the only space for teens to congregate outside the purview of parents and teachers, the recreation center is also the place for after-hours activities like drinking, drug use, and loitering.

This behavior leads the town to close the center, sending the local teens out to misbehave across the landscape. In one sequence, their unruliness interferes with the town's economic fortunes, suggesting the broader implications of failing to discipline teenagers. As evidenced by unfinished tract houses and open fields marked for construction now delayed, New Granada has failed to attract enough investors or residents. To rejuvenate their flagging economy, prominent local businessmen try to lure investors from Houston by portraying New Granada as not only a good investment but also a good place to raise a family, far better than the dirty, dangerous cities of the late 1970s. On the day the Houston investors tour the town, the closed recreation center is accidentally reopened. As the police attempt to close it back down, a violent confrontation erupts between officers and patrons, scaring away the visiting investors who witness the chaotic scene, and leading to the center's permanent closure.

The town then convenes a meeting at the junior high school to discuss New Granada's problem teens. Once the parents and other citizens are inside the school, the kids lock them in and riot in the hallways and parking lot of the school. They loot the main office and shoot guns while destroying and vandalizing everything in sight. The teens then flee toward the recreation center. A police car chasing them crashes into the building and explodes, setting the center ablaze. It burns to the ground in a symbolic and literal end to teen social life in the town.

The fiery ending highlights the problem of bored suburban teens, and their supposed propensity for violence, who lack proper recreational activities, guidance, or supervision. Rather than the placid teens of the sitcom suburb or the urban delinquents of postwar teen social problem films, the young people of New Granada are liminal figures nearly always on the verge of dangerous, sadistic acts engendered by suburban life itself. Yet they are also brimming with redemptive possibilities if only they could be directed, molded, and disciplined properly.

This was often the purpose of the recreation and youth center movement—to redeem some teens and prevent the dereliction of others. From the 1940s onward, these centers were intended to provide safe, educational spaces for redirecting teens from dangerous streets into productive activities. In the 1940s and '50s, cities built youth centers to combat juvenile delinquency.[15] President Lyndon Johnson's Great Society programs funded urban centers to help address the urban crisis, though they quickly became gateways for the incursion of law enforcement as part of the War on Crime.[16] The suburban rec center, in contrast, symbolized the height of suburban social planning through the mid-1970s, as seen most prominently with new towns like Columbia, Maryland, and Irvine, California, supposedly designed with young people in mind.[17] Yet, as a *Christian Science Monitor* film critic described it, the center in the fictional planned community of New Granada was "the only place for the kids to hang out," a space that "quickly becomes tedious, and since the 'bad' kids are lumped there with the 'good' ones, mischief occasionally brews—and the community holler for the center to be shut down."[18] Instead of keeping kids safe, the rec center mixed "good" and "bad" kids—a recurring justification for regulating suburban public spaces.

Like the film's plot, news media narratives reiterated this notion of the corruption of "good" teens by "bad" ones in recreation centers, leading parents, police, and teachers to more strictly supervise the spaces, in turn causing teens to congregate elsewhere, usually the newly ubiquitous suburban shopping mall. According to such stories, because of the centers' increasingly nefarious associations and actual criminal disruptions, many towns closed them or turned them into less teen-specific community centers.[19] The *Milwaukee Sentinel* reported that Greendale, Wisconsin, closed its recreation center in 1977 because of flagging attendance and reports of criminal activity.[20] In 1980, a Dunedin, Florida, center was opened explicitly to cater to all of the town's residents to avoid becoming an exclusively teen hangout with all that such a designation entailed.[21]

In an article about a Largo, Maryland, center, the *Washington Post* reported that a state parks and recreation commissioner had proposed changing a recreation center into a community center because "we have had a lot of problems. Some of the teen-agers are very disruptive and have done a lot of damage. . . . They have put dead cats on their [senior citizens'] cars."[22] Sponsored by civic or religious groups, many centers remained open but held little attraction for suburban teens, as the spaces became more regulated than school, home, or the mall and therefore less attractive to young people searching for spaces of their own.[23] As municipalities changed teen-oriented recreation centers into community centers, more strictly supervised remaining youth centers, or closed them altogether, suburban teens continued to search for other spaces in which to socialize, with similar consequences.[24]

The Decline of Western Civilization

The narratives, representations, and practices of the hardcore punk scene that emerged in late-1970s suburban California further marked teens as prone to malevolence and as requiring stricter regulation in the places they frequented outside the home. Yet hardcore punks did not simply conquer these spaces and leave mayhem in their wake, as teens had at the rec center. Instead, they fought for space and visibility against increasingly aggressive actions by police and business owners who sought to realize an idealized postwar suburban social order of teen conformity and productive consumptive spaces through spatial regulation of this group of dangerous teens.

Rooted in largely nonprofessional, communal performance spaces, suburban hardcore punk, as it emerged in and around Los Angeles in the late 1970s, was not a commercial venture. It was a music form produced by suburban teens and young adults for an audience of their peers who were mostly local, a genre that both built on their privilege to perform music outside a profit motive and decried that privilege as culturally suffocating.[25] The music and its social scene were public manifestations of suburban teenagers' disaffection with what they perceived as the bland, predictable lives that parents, teachers, and mass culture sold to them as a fulfilling American ideal. This was not the world hardcore punks experienced. Instead of the loving homes, supportive parents, and social acceptance found in 1950s rerun sitcoms and their 1970s counterparts such as *The Brady Bunch* and *Family*, they observed a suburban culture marked by malign neglect and often shattered by abuse, alcoholism, and divorce—what filmmaker Penelope Spheeris called "the decline of Western civilization" in her 1981 documentary of the same name, about hardcore.[26] With this title and the film itself, Spheeris signaled the connection between the crisis of the family, national decline, and the intentionally conspicuous subculture of suburban hardcore punks.[27]

In their music, hardcore punks represented themselves as outcasts, though they often echoed earlier critiques of postwar suburban life. Both these punks and previous postwar critics portrayed suburban communities as stultifying havens of middlebrow pleasures and emotional repression.[28] These teens, however, experienced suburban life as its progeny, as direct outgrowths of this cultural milieu who could not leave but rejected their cultural inheritance. As such, they lived and performed in suburbs themselves until they were self-sufficient enough to escape. While there, they co-opted public spaces such as backyards, abandoned lots, basements, churches, and restaurants to play loud music, form mosh pits, and generally misbehave. Through their music and spatial practices, hardcore punks intentionally upended traditional suburban culture and provoked its authority figures to confront them.

They used their differences in dress and decorum to signal their insularity to fellow punks and opposition to outsiders, particularly parents and police.[29] By wearing leather jackets and secondhand clothes and sporting mohawks and various piercings, hardcore punks marked themselves and became objects of discipline whose successful regulation and expulsion by local authorities reaffirmed a postwar family and spatial order clearly in crisis.[30] This self-presentation strategy proved to be the crucial aspect of the emergence of suburban punks. They were identifiable public figures expressing an antisuburban viewpoint in combative public performances of aggressive, explicitly antimusical music.[31] Suburban punks, then, were mostly not performing and socializing in cloistered venues but in the very suburban places they decried. These spaces proved a hostile climate for their congregation and performance where police officers almost inevitably confronted and often arrested hardcore punks.

The first suburban hardcore song, "Out of Vogue," was recorded and released in 1978 by the Orange County, California, band Middle Class on their seven-inch, extended-play (EP) album, *Out of Vogue.*[32] In committing to wax the first suburban hardcore album, Middle Class articulated hardcore's style visually, musically, and lyrically. The band's very name and album cover rooted their music in a typical suburban milieu. The cover showed two young girls in the middle of a tree-lined street, with cars parked in driveways and on the street, and rows of houses neatly arranged along the block. The scene was utterly ordinary for Orange County in 1977. With the band name, Middle Class, in the top right corner and the album name, *Out of Vogue*, running along the bottom and toward the right, the name and title framing the girls, the scene feels both familiar and distant. The girls appear content, but the street scene looks expansive, boring, and mundane. In choosing a band name and album title, the band could not have been more didactic—the default mode of hardcore punk. They were stating their band's perspective as teenagers from the suburbs who were uncool or "out of vogue." Although Middle Class would never achieve the popularity or longevity of other influential hardcore bands such as Black Flag or the Dead Kennedys, their first EP was a milestone in suburban hardcore: these were "typical suburban teens" playing their own music about their own (terrible) lives for other teens.[33]

Putting the record on the turntable, one heard Middle Class play a fast, loud, monotonal blast of two-minute songs. After four songs, it was over before it barely started and begged multiple plays for fans who wanted to understand the nearly incomprehensible lyrics and blistering guitar riffs. When the album was played again, half-sung, half-yelled lyrics presented critiques of the middlebrow culture that surrounded the band and their audience. On the EP's title track, they sing: "We don't need no magazines / We don't need no TV / We don't want to know."[34] Clearly they eschewed bland suburban life and the latest trends of popular culture in favor of the seemingly more authentic subculture of hardcore where they didn't have to conform to popular styles or parental expectations. Describing their music in 1978, the band identified the rage at the heart of hardcore: "There is a certain amount of anger in the music but its [*sic*] kind of directionless, we're not mad at any one person, we're not mad at fascists or communists or anything like that, we're just generally mad."[35] Their comments, viewed in the context of their lyrics and music, suggested that their rage was induced by their boring, comfortable, middle-class lives in the conservative suburbs of Orange County.[36] In expressing that anger, the band created the archetypal attitude and lyrical touchstones of hardcore—alienation, disaffection, and anger—stemming from the failure of their suburban upbringing to live up to its legacy, a position that ironically mirrored conservative critiques of the family in the same period.[37]

The music and lyrics of hardcore bands like Middle Class combined the fast-paced sound and do-it-yourself production of the United Kingdom and New York City punk rock movements (epitomized in the United States by the Ramones, from Queens, New York) with the outlook of disillusioned suburban teens caught between the idealized vision of contemporaneous shows like *Eight Is Enough*,

Figure 4.2. The cover of the first suburban hardcore punk album, *Out of Vogue* (1978), by the band Middle Class, depicts the blandness and alienation of late-1970s suburban life. Courtesy of Middle Class

reruns of *Ozzie and Harriet*, and the reality of divorce, drug use, and economic stagflation.[38] Yet Steven Blush, a historian of the hardcore scene, warns that even though "hardcore was the suburban American response to the late-70s punk revolution, . . . it would be wrong to say, 'If you understand punk, you understand Hardcore.'"[39] That was because much of hardcore expressed a distinctly American, suburban perspective by adding new content and stylistic innovations to an established punk aesthetic of rebellion and misanthropy. Hardcore bands screamed, sang, and yelped about fear, rejection, anger, and depression caused by what they thought was a stifling, generic landscape and by the barely concealed dysfunction of the nuclear family.[40] To a large degree, these critiques of suburban life were not new when they emerged in hardcore lyrics. Academics, artists, filmmakers, and writers had long debunked the myth of suburban perfection (and continue to do so), and feminists had worked to demystify and change the nuclear family ideal.[41] Because of their suburban pedigree, however, hardcore punks infused their critiques with a distinctive intensity and specificity. Their dissections of the stultifying fantasy of mass cultural delights masking abusive, fractured homes came from their own experiences, which made their rebellion more powerful and more noticeable to parents and police.

Embracing middle-class mass cultural pleasures like beer and television as seemingly the only entertainment available, hardcore punks also mocked these same middle-class pastimes for their inauthenticity. In "TV Party," genre pioneers Black Flag sang sarcastically about prime-time television as the singular cultural outlet of suburban life. Lead singer Henry Rollins screams: "I wouldn't be without my TV for a day (Or even a minute) / Don't even bother to use my brain any more (There's nothing left in it)," while the rest of the band yells the names of popular shows ("*Alice! Three's Company!*").[42] In "Six Pack," the band treats beer—like television—as a staple of suburbia that mediates the banality of everyday life. Highlighting the pointlessness of comfort-obsessed middle-class life, singer Henry Rollins shouts, "Born with a bottle in his mouth / They say I'm wasted all the time / What they do is a waste of time."[43] While these topics seem likely subjects for songs by teenage boys, they also connote the particular relationship of the suburban punk to mass culture. These bands and their audiences found pleasure in drinking beer, eating junk food, and watching television as the only recreational activities available to them, empty gestures that passed the time. Simultaneously, hardcore bands mocked these hobbies as mindless, tedious, and suited to the suburban life of their middlebrow parents who solipsistically pursued self-gratification in their free time rather than genuine human connection or engaged parenting.[44] The mass culture native to suburbia did not fulfill the suburban punk's needs for the excitement, community, and cultural fulfillment at the heart of the promise of postwar suburbia.

Beyond critiquing suburban consumer culture, hardcore bands also focused on destroying the façade of perfect suburban families, and in this way they pulled off an inversion of the political handwringing from on high about the crisis of the family. In their song "Mrs. Jones," the Circle Jerks ask the eponymous parent, "Do you know what your kids are doing?" The answer, they sing: "Youngest Debbie's skipping class / Grades so poor she'll barely pass." Finally, they note: "The family ties are breaking down / There's not much to do to save them."[45] Similarly, Youth Brigade sang in 1984, "You don't understand the way we feel . . . / You say that we should not complain / You hear it over and over again / But you don't seem to realize / How uncertain you've made our lives."[46] According to these punks, their parents had expectations that could not be met and an idea of family that proved unrealistic and ultimately unproductive for those who didn't fit the mold of jock, cheerleader, or nerd. As for those who did fit the mold and did follow their parents into middle-class banality, their fates were worse. The Descendents sum up this dim view in their song "Suburban Home." Lead singer Milo Aukerman glibly intones, "I want to be stereotyped / I want to be classified / I want to be a clone / I want a suburban home."[47] Hardcore songs about fantasies of placid family life, repetitive built landscapes, and mindless mass culture presented a damning critique of suburban life delivered by suburban teens themselves. That attitude, contained in the music's lyrics and sound, would matter as hardcore punks moved into public space. They created music that voiced their antagonism and anger toward suburban culture, emotions that they also embodied through aggressive dancing and violent performances. Often the latter ended in confrontations with authorities who thought they could cure suburban teen angst through spatial regulation.

With a dearth of spaces available for hardcore performances, suburban punks created ad-hoc spaces for socializing, practicing, and performing in what became known in hardcore parlance as the "scene." Peter Belsito and Bob Davis, documenting the scene in their 1983 book, *Hardcore California*, described the situation for suburban Los Angeles punks in the late 1970s: "Kids in L.A. have no real physical center to hang out in. Everything is spread out in endless suburbs. There's a constant feeling of dislocation."[48] That dislocation invited the purveyors of hardcore to commandeer spaces and make them their own, at least temporarily. These spaces were not large venues and, for the most part, not the traditional rock clubs that were part of the burgeoning music scene on Los Angeles's Sunset Strip, particularly as those clubs refused to book hardcore shows because of their reputation for violence and property destruction.[49] Instead, hardcore bands and their fans frequented house parties, church basements, recreation centers, beach parties, their own makeshift "clubs" in local restaurants, and any another space they could seize to give place to their scene. Sociologist Donna Gaines argues that for hardcore punks, "the general idea was to do it yourself, to create immediate rupture, quick community, in a place you could call your own."[50]

However, creating that quick, on-the-spot community was not without its consequences. Because of their unusual locations, the violent nature of the performances, and the lyrical antagonism, hardcore shows invited closer scrutiny by police. In their own zines, punks noted the prevalence of violent confrontations

Figure 4.3. The cover of this issue of the punk zine *Flipside* (Volume 36 [1982]) maps the sprawling suburban locales of the hardcore scene outside Los Angeles. Internet Archive (CC BY 3.0).

at shows, usually blaming club owners and police for instigating them.[51] In his zine *The Big Takeover*, punk journalist Jack Rabid described his experience at a Black Flag show in 1980 at the Starwood, a small hardcore club in California: "I remember driving back by myself to Santa Barbara that night in my parent's little Chevette, my head bleeding all over the seats" from the slam-dancing and being assaulted by police attempting to break up the show.[52] In the introduction to the December 1980 issue of the foundational punk zine *Flipside*, the author bemoans a spate of conflicts caused by police who refused to let fans enjoy the show and leave peacefully. Instead, officers broke up the show mid-performance, only heightening the tension.[53] In its January–February 1983 issue, punk zine *MaximumRockNRoll* (*MRR*), under the satirical headline "Stop the Presses! Late Bulletin! RIOT ON THE SUNSET STRIP!!!", reported, "Hollywood police swept down on and tried to close yet another punk gig and hundreds of punks fought back."[54] In fanzine narratives of police confrontations, punks blamed police who did not understand their behavior and would not allow punks to police themselves. *MRR* argued that the show that ended in a riot was "orderly, by any standards, and that it was just another case of police harassment of punks in Southern California."[55] For punk media, this was the scene's rallying cry. The crisis was not teen behavior but aggressive police harassment that it made it difficult to cultivate the scene.

Mainstream media saw the confrontations between punks and police differently. The *New York Times* rock critic John Rockwell promoted the hardcore scene as artistically valid but essentially violent. He described the viciousness of the scene as "sometimes diffused by parody, welcomed as cathartic, or explained away as outside agitation (i.e., visitors to Hollywood clubs from beach towns that most people think are part of L.A. in the first place). But at other times, the violence simply seems to define the hardcore scene."[56] Likewise, Stephen Braun, in a *Los Angeles Times* article titled "Battle over Punk Rock Club Reflects Rift in Values," noted: "Confrontations have become weekend occurrences outside Cathay de Grande, a Chinese restaurant in Hollywood that gave up on subgum and fried rice three years ago, replacing its menu with punk rock shows four nights a week."[57] He continued, "Clubs featuring punk rock tend to have short life spans in the Los Angeles area. Most have closed under public and official pressure." Ultimately, both hardcore zines and the mainstream press linked the scene to violence in public areas, thereby associating hardcore not just with violence but with confrontations with police. These associations not only connected teens with the potential for disruptive or even violent behavior, but would also buttress moves by police and mall owners to make it challenging for teens to congregate in public.

The hardcore scene's violent reputation made it difficult to book shows at legitimate venues. Instead, fans moved the scene to more marginal suburban spaces, which eventually led to its erosion.[58] Even the most popular and acclaimed bands, such as Black Flag and the Circle Jerks, had trouble booking shows at the few remaining legitimate punk rock clubs "due to radical rock shows' notorious, if slightly exaggerated reputation for vandalism and encounters with the police."[59] Instead, according to Steven Blush, shows went down in "marginal sites in low rent 'hoods'— usually a VFW hall, church basement, or dilapidated warehouse."[60] In moving to these sites, punks fomented hardcore as a suburban scene by moving further into the communities where many of its musicians and fans lived and where clashes with police were likely.

One of the most notorious nodes of hardcore was the Church, an abandoned house of worship in Hermosa Beach, California. Black Flag made this their rehearsal space and makeshift apartment, living alongside runaways and misfits who joined the hardcore scene.[61] A writer in *Flipside* said of the Church, "You gotta head for the suburbs. The Church is the best place to see and feel punk rock, or else those one off gigs that we go all out to thrash the hall."[62] In *The Decline of Western Civilization*, the Church is shown to be a graffiti-covered basement with small closets that band members slept in. In that way, the Church was a typical hardcore space. It was cheap and small and was used by the scene for only a short time before someone expelled the punks. At the Church, the landlord evicted Black Flag and their compatriots for making too much noise. They moved to the Worm Hole, a space in Hermosa Beach where, eventually, the town council ran them out because of the large numbers of vagrants and runaways that congregated outside.[63] Spaces like the Church and the Worm Hole became familiar haunts that exemplified and extended representations of hardcore punks as dangerous teens who were out of control in public spaces, representations that raised the ire of local police departments.

Beyond infamous spots like the Church, some evidence of other scene spaces can be found in hardcore zines and show flyers dating from the late 1970s through the mid-1980s.[64] This evidence reveals that the hardcore scene occurred in varied and often fleeting locations because of its notoriety. Bands and fans put on shows at short-lived clubs as well as restaurants-cum–punk rock venues on the outskirts of Los Angeles and San Francisco. Regular sites included the Hong Kong Café and Mabuhay Gardens, the latter a Filipino restaurant that periodically opened and closed because of the disturbances caused by punks.[65] Other flyers simply identify the location of a show with an address. A flyer for a show in 1979 identified the venue only as 5629 Hollister Avenue in Goleta, California. Currently the location of a car dealership on a busy street, in the 1980s it was probably the address of a small hall, apartment complex clubhouse, or even a vacant lot where punks put on a show. These documents suggest the hardcore scene's transience, stemming from its reputation for violence and desire to avoid the police. That desire was nearly impossible to meet, however, for place-bound local teens dealing with suburban cops who often had little else to do but bust up punk gatherings. Ultimately, many punks got tired of police harassment and they quit or left, which ultimately minimized the presence of the hardcore scene in suburban spaces.

The story of hardcore punk in the suburbs symbolized the changing perception of teens in public space. Even though their style and music intentionally stood out from their suburban surroundings and often precipitated conflict, the policing of punks signaled a more general approach to teens and their misbehavior in public. Parents and police addressed these antisocial teens sporting mohawks, unusual piercings, and torn jeans as an easily identifiable manifestation of social disorder borne of the civil rights and cultural revolutions of the previous twenty years. Their attempts to bring order out of chaos and reverse cultural degradation by policing hardcore punks were part of a broader strategy to reform the suburban teen through spatial regulation that would safeguard public space and return vulnerable teens to the sanctuary of the home.

Through the 1980s, teens who were not hardcore punks or willing to abandon suburban living had fewer places to congregate in public space. Both licit spaces such as the recreation center and illicit ones like abandoned housing and appropriated venues were largely shut down by municipal authorities. And so the teens who stayed in their suburban locales were left with little choice but to frequent the suburban mall—the central and seemingly safest public space that welcomed everyone as a consumer.

Mecca for Teens

Developed and marketed in the postwar United States as the primary place for shopping, socializing, and participating in suburban public life, the shopping mall had by the late 1970s become the central space of a decentralized American landscape.[66] Indeed, during the shopping center–building boom of the 1970s and '80s, the mall became synonymous with American suburban life. During the boom, news media depicted the extended area of the newly ubiquitous shopping mall as the space that not only served shoppers but filled a particular void for suburban teens—a "mecca for teens" that was "more home than home."[67] The fourteen thousand new shopping centers constructed in the 1980s offered amusements and other services ranging from fast food and arcade games to movie multiplexes and record stores all seemingly tailored to teen interests at a moment when the number and capacity of other spaces and pursuits were limited.[68] Other parts of the mall, like atriums and parking lots, offered venues for activities beyond shopping, such as drinking alcohol, making out, having sex, skateboarding, or even just congregating beyond the watchful eye of parents and teachers.

Still, the shopping center was not entirely unregulated, just less so than school or home, and so it seemed to represent a satisfying compromise for teens, parents, and police. Parents, in fact, understood the mall as safe compared to other public spaces. A mother from suburban Syracuse echoed this point in a 1988 newspaper interview, "Part of me says when you get a lot of kids together it's not a healthy thing. The other part says they have to have someplace to go that's not on the street corner. At least it's well lit. I know she won't get raped."[69] On its face, the mall of the 1980s seemed a safer public space for teens than a street corner, makeshift punk club, a construction site for new housing, or even a recreation center. Yet in emphasizing teenagers' disruptive, transgressive, and even criminal conduct, the mall's elaboration in the news media and popular culture associated the shopping center with danger not only for teenagers but because of them.

According to bygone notions in the media and popular culture, the suburb was simply a spatial articulation of traditional family values where public space was safe and the public teen was a good citizen vulnerable only to outside (read: urban) influences. Popular culture texts like the movie *Fast Times at Ridgemont High* subverted such ideas by offering the mall as home to multiple transgressions presented as quotidian acts.[70] The film presented scalping concert tickets as a legitimate enterprise for teens alongside customary mall work, like taking tickets for the Cineplex or waiting tables at the pizzeria; it thus reframed as imperiled and imperiling the American teen and the shopping mall going into a decade of massive growth for suburban shopping centers.

Most prevalent in the film are sex and sexuality as a naturally occurring part of mall space, even as the reason for some to visit or work in the mall. During her shift as a waitress at the pizza shop, Stacy (played by Jennifer Jason Leigh) expresses her frustration over having to sling pizza slices in a space where her peers can't see her. She glumly intones to her slightly older and more sexually experi-enced coworker Linda (Phoebe Cates), "You told me I would get a boyfriend working in the mall." Later, Linda prods Stacy about losing her virginity: "What are you waiting for? You are fifteen already." Soon after that conversation, an older customer at Perry's asks Stacy out. Ron Johnson, a so-called "fox," does not become her boyfriend. Instead, they go on one date, which ends up inside the dugout of a Little League field where twenty-six-year-old Ron deflowers fifteen-year-old Stacy. The scene is presented without a hint of judgment about this ille-gal tryst. Later in the film, Stacy has sex with a classmate, causing her to become pregnant and have an abortion—with no involvement from parents, teachers, or even the baby's father. The film depicts all of these incidents matter-of-factly, suggesting not only the normalcy but also the inevitability of suburban teen sex-uality given the opportunities afforded by the seemingly unregulated Ridgemont Shopping Center. The film, too, contributed to an emerging cultural logic that justified increased oversight and discipline of mall space to protect teens, in large part, from other teens.

Depictions in the news media also suggested the shopping center was both advantageous and dangerous for its teen patrons because it afforded freedom of movement and spaces for sexual activity, drinking, and drug use. *Washington Post* columnist Bob Levey wrote of the liminality of the shopping mall space in his 1981 article "Teens View Center as 'Their' Community." The first half of the article promoted the safety, fun, and sense of community the mall provided for teens who had few other places to congregate. Levey quoted Steve Rader, age fifteen, as saying he would be at the mall day after day because "this is like a community of friends for me. This is where I feel comfortable."[71] Levey portrayed Rader as legitimately frequenting the mall: he worked there and spent money while hanging out with friends he already knew—all sanctioned activities.

But later in the article, Levey identified the "dark side" of the mall as a "teen mecca." "According to Montgomery County, Maryland police," Levey wrote, "the plaza's Lot 19—a parking area along the northwestern edge of the shopping cen-ter—is notorious as a nighttime gathering place for young drinkers, or vandals, or both."[72] With many of the community's teens at the mall, crime and rowdy behavior were also present. Levey then argued that without an increase in secu-rity personnel, the Montgomery Mall, and others like it, would continue to see fights and other disruptions of mall spaces. According to this logic, the presence of the "good" teen, like Steve Rader, alongside the drinking rabble-rousers in the parking lot would cause Steve to move from productive citizen to a dangerous presence—providing further demonstration that suburban families were failing at bringing up "normal" teens who could resist transgressive suburban subcultures.

The ubiquity of teens in malls gave rise to an effort by the news media to name the phenomenon; ultimately they settled on dubbing teen denizens of the shopping center "mallrats." Although any teen at the mall could be assumed a mallrat, not every teen was, according to security guards and mallrats themselves. Rather, a mallrat was someone who, "thanks to two 20th century phenomena— the shopping center and the computer chip . . . may never again know the heat of summer. Instead, they may become what some Albany security guards call 'mall rats,' taking up seasonal residence in shopping malls, living on soda, ice cream and fast food and spending uncounted hours in air-conditioned arcades."[73] Mallrats were essentially teens who spent most of their free time in the mall with no particular agenda other than "hanging out" and playing arcade games. As the *Washington Post* described mallrats, "They shift from place to place, moving in small knots, unnoticed by the average shopper," and "gather in the sorts of numbers that once collected at drive-in diners and drive-in theaters. And, though most of the kids tend to be well-behaved, they bring with them fights, thefts, noise and drugs."[74] The naming of the mallrat consolidated and made legible under a single moniker the image of disruptive patrons without an agenda, prone to misbehavior and disruptive to the mall's economic and social order. This label thus suggested that teens were an invasive species taking advantage of their environment as parasites and would leave only by being forcibly removed. Still, teen misbehavior posed a dilemma for mall owners in that these customers were dangerous to the primary commercial purpose of the mall, yet also vital to that purpose as more of them flocked to malls as a refuge where they would inevitably spend money.

Pac-Man Fever and Arcade Addicts

One possible solution to the problem of unruly teens in shopping malls was to give them a place of their own in the mall where they could spend their money and would not disrupt the rest of the shopping center: the video game arcade. Mall owners and managers located arcades away from anchor stores or higher-end shops so as to sequester teens in a contained area of the mall. The video game arcade, then, was part of the broader promise of suburban shopping spaces to both protect and safely contain teenagers while allowing mall businesses to make money by providing the goods and services essential to the era's middle-class suburban lifestyle. The checkered history of arcades, especially in shopping centers, however, tells a different story. The video game arcade of the 1980s moved from being a way to contain public teens to another home for teen misbehavior and further justification for mall owners, parents, teachers, and town officials to regulate or even ban the arcades. In turn, the increased policing of suburban public space not only facilitated the movement of video games and their players into the home, but also virtually erased the teen-oriented suburban arcade by the end of the 1990s.[75]

Starting in the mid-1970s, coin-operated electronic video games began to crop up in various public spaces, to the delight of teenagers and adults alike. Kids after school and businessmen on lunch breaks found standalone machines or small clusters of game cabinets in pizzerias, convenience stores, laundromats, and bars.[76] As the industry matured and more games became available, aggregating the games in one space in the fashion of earlier urban pinball arcades provided a way to minimize costs and maximize profits by focusing on the increasingly popular games.[77]

In the suburbs, this meant the introduction of arcades into established retail spaces such as shopping malls, where teens were already gathering.[78] However, mall owners and parents quickly realized that clustering teens in one space, while keeping them from disrupting other mall spaces, could also lead to security problems, which they had sought to curb.[79] For this reason, shopping centers required arcade owners and operators to implement strict rules to safeguard arcade space.[80] These rules aimed to stop "good" teens from becoming "bad" and to reform others by channeling their behavior toward consumption and away from corruption. Some of the rules, like prohibiting alcohol and gambling, were designed to stop the transgressive behavior associated with urban pool halls and pinball arcades, the antecedents of video game arcades.[81] Other rules limiting eating, smoking, and loitering mirrored those aimed at curbing teen behavior in mall space more generally. Spaceport, a chain of shopping mall arcades, made these points clear in its employee-training video from 1981. The narrator emphasized that employees should use a polite but firm tone when enforcing the rules, particularly those concerning behavior within the arcade and lingering around its entrance lest they alienate a potential consumer. The video shows still photos of employees breaking up a group of young men hanging outside the arcade while a voiceover reminds them never to use physical force but to call security or police should the patrons resist.[82] The video makes clear that teens are the arcade's primary patrons as well as the most likely culprits in violating the rules, a paradox requiring a deft touch by employees in sorting good teens from bad.

However, as one arcade operator hopefully noted, "There isn't a single kid who leaves here with enough money to go out and buy dope"—articulating the logic of consumer-led cultural reform at the heart of mall and arcade security changes.[83]

An alternative to the mall arcade packed with teens was the family-friendly arcade popularized by Pizza Time Entertainment's Chuck E. Cheese restaurant and arcade. The original, opened in San Jose, California, in 1977 by Atari founder Nolan Bushnell, promoted its safe environs, wide variety of games, and cheap pizza. Businesses like Chuck E. Cheese, geared toward a wholesome experience, attempted to associate the arcade with families and safety and not unruly teenagers. However, for most of the 1980s, the mall arcade proved far more popular than its family-friendly counterpart because teens did not go there and parents could suffer only so many hours spent eating bad pizza and listening to the blaring sounds of video games and animatronic bands.[84] By 1986, only a year after recording $150 million in sales, Chuck E. Cheese owner Bushnell filed for Chapter 11 bankruptcy as most of the industry suffered a lull.[85] Still, thousands of standalone and mall arcades continued catering to teens through the mid-1980s after an initial growth spurt that saw sales of arcade video game machines grow from $50 million in 1978 to about $900 million in 1982.[86] Arcade game releases peaked in 1989, only to fall nearly continuously until 2013 with the emergence of adult-oriented arcades and resurrection of Chuck E. Cheese–style outlets.[87]

In this respect, teen-oriented arcades, like shopping malls, were victims of their own success. In news articles, the question was not whether teens in arcades would be disruptive but rather how disruptive they would be given the large numbers of teen patrons, so-called "arcade addicts." Local officials feared that "adequate supervision would not be provided and the place would become a hangout for teen-agers who would cause problems for police."[88] According to the news media, these officials were right. "In town after town, local officials are struggling to cope with a craze that has swept the country: Arcade videogames that gobble up the time and money of America's teenagers."[89] A new arcade in the Plaza Camino Real shopping center in Carlsbad, California, dramatically increased complaints about teen behavior. Teen patrons began gathering near an adjacent bookstore, blocking its entrance, and also congregating at a bank of telephones, "inhibit[ing] their use by mall customers." "A day does not go by," the mall manager complained, "that customers do not call this office complaining of the arcade and its patrons."[90]

Teen troubles went beyond disruptive behavior as the news and popular culture presented players as increasingly addicted to the games. Films such as the horror anthology *Nightmares* and the science fiction adventure *The Last Starfighter* portrayed video games as leading to trance-inducing addictions capable of disrupting otherwise normal lives.[91] Most visibly, in April 1982, *Time* named "Pac-Man Fever" the most prominent hazard of the arcade, while the *Washington Post* asked whether "Pac-Man thumb [was] the anti-social disease of the '80s."[92] These and other observers argued that the game was so fun and addictive that it struck players with an unbreakable fever for more, leading hopelessly devoted young fans to engage with all things Pac-Man to the detriment of homework and their social lives. Whether a dedication or a fever, playing the game made Pac-Man the most profitable and visible arcade game of the early 1980s. *Time* estimated the game and its associated properties generated $1 billion in fifteen months, rivaling the *Star Wars* film franchise in revenue and visibility.[93] The game was even immortalized with a Saturday morning cartoon, a cereal, numerous spin-off games such as Ms. Pac-Man, and a hit single, "Pac-Man Fever," written and performed by Buckner and Garcia that reached number 9 on the *Billboard* charts in 1982. Addiction to the game became a central concern of parents, teachers, and culture critics who argued that it compelled teen players to loiter at the arcade and paved the way to their dangerous behavior there. A parent from Centereach, Long Island, argued, "They mesmerize our children, they addict them and force them to mindlessly pour one quarter after another into the slots. We see 15-year-olds playing these games at 10:30 on school nights and during school hours. We want them out of our town."[94] The games were not simply popular but were an addiction that critics saw as a real danger to schoolwork and a healthy moral life, a threat that could best be addressed through stricter control of arcade space.

Despite the implementation of strict rules and attempts at rigid enforcement to maintain order among mallrats and arcade addicts, teens did continue to congregate, spend money, loiter, and cause trouble in malls and arcades. A manager of three malls in Wichita, Kansas, said, "There've been times when we're sorry we have a game room. At other times, we're pleased they have somewhere to go. Occasionally we have to use a little persuasion on them from the security police. We had to make an example out of two or three of the real troublemakers. The rest just come to enjoy themselves, and they do spend some money."[95] This fundamental paradox of the video game arcade in the shopping mall of the 1970s and '80s exemplified the larger contemporary recoding of suburban public space. Even when teens were largely removed or distracted from other public spaces, including malls, they created security problems in these new, supposedly safe spaces. These troubles in turn created a new understanding of safe space that did not include teenagers or required new strategies for properly policing teens within it, and led to greater supervision of everyone who entered mall space.

Even lighthearted cinematic fare like *Pinball Summer* (1980) and *Joysticks* (1983) showed the arcade space as home to teenage debauchery.[96] Part of an exploding exploitation genre that sought to attract a teenage audience, these films featured supposed fads—like video games or roller derby—liberal use of foul language, and depictions of sexuality focused mostly on female nudity, as seen most prominently in the *Porky's* series. Although they were a small part of this kind of fare in the 1980s, arcade movies made explicit connections between video game arcades and transgressive suburban teen behavior already visible in arcades and the news. Comically amplified to appeal to their teen audiences, these movies suggested that the concerns of parents, mall operators, and town administrators were exaggerated. However, by trafficking in the standard motifs of 1980s exploitation movies while making light of the colorful media image of the video game arcade, they also elaborated on those narratives, preserving and promoting the arcade's association with teen sex, substance abuse, and all-around bad behavior.

In *Joysticks*, teen customers and employees of Bailey's arcade must defend themselves against concerned parents and business owners who object to patrons' activities. The actual space of Bailey's arcade is presented as capable of altering the behavior of its patrons and employees, turning all who enter into free-wheeling bacchanalians. All of the characters—including skilled game players and ostensible heroes Jefferson and Eugene, nerd employee Jonathan Andrew McDorfus, and antisocial punk King Vidiot (a clear allusion to the hardcore scene)—enjoy sex, drugs, and alcohol as a result of their association with the arcade and one another. The arcade's main critic, Joseph Rutter (Joe Don Baker), agitates for its closure by emphasizing the place's lurid reputation. On entering Bailey's arcade, he claims, "you are hit by a stench of filth that covers the premises." Portraying himself as a concerned parent of a wholesome teen customer of the arcade, he declares that what happens there every day is a testament to moral decay in society. Exaggerating the concerns of real parents and conservative critics and politicians about family decline, Rutter argues that the arcade is a breeding ground for morally detrimental behavior.

Ultimately, the teens at Bailey's don't so much defend their behavior or the sanctity of the arcade space as deflect responsibility. Like justifications provided by mallrats about why they misbehave, the main characters rationalize their behavior. They claim they were forced to misbehave in the arcade. With no other outlet besides hanging out at the mall, the 7-Eleven convenience store, or the arcade, they plead that losing the arcade would further limit their options to congregate in suburban public space and actually lead to continued bad behavior. While the film was not intended as a realistic portrayal, its predominant images conformed to those imagined by the arcade's critics and disseminated in the news media. In that formulation, arcades were teen hangouts that endangered "good" teens by putting them in proximity to "bad" ones. Despite the filmmakers' attempts to present arcade hijinks in the film as essentially harmless, *Joysticks* echoed and enhanced visions of transgressive teens in public, further associating the arcade with poor teen behavior and facilitating movements to more closely police it.

Other texts made similar associations between poor behavior and the video game arcade, including allusions to the hardcore punk scene of greater Los Angeles in the early 1980s. Black Randy and the Metrosquad released their song "I Slept in an Arcade" in 1979.[97] The song recounts the peripatetic lifestyle of a punk rocker who rubs elbows in Los Angeles with porn stars and fights with police but, ultimately, is homeless, finding a place to sleep only in an arcade. The song reinforced the association of the arcade with degenerate teens, in this case notorious hardcore punks like those in Black Flag and the Germs, while also suggesting that the arcade was a home for these disaffected teenagers. Similarly, the Canadian Broadcasting Corporation radio anthology series *Nightfall* broadcast a story entitled "No Quarter" on March 4, 1983. "No Quarter" follows a story line similar to that in the film *Nightmares*, in which a teen listens to punk rock on his Walkman as he masters the games at his arcade and eventually gets addicted to them. When shown, then, the arcade was framed as home to addictive games and as socially dangerous. Taken together, these texts hardened the link between teenagers and their participation in seemingly dangerous subcultures in the central spaces of suburban life that called forth new security practices to address social problems.

Videomaniacs and the Public Interest

The seemingly addictive power of video games and the potential moral and social hazards of the arcade space inspired protests and regulatory responses from parents, teachers, town administrators, and mall owners. The immediate goal of each group was to prevent disruptive behavior in the spaces or close them down if they could not. Business owners and municipalities, for their part, created new policies and practices to focus teens on spending money, and parents and teachers sought to reform teen behavior through new regimes that would ideally bring teens back into the suburban home. Further, the suburbanites' fear of and for teenagers in that era motivated them to increase surveillance and scrutiny of public spaces, which meant that spaces like the mall exhibited fewer of the hallmarks of civic public space, and furthered the local dominion produced through their Nimby protests and responses to criminal threats happening at the same moment.

Most states empowered municipalities to regulate businesses and impose zoning within their borders, including specific ordinances regarding coin-operated gaming establishments. In 1984, Bloomfield, New Jersey, for example, required arcades that sought to add more than twenty gaming machines to an arcade to employ professional security guards who had to be off-duty police officers.[98] The town council passed the law in part to deal with crime in and around the arcade, including bicycle thefts and graffiti. While the latter part of the ordinance requiring off-duty police to work as security guards was struck down by the New Jersey Supreme Court, the court did find the requirement of security personnel was "a reasonable measure to protect the public interest," including the safety of "video arcade patrons." In this way, the court articulated the same regulatory logic as parents and mall owners in addressing teen behavior.[99] In 1983, Vienna, Virginia, banned businesses from having more than three video game machines, because "parents are worried about kids wasting money, staying out of school and 'hanging out' around the popular machines."[100] Other cities, such as Palm Springs, California, had local ordinances that prevented establishments from having more than four video games to prevent the congregation of teen patrons.[101] Similarly, San Gabriel, California, passed a moratorium on issuing arcade licenses pending investigation into the effects on "public health" of video game arcades.[102] The lengths to which these municipalities went to police arcades and slow their growth demonstrated the power of two images in the suburban public consciousness: the out-of-control teen and the arcade addict as public menaces who needed close scrutiny on the suburban landscape lest they corrupt other teens and degrade public morals.

Other communities moved to ban arcades or limit access to patrons over seventeen in order to combat the risks associated with "videomaniacs."[103] Bradley, Illinois, prohibited children under age sixteen from playing video games in arcades located in shopping malls.[104] White Plains, New York, banned arcades altogether in its Galleria Mall.[105] Near Washington, D.C., critics speculated that "video game arcades located near residential neighborhoods might introduce un-desirable elements into the community," a clear allusion to keeping out black teens from the adjacent city.[106] In Brookhaven, New York, experts found that "the problem is with the sleazy atmosphere that can develop around them [ar-cades], and the element of child exploitation"; while a Boston-area official ex-plained, "The games have led to major complaints. . . . There are increases in crime, pedestrian traffic, noise, and disruptive conduct."[107] These strict laws showed the power of the video game arcade in raising the specter of the public teen as victim and victimizer. Operating under the premise that teens could be both, suburban towns used new regulations to discipline teens toward produc-tive consumptive behavior or push them out of these public spaces and back into the safety of the home.

Protecting Shoppers Means Protecting Profits

Even against this backdrop of negative news reports and popular culture representations, bans proved an unwieldy and unproductive solution, particu-larly because they negatively impacted the profits of mall and arcade owners, themselves important political stakeholders in suburban communities. In lieu of all-out prohibition, these proprietors implemented private solutions to accom-modate teens and their wallets while also protecting the space and reputation of the shopping center and arcade. And so the shopping center of the 1980s and '90s experienced an overhaul in security tactics that included a move toward professionalization of personnel, introduction of technology such as closed-circuit television (CCTV) that increased scrutiny of all mall customers, and im-plementation of curfews for those under sixteen. These new policies increased surveillance of mall space for all patrons while helping push teens back into the home to play video games and hang out. In discouraging socializing among pa-trons, particularly teens, and housing business that may bring that demographic to the mall, these policies undermined the long-term viability of many shopping centers, especially as e-commerce arrived, despite the desire to protect shoppers and evict dangerous patrons.

The shopping center industry was concerned about disruptive teens primarily because of profits lost to the petty crimes they committed and the negative per-ception of malls that came with narratives of mall crime and disruption. In a November 1978 issue of *Shopping Center World*, a leading industry journal, mall owners identified shoplifting, loitering and drinking, and vandalism as their top three security concerns—all crimes predominantly associated with teenagers.[108]

Similarly, in his column from March 1979, mall security expert Dr. Harold Gluck alerted his readers to the supposed "plague . . . called shoplifting."[109] According to mall owners and security experts, teens posed a visible and disorderly presence in shopping centers that undermined the space's profit motive—a motive that was superseding the purpose, envisioned by midcentury mall designers, of serving not only as a space of commerce but also as a civic space for sprawling suburban communities.[110]

Articles in *Shopping Center World* also emphasized "loss prevention" in addressing insurance liability, the costs of hiring and training staff, preventing theft, fire-proofing, and effectively lighting walkways and parking lots to avoid lawsuits.[111] The journal's security writers, including Dr. Harold Gluck and retired professional thief Mike McCaffrey, sought to combat the notion that the aimless, shoplifting teenager was the most dangerous threat to the bottom line while still addressing the highly visible threat of the disruptive teenager. Gluck emphasized that it was professional thieves who were more dangerous because they were looking to live off their booty, whereas the teen shoplifter stole for a cheap thrill or to get the latest fashion.[112] In trying to convince shopping center executives of numerous, less visible but high-risk threats, *Shopping Center World* acknowledged the pervasiveness of the disruptive teen and loitering mallrat images among its audience of mall and store owners, and this reinforcement helped orient the evolving security policies of mall owners in the 1980s around teens.

With both the nuisance of mallrats and the threat of professional thieves in mind, mall owners and operators shifted their security tactics and strategies to providing a comprehensive response that would ideally handle both visible social problems and less visible but more costly threats simultaneously. The authors of *Shopping Center World* urged mall owners to make their security teams larger, more professionalized, and more technologically advanced. William R. Brown, in the article "Protecting Shoppers Means Protecting Profits," emphasized the use of CCTV monitoring to prevent crime, provide evidence for prosecution, and to monitor the shopping center more effectively and efficiently for concerning, if not explicitly illegal, behavior.[113] This was a new use of CCTV, as it had not begun as surveillance technology. Rather, cable television pioneers developed the technology to provide broadcast TV access to low-lying areas and urban apartment and hotel dwellers who could not receive a direct, over-the-air signal.[114] Indeed, through the 1970s, CCTV was mostly an addendum to broadcast and cable television programming, such as sporting events shown in bars, or speeches and sermons put on screens for overflow crowds.[115] In the 1974 edition of the

Closed-Circuit Television Handbook, author Leon Wortman acknowledged the use of CCTV for security, among numerous other purposes. Yet he mentioned the security-related use of this technology only for policing the gates and other entry points for industrial manufacturing sites.[116] He did not suggest or acknowledge commercial security use in shops or malls to regulate spaces open to the public.

Yet, by the end of the 1980s, shopping centers had adopted CCTV nearly universally as the technology got cheaper and more effective in recording images while making the policing of mall space more efficient.[117] Although the efficacy of CCTV surveillance in stopping crime is difficult to assess, the presence of cameras, functional or not, suggested constant surveillance and encouraged patrons to discipline themselves lest they be caught on camera breaking mall rules or the law.[118] While some courts have found CCTV surveillance tantamount to police officers moving in and watching the public, the use of the technology is actually quite different. It allows a small number of personnel to monitor the many spaces of the mall almost at the same time from a central location while also recording behavior for possible criminal prosecution or banning from the mall—making possible a much more comprehensive canvass of the space than a few police officers walking a beat could effect.[119] Initiated in large part in response to disruptive teens, this advance changed the very nature of mall space as patrons came to understand that they were likely being watched. While this awareness might have enhanced a sense of safety for some, for many it discouraged free association and expression in the heavily policed, quasi-public space of the mall.[120]

Beyond new technologies like CCTV, the security writers for *Shopping Center World* stressed the importance of hiring well-trained, professional security workers in sufficient numbers to be visible throughout mall space, rather than the poorly trained and badly paid forces of the previous era.[121] Seasoned thief—turned-columnist Mike McCaffrey pleaded for a new kind of security force by emphasizing the constant threat from thieves: "Remember, at all times, that your store is under surveillance by someone who knows how to steal, perhaps even someone who is a professional and [as] good at theft as I was."[122] The journal's staff attempted to shift industry attitudes to favor practices and new tactics for regulating mall space to prevent both teen misbehavior and the costlier damage being done by professional criminals.

The popular security manual *Principles of Security* explained best practices in retail security, including private security education. It advises a multistep screening process for hiring guards, including a background check, honesty test, credit check, and psychological evaluation. Once hired, the authors recommend, staff to be licensed for weapon use should undergo a program including at least thirty hours of firearms training.[123] Although the industry attempted to create a more professional and efficient security force, this goal was not always met in shopping centers in the 1980s. In 1988, *U.S. News & World Report* noted a spate of crimes committed by security guards, including theft, murder, rape, and kidnapping.[124] Security experts warned that despite the move toward better training and background checks, "For $3.35 an hour, you're not going to get a West Point cadet."[125]

Ultimately, the shift in mall security continued to move the indoor shopping mall away from the original conception of a central space that not only housed stores but also served the community through public gatherings and cultural performances.[126] With Larry Smith, visionary mall designer Victor Gruen had written in 1960 that proper mall planning "also brings into being community facilities, such as auditoriums and meeting rooms. This is done with the express intention of creating an environment which, if properly utilized, will establish the shopping center as the focal point for the life of a community or a number of communities."[127] Gruen and Smith continued that shopping center security would function as a "public relations" service, helping customers find parking and load their vehicles rather than preventing crime.[128]

Instead, the 1980s mall exhibited a privatist ethic in policing its seemingly open space by using professional, private security forces working at the behest of mall and store owners to "get tough on teenage rowdies" and to promote shopping rather than loitering.[129] This step-up in mall security and the parallel rise in private neighborhood security helped private personnel to surpass public law enforcement officers in number during the 1980s.[130] Security expert Anthony N. Potter wrote in 1983 of the change in shopping center security, "Today, the walls of my office are lined with bookcases containing over 1,200 volumes on private security, a knowledge explosion that is symbolic of the growth of the industry to the point where there are now two security officers for every law enforcement officer in the United States." Revenues for private security firms increased 12 percent a year, and the total number of security guards rose 300 percent from 1969 to 1988.[131] The *Hallcrest Report II*, a 1990 survey of private security, noted that at the end of the 1980s, "private security is more than twice the size of federal, state, and local law enforcement combined."[132] In a 1989 article in *Shopping Center World*, Robert Bond argued that shoppers were feeling safe again because of the revolution in shopping center security over the previous decade. While new security measures may have made customers feel safe and possibly protected the bottom line, they more closely policed suburban space, making more clear to patrons that mall space was not as free and open as government-owned and -regulated public spaces.[133] Though intended to reduce the presence and activity of suburban teens in the mall and curb crime, these measures also had the effects of subjecting all mall patrons to increased scrutiny and encouraging rule adherence through panoptically induced self-discipline.

Despite the advances in mall security, the problem of the disruptive mall teen did not go away in the 1990s. The complaints from store and mall owners as well as shoppers about teen behavior at the mall remained largely the same as those about the 1980s mallrat—loitering, drinking, vandalism, and general disruption.[134] Still, shopping center owners were in a quandary as they continued to court lucrative young consumers without eroding the image of the mall as safe for other customers. Before the full advent of online shopping in the twenty-first century, teens represented a huge share of consumer spending, preferred visiting the mall to shop, and spent upward of $100 billion there by 1996.[135] Stuck between addressing continuing security issues and welcoming teens crucial to the bottom line, some shopping mall owners created curfews for teen patrons to augment larger numbers of better-trained security personnel. The curfews were designed, like earlier measures, to keep teens coming to the mall but focus them on shopping by requiring adult escorts on weekend nights. While not the first to institute a curfew, the Mall of America, then the nation's largest shopping center, implemented a new rule to better regulate the approximately three thousand teens who visited the mall each weekend and to combat an image of the mall as "Fight City."[136] Maureen Busch, Mall of America's associate general manager, argued, "They fight, use bad language and often intimidate and disrupt guests. The potential exists for even more serious incidents to occur. We have a responsibility to take action."[137]

To meet this responsibility, the mall required anyone under sixteen to be accompanied by a parent or someone over twenty-one after 6 PM, Friday–Sunday, while also adding thirty people to its security force. In total, it employed 150 security officers who manned 140 closed circuit television cameras while providing 130 emergency call boxes for patrons.[138] In addition to raising thorny questions about First Amendment rights to assemble in "public," the policy was risky as this was "an extreme measure to control teenagers, who are also valued customers."[139] One teen remarked that she would not be caught dead with her parents at the mall.[140] Others felt the curfew was an overreach that punished good kids because of the behaviors of a small number of teens.[141] An editorial from *USA Today* chastised the mall owners: "The curfew, legal or not, is a poor solution that sends the wrong message to kids. After all, we're talking about the Mall of America here. Not the Mall of Albania."[142] The Mall of America even went as far as to hire a group of "Mighty Moms" and later "Dedicated Dads" to help enforce mall policy and de-escalate conflicts.[143]

Implementation of the curfew at the Mall of America built on a growing trend of city and municipal curfews for teens. By the mid-1990s, hundreds of America's biggest cities, including Minneapolis, had youth curfew laws targeting violence, drug trafficking, gang activity, and truancy; more than one thousand smaller jurisdictions had similar laws.[144] However, those laws, and their shopping mall iterations, were criticized over unfair application of the rules, with the most prominent critique being that law enforcement and security personnel used the curfew to racially profile and disproportionately detain teenagers of color. As the new curfew was announced at the Mall of America, civil rights leaders criticized such action, while young black patrons expressed anger, feeling they were the target of the new rule and noting how they were already being followed once they entered individual mall stores.[145] Gary Sudduth, president of the Minneapolis Urban League, remarked upon hearing of the possibility of a curfew, "Given the mall's earlier attempt to restrict bus access to its site, we can only conclude that racism is playing a role here. It seems to us that the Mall of America believes that children of color will not have a parent—or a car—readily available for their visit to the mall. Therefore, they believe, the new policy requiring the presence of a parent will reduce the number of non-white young people in the mall in the early evening."[146] Skepticism of the curfew was well founded. In 1996, when the curfew rule was instituted, a *New York Times* article dubbed Minneapolis "Murderapolis" and noted that the city's "idyllic image has been shattered by violence, with gang turf wars and drive-by shootings on streets where children play games of kick-the-can."[147] In that context, it was not hard to imagine mall security using the curfew to racially profile mall patrons more overtly in order to prevent the mall being associated with Minneapolis's violent reputation. Further, the fear that the curfew would be a tool of racial profiling also came from the well-documented experiences of black shoppers and patrons who experienced discriminatory treatment in retail establishments, often through the implementation of race-neutral policies.[148]

Despite protests and fears of declining profits, the Mall of America continued with these new policies as the owners believed "security is marketing."[149] Almost immediately, the mall saw fewer fights between teens.[150] At the same time, sales of teen apparel rose suggesting that the new policies focused teens who did go to the mall on shopping rather than carousing.[151] A year later, a security official representing the ownership group reported to the International Council of Shopping Center's security conference that traffic decreased one percent, but sales noticeably increased on both Friday and Saturday. She also noted, "In the nine months before the new policy, we had 391 arrests of people under 17 years of age on Fridays and Saturdays; since then we've had just one child arrested."[152] Mall spokesperson Teresa McFarland told the press, the policy was an unmitigated success.[153] Store owners, too, were largely pleased. Benjamin King, owner of a jewelry store on the east side of the mall where teenagers usually congregated, said, "It's been phenomenal for us. . . . Before, 30 or 40 kids would be outside the front door. Kids would be throwing each other up against the glass, roughhousing, name-calling, and getting loud."[154] Five years later, mall officials still called the policy a success. "There were literally thousands of unsupervised kids. Now it's a completely different place, and the families are back."[155] Perhaps unsurprisingly, the megamall's success at increasing profit and reducing disruption spurred a movement of other shopping centers to implement curfews to deal with disruptive teen patrons.[156]

By the end of the 1990s, shopping center owners continued to increase their policing of mall space and scrutiny of patrons in an effort to maintain the image of safety and therefore profitability. As with the privatization of neighborhood and home security, the intensified policing of quasi-public space like the Mall of America was done according to parochial concerns and had similar racial effects by reinstating segregationist practices through more covert and insidious methods to promote a secure, white consumerist space.[157] For suburban teens, this meant returning to the presumed safety of the home; going to the mall to actually shop, often more frequently in the company of adults; or counting on mall security to not see them as a threat.[158]

Despite a resurgence in arcade revenues in the late 1980s, standalone and mall arcades mostly disappeared from the suburban landscape in the 1990s. The implementation of new regulatory practices in suburban public spaces coincided with the decline of the video arcade market and the upswing in the sales of home video game systems, helping to draw teens back into the home as mall and community forces were encouraging them to leave public space.[159] For game players, their home system was technologically superior, and, for parents, morally preferable as they could better watch their children. The disappearance of arcades and the forced withdrawal of teens from suburban public space signaled the more explicit orientation of public space toward private interests.

The home arcade alleviated the social and moral dilemmas of the mall arcade by transferring the powers of oversight and regulation back to parents while allowing the arcade industry to reform itself. Many arcades became family-friendly and chose not to court a large teen audience.[160] In 1989, an operator of a North Carolina mall said of the arcade in his shopping center, "The emphasis isn't on teenage boys anymore. We have something for mom, we have something for dad, something for children. We have something for everyone."[161] These venues also benefited from the new shopping center security practices that helped make arcades safer. By the end of the 1980s, video arcades had "made a comeback in malls after having been dropped by many centers in the early 1980s because of the sometimes unruly behavior of teenage patrons."[162] Yet, just as many casual gaming venues such as bars and convenience stores had been replaced by the arcade in the late 1970s and early '80s, the family-friendly arcade eclipsed the teen-friendly version, and that version has yet to return to the height of its popularity in the early 1980s.

Real teen behavior and its elaboration and exaggeration in news media and popular culture produced suburban public space as dangerous both to and because of teens. In these places, teens drank, smoked, gambled, had sex, and generally caused disturbances for citizens, police, and members of their own social group. The response to teenagers' presence in suburban public spaces facilitated a new policing of public space that attempted to reform teens or exile them from those spaces and reintegrate them into the home. In doing so, this spatial regulation was part of a new era of privatized policing of public space in which private police forces outnumbered municipal, state, and federal law enforcement and subjected those who move through that space to increased scrutiny by private security.

At recreation centers designed for teenagers, actual incidents of violence and substance abuse, and their narrativization in news media and such films as *Over the Edge*, associated these spaces with transgressive behavior. This depiction helped bring about the closure or reorientation of recreation centers across the country in the 1980s. Similarly, though not associated with any single space, the suburban hardcore punk scene caused a parallel surge in the policing of public space. In their music and public performances, punks themselves produced their scene as violent and antisuburban. News stories enhanced this image with tales of aggressive dancing and antisocial behavior. Although director Penelope Spheeris sought to contextualize their behavior in *The Decline of Western Civilization* and *Suburbia*, her films largely reinforced the notion of the suburban hardcore punk scene as antisocial. These images enabled police and municipalities to regulate the scene out of suburbia. Continually harassed at live performances and pushed to sites on the margins of public life, many hardcore punks left the suburbs for more amenable spaces in major American cities where their scene would not be considered such an aberration.

The teen havens of the shopping mall and the arcade changed as well. Mallrats and arcade addicts' transgressive behavior and its representations in the news media and popular culture marked them as dangerous and endangered figures. Municipalities and mall owners responded to these seemingly malevolent teens with new measures to protect "good" teens as well as other shoppers who were making legitimate use of mall space. Many towns passed restrictive ordinances regulating video game arcades, while mall owners professionalized their security forces and modernized their surveillance technology. As a result, the new regulations of space largely erased teens from suburban public life and also subverted the very notion of suburban public space itself.[163] Ultimately, the responses to teenagers in public space normalized the stricter surveillance of that space. Together, these responses epitomized suburban values in valorizing private property rights and extragovernmental solutions to social dilemmas while showing little regard for public goods such as open, democratic space.[164]

Suburban parents, though occasionally troubled by the content of video games, were happy to welcome their children back into the home, where they could be guided in their popular culture choices and segregated from large groups of teens thought to be bad influences.[165] Teens could play a vast array of games and avoid the possible hazards posed by other teens or police harassment in public space. This endorsement of parental guidance of teens at home was undergirded by the stricter policing of suburban public space, thus aligning the priorities of families and mall owners as to the regulation of public space. These actions complemented suburban desires for increasingly noncivic pursuits with regard to everything from endorsing school choice to Nimby resistance to trash incinerators and nuclear power plants.[166]

However, as many teens made the home their central space of recreation, it was not necessarily as safe as parents might have hoped. The following chapter explores how parents and culture critics came to see the popular culture products coming into the suburban home as undermining parental power and the sanctity of the home. This reaction helped bring about new regulations—of the home itself.

Chapter Five

Parental Advisory—Explicit Content

Popular Occulture and (Re)Possessing the Suburban Home

In the fall of 1987, United States Surgeon General C. Everett Koop delivered the keynote address to the Parents' Music Resource Center (PMRC) symposium.[1] Formed in 1985, the PMRC worked to raise awareness of the dangers of popular culture products for young audiences. Koop's address to the group, "Raised on Rock 'n' Roll: The Sound and the Fury," emphasized, as a public health issue, the moral and social dangers of popular culture, particularly those posed by heavy metal music and pornography.[2] The surgeon general told his audience of concerned parents that these products led directly to premarital sex, violent behavior, and occult worship. Koop argued that hazardous products were no longer relegated to the periphery of American consumer culture but brought directly into the home by industries motivated by money rather than morals. At the dawn of the 1980s, MTV, and cable television more generally, supplied a wider variety of less regulated content into the home, particularly suburban homes where families could afford the luxury of cable service.[3] Largely bypassing parental censors, these new outlets created a problem for a generation of parents raised with a more limited set of highly regulated media.[4] "Now we have rock videos without control and frequently viewed without parents even being aware," Koop lamented. "Many that I have seen are senseless violence with senseless pornography to the beat of rock music."[5] Consequently, Koop argued, music and music videos encouraged deviant and dangerous activity made all the more hazardous because parents were unaware of and unable to cope with the avalanche of material coming straight into the home.[6]

For Koop, and the concerned parents he was speaking to, the debate about media effects was not simply a political argument. Beginning in the early 1980s, murders and suicides allegedly caused by satanic and occult messages in popular products emerged in the news media and popular culture as visible threats to suburban American youth. Parents and culture critics located the origin of occult danger in role-playing games like *Dungeons & Dragons* (*D&D*) in which players supposedly conflated their real and game lives. For other tragedies, they blamed heavy metal bands for compelling listeners to act violently. In one case, an avowed worshipper of Satan and a "Knight of the Black Circle" blasted the music as he killed another Long Island teen in 1984, whereas in other instances, in 1985 and 1986, three young men who committed suicide were supposedly inspired by their favorite heavy metal artists, Judas Priest and Ozzy Osbourne.[7]

These initial cases highlighted not just the danger of occult products but their intrusion into suburban homes with dire effects on a family unit already understood to be in crisis. These families had imagined their homes as sanctuaries from dangerous influences like those seen in public places such as the shopping mall and the arcade.

This approach contrasted with the ways politicians and other culture warriors addressed black families, black popular culture, and urban life in the same era, betraying their largely suburban concerns. The so-called "problem of the black family," articulated in the Moynihan Report (1965) and concretized in public policy and popular culture, was simply viewed differently by the culture warriors of the 1980s. They sought to protect or redeem suburban families in the face of a supposed onslaught of pornography, violence, and occultism. In contrast, politicians and culture critics often saw the black family as a lost cause and black popular culture as something to defend consumers against.[8] As Tricia Rose explains in in the context of hip hop: "Hip hop's violence is criticized at a heightened level and on different grounds from the vast array of violent images in American culture. . . . While heavy metal and other nonblack musical forms that contain substantial levels of violent imagery are likewise challenged by antiviolence critics, the operative assumption is that the music and its violence-peddling creators will negatively influence otherwise innocent listeners."[9]

When the problems facing urban families of color were addressed, it was largely as a regulatory function of the state through the Wars on Poverty and

Crime.[10] Law enforcement, family services, and other state agencies did not empower black families, in practice or rhetoric, as they did white suburbanites. They subjected them to the power of the state or punitively left them initially to "benign neglect" and later to "personal responsibility."[11] From the framing of rap as a social problem to the scourges of "black on black" crime, the "culture of dependency," and "welfare queens," along with the continued demonization of black mothers, politicians and culture warriors did not imagine the city or its inhabitants, largely people of color, as redeemable and therefore part of the moral restoration they sought in late-twentieth-century America.[12] Their approach to white, suburban families was far different. Rather than excoriation, President Ronald Reagan and other culture warriors extolled their virtues and empowered them to act without state interference. Historian of welfare policy and the family Marissa Chappell succinctly notes: "The 'traditional family' that antiwelfare conservatives like those in the Reagan administration celebrated, then, was race- and class-specific," meaning, they venerated the white suburban middle class.[13]

This difference can be seen in the suburban focus of culture warriors and concerned parents in response to the incidents noted above and the social trends they represented. Those events and trends fused the occult and morality concerns of the broader culture wars of the 1980s and '90s with fears about the decline of the white, suburban nuclear family as these groups sought to "resurrect" a nostalgic vision of home and family centered in the suburbs.[14]

These groups battled the liberalization of cultural mores in the aftermath of the upheavals of the 1960s by promoting a particular vision of Judeo-Christian ideology to ameliorate perceived moral crises such as abortion, divorce, homosexuality, and pornography.[15] As historian of the family Robert Self argues, "In the second half of the 1970s, conservative evangelicals created a furor over the state of the American family without precedent in the twentieth century. . . . [E]vangelicals, led by right-wing fundamentalists, raised the specter of family breakdown as national ruination."[16] Groups such as James Dobson's Focus on the Family, Pat Robertson's Christian Coalition, Randall Terry's Operation Rescue, and Jerry Falwell's Moral Majority used direct-mail literature and televised preaching (on expanding satellite and cable networks) to raise consciousness and spur action.[17] Christian evangelicals not only participated in full-throated critiques of popular culture as deleterious to young consumers but also buttressed personal and family action, not government intervention, as the key to protecting youth.

Concerned suburban parents, then, found common cause with a vast, diverse movement that voiced moral concerns about the content of all manner of popular media. Together, the various components of this movement identified these cultural dangers as the causes of tragic outcomes for teens in the 1980s and '90s and promoted family action as the proper response. In doing so, concerned suburban parents and culture warriors echoed the broader conservative ethos of the era that endorsed family values. President Reagan promoted this view in 1985: "Let's give our children back their childhood. Let's give them the support all children need— the support of traditional values like family, faith, hope, charity, and freedom."[18] The culture wars, then, helped to make social ills and family tragedies more visible and to make them appear the consequences of dangerous media, just as Reagan and other culture warriors reinforced the idea that families, not government, must address those threats in an era of moral crisis that played out in suburban homes.[19]

In their legal battles, advisory literature for parents, congressional testimony, and media appearances, concerned parents marked occult, sexual, and violent hazards posed by cultural texts as real and imminent, produced and distributed by an amoral culture industry, and linked conclusively to violent, transgressive behavior among vulnerable suburban audiences. Working within the broad parameters of the culture wars, concerned parents carved out a pragmatic cultural politics mostly devoid of the ideological attachments of culture warriors on the right such as Bob Larson and Jerry Falwell, or those on the left such as the American Civil Liberties Union. Through their focus on pragmatic, local solutions in defense of the American family's sanctuary—the suburban home—they were able to craft a powerful, conservative cultural critique, while trying to position themselves as being outside traditional politics or ideological constraints. As with their responses to environmental threats and crime, organizations like the PMRC and others emphasized parental empowerment rather than solutions achieved via legislation or the courts (even though their efforts were often abetted by the government). Further, in focusing on their particularly suburban concerns, they addressed a household under siege, rather than one beyond redemption or part of an already desecrated moral landscape in the city.[20] Frightened by the increasing visibility of suicide, substance abuse, and other social ills in suburban locales unaccustomed to the visibility of social disorder, parents for the most part located the causes and solutions to these problems not in the realms of medicine, science, education, or public policy but in proper consumer culture choices—including those available at the nearest shopping mall.

Together, family values conservatives and commonsense-oriented concerned parents articulated the notion that teen suicide and occultism could be prevented by keeping adolescents from playing *D&D* or listening to Marilyn Manson. This view was part of the broader conservative cultural politics of the Reagan revolution. Reagan himself explicitly articulated a new vision of social reform in 1982 when he said his administration would be "reducing the role of the Federal Government in all its many dimensions" in order to "leave to private initiative all the functions that individuals can perform privately."[21] Accordingly, spending on social welfare programs occupied a smaller share of federal spending and gross domestic product in 1985 than in 1981, with those most in need left without, while suburban parents were left to their own devices in addressing their particular fears.[22] Initiatives addressing pressing social issues were handled through advocacy and consciousness raising rather than through structural solutions that policymaking and budget earmarks could have achieved for a broader swath of citizens. Most famously, First Lady Nancy Reagan undertook the "Just Say No" to drugs campaign, which was emblematic of the Reagan administration's approach. To eliminate demand and destroy the illicit drug markets, she encouraged kids simply to refuse drugs.[23] President Reagan seconded this call: "By educating our children about the dangers of drugs, we're going to dry up the drug market and kick the dope peddlers right out of this country. Every time Nancy and I meet this country's wonderful young people, we feel more confident that we are going to win this battle."[24] Yet "Just Say No" did nearly nothing to address why kids took drugs or how they entered their communities.[25] In addition to the rhetoric, the 1986 federal budget called for reduced spending on treatment and education while increasing the enforcement allocation to $1.8 billion; the stepped-up policing that resulted disproportionately impacted urban communities of color and did not effectively lessen demand for or use of drugs.[26] By promoting privatism and voluntary citizen activism, the Reagan administration empowered concerned parents, mostly white and suburban, who traced the danger facing their kids to popular culture in the home. This orientation also marginalized solutions that could have helped more youths in danger from depression, drug abuse, suicide, and teen pregnancy, further undermined the idea of effective state social policy, and eventually became the central rationale for federal spending that empowered religious groups and individual families to address social issues, as seen in George W. Bush's faith-based initiatives.[27]

In that cultural climate, the suburban home, once thought to be a safe haven from the perils of public space (as previous chapters show), was actually itself the site of danger from a new "environmental" threat.[28] This perspective enabled suburbanites to fashion the home and the suburb as desanctified spaces that corporations and government could not or would not protect. By positing the home and its inhabitants as also under siege from dangerous popular culture products, these movements, and the parents they inculcated, produced volumes of material that valorized and buttressed suburban power and cultural authority. This productive victimization allowed many suburbanites to reassert power over the home while cementing their concerns in debates about morality and culture as dominant. And, like strategies in fighting crime and environmental hazard during the same period, this approach to emerging threats was central to suburban identity, values, and power. The claims of victimization—in this case, the breaching of the home with dangerous products and immoral influences—and the authority derived from that victimization were part and parcel of the idea of the suburb at the end of the twentieth century.

Satan in the Suburbs

In 1984, New York City newspapers reported that Ricky Kasso and James Troiano allegedly murdered their friend Gary Lauwers and mutilated his body as part of a satanic sacrifice in Northport on the north shore of Long Island. According to law enforcement, Kasso tortured Lauwers after a botched drug deal and forced him to repeatedly say, "I love Satan."[29] Just a day after the murder, lead detective Lieutenant Robert Dunn further underlined the occult associations of the murder. "This was a sacrificial killing," Dunn insisted. "They built a roaring fire in a field near the woods. They cut the sleeves out of his shirt and burned them and they took his socks off and burned them. I don't know what this is supposed to mean, but this is what they did. It's pure Satanism."[30] News media portrayed the population of the serene, middle-class community of Northport as stunned by the murder.[31] One resident said, "There are exotic things that happen in Manhattan, but they don't happen in Northport," while another claimed, "We've never seen any bad disturbances, nothing like this. It's shocking—the three boys are from the town itself."[32] Bad things happened—just not in Northport. In the era of the culture wars, something more nefarious must have been to blame.

To explain how a safe community of tree-lined streets could be home to such a horrific crime, police contended that members of a satanic cult called Knights of the Black Circle had for nearly three years been using and selling drugs while listening to the supposedly dark influences of heavy metal in the Aztakea Woods.

The television newsmagazine 20/20 claimed the murder was linked to satanism and rock music and symbolized a growing number of teen satanists who were committing heinous acts like sacrificing hundreds of dogs.[33] Local news reports indicated that despite hailing from good homes with significant advantages, the members of the alleged cult had fallen into lives of drug abuse while "hanging out" listening to heavy metal.[34] These articles highlighted the teens' love of heavy metal as setting them apart from their college-bound peers and putting them on a course for drug abuse and Satan worship. Later, as the legal case against James Troiano concluded with a not-guilty verdict, police and the news media acknowledged that the murder had been about nothing more than drug deals and drug abuse.[35] Yet the associations of the murder with heavy metal and satanism persisted rather than there being a sustained public discussion about why these privileged young men bought, sold, and used drugs.

By the time of Lauwers's murder in 1984, satanism and the occult had already emerged as a national news topic following the high-profile Charles Manson family murders in the late 1960s and films like *The Exorcist* (1973), *The Omen* (1976), and *The Amityville Horror* (1979), among dozens of other occult-themed movies. Further, the era saw the flowering of various other pagan or satanist cults, including Jim Jones's People's Temple, as Americans searched for meaning through "psychic self-improvement" in various "therapeutic" programs, religions, and belief systems.[36] As Americans searched for meaning in and beyond mainline religions, politically active evangelical Christians identified this shift as a sign of increasing satanic and occult influence. Engaged in a war against these forces and the cultural shifts that enabled them, early Christian televangelists and conservative culture critics fueled fear of cults and satanism that they alleged were secretly infiltrating seemingly safe communities.[37] By the early 1980s, occult fears had been stoked to such an extent that even mainstream corporations found themselves accused of hiding satanic imagery in their logos. Consumer products megalith Procter & Gamble (P&G) had to defend its trademark—a man in the moon surrounded by thirteen stars—against rumors that it was a secret symbol of Satan—a story reported as being repeated mostly at church on Sunday.[38] By the spring of 1982, P&G was fielding some twelve thousand queries each month about its relationship to the devil.[39] As it turned out, persons affiliated with competing companies had spread most of the rumors. Yet the allusion to devil worship had great cultural currency. It seemed not only possible but likely that a mainstream brand like Procter & Gamble—associated with deodorant, diapers, and food—could be run by satanists trying to recruit its customers.

The emergence of heavy metal as a mainstream music genre in the 1980s inflamed culture warriors' concerns about the occult.[40] These associations dogged the genre from its development and grew as it fragmented into numerous subgenres, including death metal, black metal, and grindcore, that explicitly traded in dark imagery.[41] Some artists, such as W.A.S.P. and Slayer, capitalized on these associations by using occult imagery and referring explicitly to devil worship. Others, like Judas Priest or even hard rock bands like KISS, were assailed as demonic because of their dark clothing, stage theatrics, and vaguely religious imagery.[42] By the 1980s, driven in large part by Christian evangelicals, the broad understanding of heavy metal was as gloomy, disturbing, and a marker of the infiltration of occultism into American popular culture, available to any consumer with eight dollars for an album.[43] Identifying an album or other product as satanic or occultural communicated something more broadly about moral degradation for a postwar US population bred to understand the nation as divinely blessed and morally centered.[44] The problem was not that satanism existed but that it was available at the mall to corrupt young minds and erode the moral fabric of America.

In April 1985, during their introductory news conference, the PMRC gave voice to the burgeoning notion of heavy metal as promoting the occult. The organization pointed to two songs of its "filthy fifteen" as representing the pervasive occult influence in popular music and hoped for an "O" rating for records with occult themes.[45] Two years later, ABCs popular newsmagazine *20/20* fueled the controversy by also suggesting causal links between suicide and metal fandom.[46] In the cultural environment of the 1980s, police, parents, and the news media found occultism and its most fearful strain, satanism, a more believable cause of murder than such far likelier causes as the boys' health and home environment.

In the Northport case, the boys' known love of heavy metal intersected with the broader fears of occult worship. In the months preceding the crime, Ricky Kasso was cited for stealing a skull and hand from a Northport cemetery crypt—apparent evidence of a Satanic ritual.[47] In the woods where these rituals purportedly took place, reporters and police found graffiti honoring the teens' favorite artists—Ozzy Osbourne, Black Sabbath, and AC/DC; hence the name of the alleged cult, Knights of the Black Circle (vinyl records). After expressing disbelief at the depravity of the crime, lead detective Robert Dunn insisted that rock videos glorifying satanic rituals were an important influence on the killers.[48] To police and the news media, the depravity of the murder itself (in which Gary Lauwers's body was mutilated and partially burned) and their love of heavy metal could only mean that Satan was at work. By 1984, Satan had come to the suburbs.

Bothered about *Dungeons & Dragons*

Developing alongside fears of the occult in heavy metal was a new threat from *Dungeons & Dragons*, a fantasy role-playing game (RPG) invented in 1974 that reached a peak of popularity in the 1980s. In the game, players create characters and are led on adventures by a dungeon master who creates an adventure campaign for the players to complete.[49] With its focus on imaginary worlds, magical spells, and mystical imagery, the game and its imitators became targets for parents who feared children would be inextricably absorbed in an occult fantasy. Spurred by incidents of players "becoming" their game characters in real life, and subsequent portrayals in news and popular culture, concerned parents insisted that the game's occult powers compelled players to act out the game with deadly consequences. Conservative culture critic Thomas Radecki summed up these fears in 1985: "There is no doubt in my mind that the game *Dungeons & Dragons* is causing young men to kill themselves and others."[50] Played in suburban basements and bedrooms, games like *D&D* represented another moral and possibly mortal threat that gave suburbanites further impetus to police the boundaries of their homes.

Radecki and others held to such beliefs because of the well-publicized deaths of role-playing game enthusiasts such as James Dallas Egbert that reinforced culture warriors' suspicion about popular occulture. A child prodigy and avid *D&D* player, Egbert vanished while attending Michigan State University as a fifteen-year-old freshman in 1979. Upon his disappearance, his parents and university authorities feared that he had attempted to live out his fantasy life in a network of dangerous steam tunnels beneath the campus. He had indeed ventured into the steam tunnels but not at the behest of any dungeon master or to fulfill a wish. Pressure to succeed in his courses and difficulty fitting in with his older colleagues had triggered depression. He fled to Louisiana to start over away from college and his family, but eventually killed himself there in 1980. Egbert's story was emblematic of an increasing focus on occult products as the cause of suicide, rather than the more likely reason that he suffered from untreated clinical depression, a mode of thinking about social ills that would become policy during the Reagan-Bush years.

When his parents hired private investigator William Dear to find James, they emphasized that their son had often played *D&D*. Dear then offered that Egbert had entered the tunnels as part of a role-playing game.[51] This theory was picked up by the Michigan State University campus newspaper, the *State News*, and eventually by the national news media. After doubts began to emerge about the *D&D* theory, newspapers still continued to suggest it as the cause of Egbert's disappearance. Even three years after his death, the *Washington Post* still connected his disappearance to role-playing games: "Although *D&D* has been in existence for a decade, it was not until 1979 that the game caught the attention of the nation in a spectacular way: a Michigan State University student disappeared for almost a month in a 10-mile network of steam tunnels under the campus where he and some friends would act out rounds of the game in an atypical fashion (it is normally played indoors with paper and pencils). This rather bizarre example of fantasy role-playing seemed all the more weird a year later when the student, James Egbert, committed suicide."[52] Despite the reporter's efforts to demystify the dangers of *D&D*, players were consistently linked to narratives of suicide and danger brought on by occult influences in the games they played, rather than to complex, personal causes of depression and suicide. Such causal linkages suggested that the way to protect young suburbanites was to police their consumption of media.

A novel, Rona Jaffe's *Mazes and Monsters*, and movie, based on Egbert's "story," reinforced and widely reproduced the notion that his suicide was caused by his addictive love of *D&D*.[53] Aired on CBS in 1982 (and ironically coproduced by Procter & Gamble), the movie tracked Robbie Wheeling as he transferred to fictional Grant College to start over after becoming addicted to the game *Mazes and Monsters*. By all appearances, Robbie is a normal college student. He attends classes and has a girlfriend. Yet, slowly, he is drawn back into playing the game because of its demonic hold on its players. Playing day and night with the game's dark forces, Robbie can no longer distinguish it from his real life. He hallucinates that he has become his game character, a cleric. To achieve his character's final goal of getting to the "great hall," Robbie believes he must jump from the top of the World Trade Center. Even though his friends are able to stop him, the end of the film shows Robbie living out the rest of his life in an institution, precluding what would have been the promising middle-class life that his parents had envisioned for him and that likely would have been his if not for the harmful influence of *Mazes and Monsters*.

The story of Robbie/Egbert served as a cautionary tale about role-playing games and occult worship. It provided a vivid and explicit explanation for self-destructive behavior free of any sense of the psychological complexity of hallucinations and suicide attempts. In the first chapter of her novel, Jaffe directly addresses concerned parents and not her presumed audience of teen readers. "Perhaps what was most disturbing about this case was something that was on every parent's mind," she writes. "These players, the ones who had gone too far and the one who had disappeared, could be anybody's kids; bright young college students . . . given the American Dream and rejecting it to live in a fantasy world of invented terrors."[54] Jaffe evidently believed that basing her novel on a supposedly true story about an average suburban kid lent her cautionary retelling greater credibility. It was not simply an author's fantastical creation but a story about a real young man seduced by the occult to act dangerously. Both the book and the film advanced the argument that role-playing games are based on occult fantasies designed to be all-consuming adventures that shut out "real life" and derail otherwise normal lives. *Mazes and Monsters* brought the fears of the occult and role-playing games straight into suburban households, casting doubt on the games many teens loved and justifying parents' fears and desires about making their homes safe.

Just after *Mazes and Monsters* aired, another "true" story attested to the sinister occult influence of *Dungeons & Dragons*. In 1983, L. "Bink" Pulling III, a Norfolk, Virginia, teenager, committed suicide supposedly on the orders of his dungeon master. Although his story received news coverage, it was the organization created by his parents that exemplified the cultural politics of concerned suburban parents of the 1980s. Bothered About *Dungeons & Dragons* (BADD) was created to raise consciousness about the dangers of *D&D* so that other parents could protect their children from Bink's fate.[55] In their introductory letter to the public, Pat Pulling and her husband wrote, "We are concerned with violent forms of entertainment such as: violent occult-related rock music, role-playing games that utilize occult mythology and the worship of occult gods in role playing situations like *Dungeons & Dragons*, teen Satanism involving murder and suicide."[56] The Pullings believed their organization was "influential in the restoration of respect for human life" in that it acted as "a referral system for people who need help regarding entertainment violence issues."[57] Rather than lobbying or otherwise prevailing upon government to regulate these products, the Pullings made BADD an information clearinghouse for publications that highlighted the scourge of the occult, including booklets on witchcraft and satanism and an educational video on the dangers of *Dungeons & Dragons*.[58] Within the broader framework of Christian culture warriors' concerns about the erosion of family values and the Reagan-era politics of personal responsibility, BADD emphasized parental knowledge and involvement in the hope of restoring "traditional values" in the home, rather than medicalization and treatment for teens suffering from depression and suicidal thoughts. In assuming both the inundation of the home with new pop culture products and the ability of concerned parents to police those choices, the organization's members made clear the limited, suburban scope of their activism.

In 1985, role-playing games and their supposed occult associations were thrust further into the spotlight on the highly rated CBS newsmagazine *60 Minutes*. In his introduction to the segment, correspondent Ed Bradley connected the game directly to dangerous activities among its teen audiences. "*D&D*. It's popular with kids from grammar school on up. Not so with adults who think it's been connected to a number of suicides and murders."[59] The program then cuts to teenagers hunched over a table in a basement as Bradley informs the audience that the game is filled with goblins, thieves, and spirits. He then lists the murders and suicides of teenage *D&D* players: "Timothy Greiss, twenty-one, shotgun suicide. The detective report noted the *D&D* game became a reality. Irving 'Bink' Pulling, sixteen. A suicide. Daniel and Stephen Irwin, sixteen and twelve. A murder and a suicide. Police said they were obsessed with the game. James Alan Kirby, fourteen years old, charged with killing his junior high school principal and wounding three other people. Police are blaming *D&D*." No effort is made to explain or contextualize these tragic acts beyond the victims' associations with the game. Instead, what Bradley's comments reflected was the seeming consensus that role-playing games were central to teen social issues like alcohol abuse, depression, murder, and suicide. As in the Egbert case, news and law enforcement in the cases Bradley highlighted offered *D&D* as a simple and lone cause. Ed Bradley seemed to concur, noting that a Connecticut town would hold a discussion among its citizens to specifically address the dangers of *D&D* after the suicide of a thirteen-year-old boy there. Given the opportunity to defend themselves, Dieter Stern, head of public relations for game makers Gary Gygax and TSR Inc., suggested that aberrant behavior could be caused by any number of factors.[60] However, the last word in the segment went to Pat Pulling, who recounted the suicide of her son and the ways in which the game endangered its players. The viewer was thus left with the sense that Satan was in the basement waiting to kill your children and that the only remedy was to avoid buying or playing the game. Such suburban solutions to social ills brought to life the Reagan era's ethic of privatism and family responsibility for social problems whereby proper consumer culture choices lead to a healthy and moral life.

Figure 5.1. A mid-1980s pamphlet about the myriad dangers posed by the supposedly occult influences of *Dungeons & Dragons.* Internet Archive.

Parents versus Heavy Metal

In the midst of parental campaigns against the influences of the occult in popular culture, three young men, supposedly under the subliminal sway of heavy metal, killed themselves. On October 27, 1984, nineteen-year-old John McCollum shot himself in the head while allegedly listening to Ozzy Osbourne.[61] Just over a year later, on December 23, 1985, James Vance, twenty, and Raymond Belknap, eighteen, went to a church playground and committed suicide with a shotgun, reportedly at the subliminal urging of their favorite band Judas Priest.[62] The parents of McCollum, Vance, and Belknap filed wrongful death suits against these artists and their record labels, arguing that Judas Priest and Ozzy Osbourne encouraged their sons to shoot themselves. These lawsuits and their

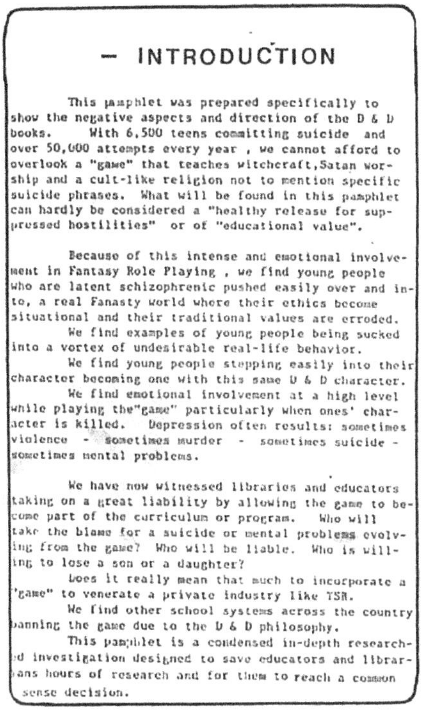

— INTRODUCTION

This pamphlet was prepared specifically to show the negative aspects and direction of the D & D books. With 6,500 teens committing suicide and over 50,000 attempts every year, we cannot afford to overlook a "game" that teaches witchcraft, Satan worship and a cult-like religion not to mention specific suicide phrases. What will be found in this pamphlet can hardly be considered a "healthy release for suppressed hostilities" or of "educational value".

Because of this intense and emotional involvement in Fantasy Role Playing, we find young people who are latent schizophrenic pushed easily over and into, a real Fanasty world where their ethics become situational and their traditional values are erroded.

We find examples of young people being sucked into a vortex of undesirable real-life behavior.

We find young people stepping easily into their character becoming one with this same D & D character.

We find emotional involvement at a high level while playing the"game" particularly when ones' character is killed. Depression often results: sometimes violence - sometimes murder - sometimes suicide - sometimes mental problems.

We have now witnessed libraries and educators taking on a great liability by allowing the game to become part of the curriculum or program. Who will take the blame for a suicide or mental problems evolving from the game? Who will be liable. Who is willing to lose a son or a daughter?

Does it really mean that much to incorporate a "game" to venerate a private industry like TSR.

We find other school systems across the country banning the game due to the D & D philosophy.

This pamphlet is a condensed in-depth researched investigation designed to save educators and librarians hours of research and for them to reach a common sense decision.

Figure 5.2. The authors of a pamphlet about *Dungeons & Dragons* speciously argue that *D&D* and other fantasy and role-playing games are causing teen suicides.

portrayal in the news media provided evidence for the fears of popular occulture and legitimized the sense that the music could unduly influence its substantially teen audience with tragic implications. Further, the lawsuits marginalized the emotional distress that likely led to these tragedies and distracted attention away from exploring the causes of a general rise in the teen suicide rate in the 1980s.[63] This framework for understanding teen mental health prioritized and empowered suburban parents who could police their homes and, if needed, afford the medical care for their children; at the same time it buttressed the political argument for defunding of social programs beyond the wars on crime and drugs. Lastly, the failure of these parents to win their cases helped demonstrate why groups like the PMRC helped suburban parents turn inward for solutions and rely on the privileges of class, race, and location rather than seek unlikely redress through government or the courts.

Jack McCollum sued CBS Records and Ozzy Osbourne, alleging that his son's suicide was encouraged by Osbourne's song "Suicide Solution."[64] Osbourne claimed that the song was antisuicide, as he had written it about the alcohol-related death of his friend AC/DC singer Bon Scott. James McKenna, the lawyer retained by the parents of James Vance and Raymond Belknap to represent them in their suit against Judas Priest, argued that "the suggestive lyrics combined with the continuous beat and rhythmic nonchanging intonation of the music combined to induce . . . the plaintiff into believing the answer to life was death."[65] In both cases, the parents saw the music of heavy metal artists as Trojan horses, sneaking into their homes under the guise of legitimate entertainment and tricking their sons into killing themselves to fulfill the wishes of these supposedly satanic artists. In each instance, the plaintiffs alleged that coded messages could be found by playing the records backward. In the Osbourne case, the plaintiffs alleged that masked lyrics on "Suicide Solution" encouraged listeners to grab a gun and shoot themselves, while lawyers in the Judas Priest case claimed the band attempted to control their audience's minds through similarly hidden messages.[66] What became clear was that no subliminal or masked messages appeared on the records. Judas Priest singer Rob Halford joked that if his band had a secret message, it would be to buy more records. In the ruling opinion of the Osbourne case, Judge H. Walter Croskey found that Osbourne's song did not contain the "call to action" the law required to hold him liable.[67] However, the judge implied that he agreed with what culture critics and concerned parents had claimed about heavy metal: "An alarming number of (primarily) heavy metal and mainstream stars sing about suicide as one way to deal with problems; some almost seem to promote it."[68]

Even though the bands ultimately won the cases, news coverage and even Judge Croskey's opinion echoed and extended the common sense that heavy metal was intimately linked to the promotion of suicide, especially through secret, possibly satanic messages.[69] In each case, critics contended that secret messages could be decoded only by true fans through multiple periods of close listening.[70] Rock critic Jon Pareles argued that masking lyrics was understood as dangerous because "it reaches teen-agers and seems to exclude parents—it's a great noisy unknown."[71] His argument bolstered parents' demand for printed lyric sheets and legitimated their fears of satanic coded messages entering the home without their knowledge.[72]

Moreover, to the extent that the courts failed to endorse parents' claims, these cases reinforced for them the futility of structural solutions to cultural problems in an era when parents were encouraged to see themselves, alone, as household saviors. Had the victims' families won their lawsuits, more court cases and legislation might have followed to deal with dangerous pop music.[73] Record companies and artists might even have felt compelled to censor themselves preemptively to avoid litigation or arrest. The outcome of these cases, however, demonstrated that the law could not be used to stop the distribution of these records or hold their makers accountable. Indeed, this failure to find heavy metal artists legally culpable for their fans' suicides, combined with the conservative climate of social reform in the 1980s, left concerned parents with little recourse but to find their own private solutions—policing popular culture themselves. Instead, many parents, lacking state-sponsored solutions or the time to police their children's cultural choices, were left behind.

For example, to address a spike in teen suicide, President Reagan declared June 1985 "Youth Suicide Prevention Month" but made no specific policy proposals to stem the tide of self-inflicted teen deaths.[74] Rather, he called for voluntarism and family responsibility, making clear what parents must do in the face of the threat from suicide.[75] Just two years later, a suicide epidemic would sweep across the nation, with parents, police, and government officials still looking to heavy metal as the cause and stricter parental oversight proffered as the solution.

Heavy Metal Burnouts and Suburban Suicide

On March 11, 1987, four Bergenfield, New Jersey, teenagers committed suicide by locking themselves in a closed garage with the car's engine running, thus consummating their pact to end their lives together. The news media claimed that the four dead teens had self-identified as "burnouts" or, more generally, teens with little ambition, and were drawn together by their hopelessness and love of heavy metal music.[76] With so little ambition, their love of metal led them to embrace hopelessness and commit suicide. *Newsweek* framed its story of "deeply troubled young people" and their many problems within their obsession with heavy metal.[77] The *New York Times* contrasted a "a quiet town, boring even," with teens who embraced the sentiment expressed in the title of an AC/DC live album found at the scene of the suicides: *If You Want Blood, You've Got It.*[78]

Within a week of the Bergenfield suicides, two young women in Alsip, Illinois, both fans of Metallica, killed themselves by inhaling carbon monoxide fumes in a closed garage. The Associated Press contended that the Bergenfield and Alsip suicides were not merely coincidental. The Illinois girls had been thinking about killing themselves for some time but decided to do it when they heard about the Bergenfield teens.[79] *Newsweek* argued that the Bergenfield suicide pact "triggered fears of a new and virulent form of the clusters of copycat teenage suicides that have plagued communities from Putnam County, N.Y., to Plano, Texas, in recent years."[80] Other presumed copycats included a fourteen-year-old boy who posted news clippings about the six other suicides on his bedroom wall, a teen couple in Bergenfield who attempted to use the same garage as the others had a week earlier, and an Illinois girl found dead in her car.[81] With so many incidents occurring, news organizations tried to explain the complex causes of teen suicides by pointing to lack of family and school support, and drug and alcohol abuse, among other causes.[82] Despite such responsible reporting, the broad understanding of the cause of the suburban suicide "epidemic" of the late eighties was that alienation and depression were promoted and exacerbated by the occult influences of heavy metal.

Following the 1987 rash of teen suicides, the ABC newsmagazine *20/20* ran a special edition of the show on the growing popularity of heavy metal among suburban high school kids.[83] The show consisted of multiple segments that surveyed the perspectives of fans, heavy metal artists, and critics. Despite the attempt at balance, the episode traded in hyperbolic, provocative language and imagery that further underscored the dire threats from heavy metal and the occult, as portrayed by the PMRC, "experts," and other news outlets. In her introduction to the show, host Barbara Walters claimed that heavy metal was a form of music associated with "ghoulish images, violent theatrics, and even suicide" that deserved attention. She asked, "Is there a message that may be too loud for us to hear?" suggesting that part of the danger of heavy metal was its coded messages intended for true fans that were inaccessible to parents. Correspondent Stone Phillips's voice-over suggested that what teens were really hearing were "lyrics obsessed with sex, Satanism, and even suicide. This is not mainstream rock and roll." As he spoke, images of explicit heavy metal album covers and performances were shown; Philips ended by asking if this music "may even be killing its audience." By juxtaposing musings about heavy metal lyrics with provocative visual content and citing a connection between heavy metal fandom and the suicides of the Bergenfield, New Jersey, teens (avid listeners of AC/DC) and the Alsip, Illinois, teens (fans of Metallica), Walters and Phillips strongly implied there were messages embedded in the music—intended only for the hard core teenage audience—that were mortally dangerous to this suburban audience.[84]

In spreading the word about the dangers of heavy metal, 20/20 rooted the threat in the suburban community by specifically naming the Bergenfield suicides and visiting other suburban New Jersey teens. In a set of interviews with students at Teaneck High School in Teaneck, New Jersey—all of them self-proclaimed metalheads—most showed modest ambition and expressed little care about anything other than their favorite music.[85] The students interviewed voiced a love of the music, which provided the basis for such needs as companionship and community. Sociologist Donna Gaines, in her study of the Bergenfield teens, saw no causal link between heavy metal and the suicides. Instead, she argued, these teen metalheads were suburbia's "dead-end kids," whose failures and alienation, caused in large part by crumbling family and school support systems, led to a lack of career and educational opportunities.[86] Yet Stone Phillips focused on the music and its culture. In the following segment, despite some of the hopeful sentiments about heavy metal, with the help of experts, he provided step-by-step instructions on how to "de-metal" kids in order to protect them from its dangerous messages.[87] In this pivotal moment in the program, seemingly normal, if sullen, teens were subjected to a program of "de-metaling" because their parents believed there would be an inexorable march toward suicide without this intervention.

The show ended with the countervailing but moderate views of Tipper Gore and Iron Maiden lead singer Bruce Dickinson. Gore advocated for a system in which everyone could make their own assessment, while Dickinson suggested that metal may not be the worst or even most prominent influence in teen lives. This ending exemplified the process of creating and dealing with the problem of heavy metal and the occult. The show went to great lengths to explain and promote heavy metal's many perils for young consumers but, ultimately, recommended what Tipper Gore, the PMRC, and other experts had been advocating all along: it was up to parents to be more informed and more in control. The episode promoted the danger of heavy metal and advocated parental involvement to protect suburban teens like those in Bergenfield and Teaneck. It is not difficult to imagine suburban parents, after watching the show, feeling empowered to police their children's popular culture choices, even to de-metal their children's music collection and wardrobe, fearing that otherwise they might kill themselves or join a cult. These narratives further heightened the sense of danger from the music, located the threat in the suburbs, raised the stakes for suburban parents to police their children's popular culture choices, and helped justify new regimes of discipline in the home.

Prevention Begins at Home

One of the experts claiming to help parents de-metal their kids on the *20/20* episode was Darlyne Pettinicchio. With her partner Gregory Bodenhamer, Pettinicchio had founded the Back in Control Training Center in Orange County, California, in 1976. The two worked with kids on probation and with those addicted to drugs and alcohol.[88] In the mid-1980s, parents brought punk and heavy metal to their attention. By 1985, Bodenhamer and Pettinicchio were convinced that "punk and heavy metal—particularly metal—are public enemy No. 1," United Press International reported.[89] To deal with this nationwide menace, they developed their de-metaling system to put parents, not metal bands, in control of their children's lives. They found that recommending parents deprive their children of these music genres, along with the associated clothing styles and social groups, was the most effective way of defeating the perilous messages of punk and eventually heavy metal. "What we do," Bodenhamer explained, "is train the parents to train the kids to obey the parents."[90] If parents neglected to take action, he warned, their children might become violent and even dabble in satanism. Bodenhamer published his parenting prescriptions at the height of the hysteria over the influence of heavy metal. *Back in Control: How to Get Your Children to Behave* asserted that the exercise of parental power was the only thing capable of stopping children from misbehaving and protecting them from dangerous influences that filled the void of parental authority.[91] The Back in Control system signaled the direction suburban parenting took in the '80s. Bodenhamer and Pettinicchio focused on empowering individual parents to eliminate undue influence from popular culture products and thereby address the problem in *their* home even if the societal issue went beyond their front door.

To help suburban parents, the PMRC also offered ways to empower those who felt victimized by popular culture. Most prominently, the council brought its battle to Congress in a hearing before a Senate subcommittee of the Committee on Commerce, Science, and Transportation. There, PMRC members argued vigorously that "porn rock" endangered young consumers, yet they also advocated nonlegislative solutions using the hearings as way to raise consciousness about the dangers in popular culture. Following the hearings, they created a hotline for parents to receive information about what products were dangerous to children and produced a home video, *Rising to the Challenge*, to explain the threats from popular culture and how to combat them.[92] Members also continued appearing frequently in the media, including newspapers and TV programs such as *20/20*,

60 Minutes, and *Nightwatch with Charlie Rose*.[93] Near the end of the 1980s, many members began publishing their own parenting guides, with Tipper Gore's *Raising PG Kids in an X-Rated Society* among the most prominent. In all of their efforts, PMRC leaders stressed the immediate threats that popular culture presented and the importance of parents defending their homes, because, as Tipper Gore argued, "in the hands of a few warped artists, their brand of rock music has become a Trojan horse, rolling explicit sex and violence into our homes."[94] The Trojan horse metaphor was key to understanding concerned parents' perspectives on and reactions to popular culture. The remedy, promoted by experts like Bodenhamer, the PMRC, and Tipper Gore, focused on individual, local action with parents actively vetting the popular culture choices their children made. Having failed to achieve a structural solution, concerned parents identified a suburban problem—pop culture products endangering the moral life of the home and the security of its borders—and suggested a suburban solution—local, private action that empowered parents in the home.[95]

At the hearing in the fall of 1985, parents, artists, record label representatives, and politicians jockeyed to frame the debate on explicit content in music. Artists and label officials argued that the PMRC sought to undermine First Amendment rights through government regulation, while the PMRC and subcommittee members claimed that children and families were endangered by explicit content that called for industry self-regulation. PMRC president Susan Baker echoed this sentiment in her opening statement: "Some say there is no cause for concern. We believe there is. Teen pregnancies and teenage suicide rates are at epidemic proportions today. . . . There certainly are many causes for these ills in our society, but it is our contention that the pervasive messages aimed at children which promote and glorify suicide, rape, sadomasochism, and so on, have to be numbered among the contributing factors."[96] Rather than take into account the more complex causes of teen social problems, the subcommittee and the PMRC identified the culture industries as the root cause of increasing rates of alcoholism, murder, pregnancy, and suicide among teens. This strategy followed directly from the philosophy of the Reagan administration and its supporters. As with the "Just Say No" campaign, President Reagan endorsed a voluntary program of citizen activism to prevent suicide. In June 1985, he called for "research and policies which strengthen the family unit and foster a sense of individual worth."[97] Secretary of the Department of Health and Human Services Otis R. Bowen said in 1986, "So often in the past, the nation has sought pocketbook remedies. I do not believe creating costly new bureaucracy and calling that the answer should be our goal." He continued, "The role of the family has been given too little attention in recent years."[98]

Yet, even in the face of those threats, the PMRC went to great lengths to insist that it did not want formal government involvement.[99] Even the artists who opposed the PMRC and Reagan agreed with this analysis. By the end of his testimony, Frank Zappa essentially agreed to the PMRC's proposal and with the opinion of Senator Al Gore that lyrics should be made available to consumers so they can make an informed choice.[100] Given the high stakes of these issues, such a solution made safety a privilege for families that could police popular culture effectively while offering little to those who could not. In that cultural climate, the structural deficiencies of urban education and welfare were beyond the purview of concerned parents who saw the issue as one of consumer protection and family choice.

Published in 1987, Tipper Gore's *Raising PG Kids in an X-Rated Society* was the culmination of the PMRC movement that began in 1985. It outlined not only the problems in American culture but essential strategies for parents in dealing with a growing epidemic of explicit words and images in consumer products readily available to teens. In the book, Gore first emphasized the urgency of the problem and its epidemic proportion while suggesting the need for immediate action: "Children are now bombarded with explicit messages on a scale unlike anything our culture has ever seen."[101] In describing the dangerous cultural conditions of the 1980s for children as without precedent, particularly in comparison to her youth in the 1950s, she sought to compel her readers to act. Second, Gore focused on localism, indicating that the most important and effective actions were those undertaken by parents, and underscoring her message that prevention begins at home. Each chapter addressed one problem and ended with a prescription for parents to deal with that problem; Gore called these solutions "practical means for restoring individual choice and control," a clear summary of ascendant neoliberal market logic in approaching social issues.[102] As opposed to difficult-to-achieve legislative solutions or unrealistic goals like a sudden shift in the profit incentive for companies to sell these products, her book emphasized straightforward application of parental authority. Similarly, the book was aimed at parents to the exclusion of other audiences. Gore largely did not address the artists and corporations making this material, as activism and moral shaming had little effect, in her view. Instead, she strongly suggested that parents in the home were the only ones who need do anything about the undue influence of explicit popular culture, which was clearly not on the wane. "More than any-

Figure 5.3. The cover of Tipper Gore's parenting manual for a new era of moral endangerment from popular culture. From Tipper Gore, *Raising PG Kids in an X-Rated Society* (Nashville: Abingdon Press, 1987).

thing else," she wrote, "I want this book to be a call to arms for American parents. I want to offer them the very real hope that we can reassert some control over the cultural environment in which our children are raised."[103] Lastly, Gore highlighted not only the violent and sexual imagery in popular music, particularly heavy metal satanism, "the cult of the eighties," but specifically pointed to those images causing epidemics of suicide and murder.[104]

Despite Gore's insistence on what was essentially a market solution to the problem of dangerous media, the culture industries did not entirely escape Gore's ire over what had befallen suburban middle-class children like hers—good kids corrupted by the immoral pursuit of profit. Gore chided both the culture industries and parents while emphasizing the primacy of parental action to protect children. "From *The Exorcist* to the Dungeons and Dragons, fantasy role-playing game," she confessed, "Americans chased one occult fad after another." But she stressed that parents needed to guide children's choices because "not everyone can see through the show-biz Satanism purveyed by more and more bands."[105] Still, according to Gore and the PMRC, only so much help could be provided from those outside the home. Dangerous products existed and would continue to be produced, but they need not be brought into the home, Gore explained in a section titled, "Prevention Begins at Home": "Parents, churches, synagogues, and schools can start by pointing out the dangers of negative media messages and by encouraging young people to adopt discriminating listening and viewing habits. Most important, parents should *spend time* with their children."[106] Her assessments of the hazards to children and the prescriptions for action all revolved around monitoring and safeguarding the home, situating the suburban home as in danger from a constant stream of threats and should be restored as a zone of safety, moral purity, and parental autonomy.[107] To achieve that restoration, as with combatting environmental and criminal threats, vigilance was required, "because parenting involves the home, children, and twenty-four-hour relationships."[108]

In 1987, on the heels of Gore's book and in the midst of two court cases in which heavy metal bands were accused of causing fans to kill themselves, the PMRC released a thirty-one-minute educational video for parents, *Rising to the Challenge*. The challenge, according to the video, was protecting children from dangerous messages embedded in rock-and-roll. The video detailed various threats to children—drug and alcohol abuse, suicide, graphic violence, fascination with the occult, and graphic and explicit sexuality—and, much like *Raising PG Kids in an X-Rated Society*, the film prioritized suicide and the occult over the hazards from violence and sex. Ironically, to educate parents, the PMRC was actually sending explicit material into homes where it could possibly be viewed by children. In fact, more than anything else the PMRC produced, this video thoroughly detailed the threats from popular music. It was not only more visceral in depicting the things the PMRC deplored, but it spent much more time presenting scientific data and evidence from experts to create apparent links between the seemingly vulgar products of the culture industry and teen violence, sado-masochistic sex, suicide, and Satan worship.

The video was rife with explicit imagery such as album covers, photos taken at concerts, and various promotional materials and graphic song lyrics, mostly from heavy metal bands like W.A.S.P. For example, it quotes lyrics from W.A.S.P.'s "Animal (Fuck like a Beast)" not only to demonstrate the inappropriateness of the lyrics for children but to embarrass parents with the song's graphic descriptions of sadomasochistic sex, descriptions their children would presumably listen to at home without intervention. The lyrics, spoken in a voice-over, accompanied various images from the band's videos, in which they simulated placing a woman in a meat grinder and the lead singer strutted around the stage wearing a codpiece with a saw blade in it. These images were intended not merely to make the case for album warning labels but to make clear the threat posed by popular music, specifically heavy metal, to the moral environment of the home through images and lyrics that dehumanized women. That dehumanization was of particular concern to the all-women panel that led the PMRC. From feminists like Tipper Gore to traditionalists like Susan Baker, they all agreed that these depictions of women had the power to degrade and undermine the authority of mothers in the home. The video highlighted images and lyrics that seemed so perverse that they required not just passive participation of parents in supporting PMRC initiatives like stickering, but active interest in their children's lives and the knowledge of popular culture that gave them the moral authority to act.

To further instill fear, the video connected the rise in popularity of explicit music with concomitant rises in social ills like teen suicide and pregnancy. No actual scientific evidence supported a clear causal relationship, but the narrators of the video proposed that there almost had to be a relationship between the rise in teen suicide and the popularity of metal because heavy metal bands sang about dark themes at the same time that more teens were killing themselves. A number of self-declared authorities on the dangers of popular culture appear in the video to bolster the PMRC's case by arguing that statistics showing the number of hours spent listening to music and watching MTV indicated the prominence of media in kids' lives. Each section of the video included expert testimony on the topic under review, as well as additional germane "facts." For example, during the segment on alcohol and drug abuse, the narrators say that the Beastie Boys' album *License to Ill* contains ninety-five references to drugs and alcohol, mentions that could go unnoticed without a printed lyric sheet.[109] Indeed, this near fetishizing of numbers and statistics helped evade the obligation to prove actual causation. This technique of suggesting causal links promoted a more sur-real and dangerous aura around popular music in the home and suggested the limitless ability of albums to do harm. To combat these threats, the video called for vigilance on all fronts, and, in the final segment, parents were given recommendations for immediate productive actions that could be taken. The video, like the efforts Tipper Gore and other concerned parents, made detailed claims of depravity and connected them to teen social crises, all in the service of empowering individual families to make better choices in the marketplace.

Pat Pulling, who believed her son had committed suicide at the behest of his dungeon master while playing *Dungeons & Dragons*, reemerged in 1989 with another parenting manual, *The Devil's Web: Who Is Stalking Your Children for Satan?* In the book, she pivoted from simply bringing to light the dangers of *Dungeons & Dragons* to focusing on the larger menace of satanism and occultism, of which she argued role-playing games were a significant part.[110] Pulling echoed the PMRC's fears and the sentiments of her earlier pamphlet for BADD, "Dungeons and Dragons: Witchcraft, Suicide, Violence."[111] "Young people," Pulling claimed in *The Devil's Web*, "still struggling through their formative years, are prime targets of sophisticated cult recruiters and are also vulnerable to the superficial lures of Satanism."[112] It was not necessarily that heavy metal concerts or role-playing games were doing direct harm, but rather that they warmed teens to ideas about the occult as well as drug and alcohol abuse, which would then lead to an actual initiation to drug taking and violent acts. "The games themselves did not cause the molestation, but they were the vehicle by which the molestation was carried out."[113] Adding to a growing chorus, Pulling was warning parents that popular culture products in the home like heavy metal and role-playing games could lure innocent kids out of the home into cults obsessed with violence, sex, and anarchy. Through the end of the 1980s, her organization and her book helped maintain the visibility of the alleged dangers of popular occulture and helped to establish a rationale for parents to more actively defend their homes and children from "the ever-growing web of occultism that threatens to entrap America's children," dramatically depicted on the cover of her book.[114]

This is a cultural virus

In December 1993 and March 1994, the US Senate convened Governmental Affairs Committee meetings that further exemplified the home's shift in status from moral stronghold to refuge threatened by popular culture products.[115] Committee cochairs Senators Joseph I. Lieberman (D-CT) and Herbert Kohl (D-WI)

Figure 5.4. The haunting cover of Pat Pulling's *The Devil's Web* depicts dead-eyed children under the sway of the devil. From Pat Pulling, with Kathy Cawthon, *The Devil's Web: Who Is Stalking Your Children for Satan?* (Lafayette, LA: Huntington House, 1989).

arranged the hearings in order to investigate video game–related violence and provide evidence for their proposed legislation on video game ratings. Much like the hearings on "porn rock" in 1985, these proceedings did not lead to any federal regulations. Instead, they served to inform the public about morally de-grading video game content, give parents relevant information they could use to protect young consumers, and shame video game makers into creating less "inappropriate" content and self-regulating through a ratings system to help consumers make informed choices. In his opening statement, Senator Lieberman linked the kidnapping and murder of a young girl at a slumber party to the violent and lascivious imagery in video games, particularly the "troubling realism" and strong overtones of "sexual violence" in a CD-ROM game called *Night Trap*. Subsequently, he described in detail the finishing moves known as fatalities in the game *Mortal Kombat*, and later played a video montage of those moves one after another, a succession that would not happen in the game as played. In light of this sexual and violent content, he argued, "a ratings system is the very least the video game industry can do," and he encouraged game creators to "simply stop producing the worst of this junk." Nothing less was at stake than "nurturing healthy children" as the crisis of the suburban family continued into the 1990s. As in the earlier debates over popular music, critics continued to figure the home as under siege from morally questionable material and to urge parents to better equip themselves to protect against that threat by educating themselves about the dangers, an effort facilitated by the culture industries' self-regulatory ratings. This frame for understanding the relationship between popular culture and the social ills of young consumers was central to the public's task of making sense of the final suburban tragedy of the twentieth century.

On April 20, 1999, Dylan Klebold and Eric Harris entered Columbine High School and committed the deadliest school attack to that point in US history. In the frantic and near constant coverage by the now-dominant twenty-four-hour news cycle, anchors, experts, and others speculated about how and why this tragedy had occurred.[116] Predominant among their explanations were the influences of neo-goth musician Marilyn Manson, violent video games like *Doom*, and a secret gang of teens obsessed with Nazis and the occult called the Trench Coat Mafia. And, explicitly or implicitly, the commentators also endorsed a family values cultural logic to blame the boys' parents as well; similarly, 85 percent of respondents to a Gallup poll conducted after the attack faulted the Harris and Klebold families.[117] These were unsurprising explanations in light of the "satanic panic" of the 1980s and the responses it generated, which consistently and fervently located the causes of suburban teen tragedies in popular culture and emphasized the need for parents to properly regulate media consumption to prevent these kind of calamities.

This time, it seemed, the stakes were even higher than in the 1980s, as Klebold and Harris carried out a well-planned attack using military tactics and weapons. Fearing copycats or, worse, an actual cult of Manson worshippers ready to strike again, politicians, law enforcement, news media, and parents blamed these dangerous cultural products and reaffirmed the call for parental empowerment and "family values," even though Harris himself left behind quite different explanations of his motivations. He wrote on his webpage, "Surely you will try to blame it on the clothes I wear, the music I listen to, or the way I choose to present myself but no. Do not hide behind my choices. You need to face the fact that this comes as a result of YOUR CHOICES. Parents and Teachers, YOU FUCKED UP."[118] Harris clearly understood how the culture wars worked and yet was also visibly its product: he still endorsed some of its logic by pointing the finger for his behavior at the failures of parents and teachers, in much the same way hardcore punks located the roots of their anger and frustration in their home lives. The reaction to the massacre at Columbine, then, demonstrated the ways in which the productive victimization of parents in the 1980s was successful in normalizing this cultural and political logic for understanding and addressing teen social problems, a logic that elided nuanced explanations of teen behavior and pinned blame on the cultural products allowed into the home that were poisoning its inhabitants.

In just the first few days after the attack, articles constantly referenced "gothic" clothing, the music of Marilyn Manson, or violent video games in describing Harris and Klebold as outcasts.[119] The Associated Press's coverage of the massacre began typically: "They are called the 'Trench Coat Mafia,' a group of about 10 students who wear long black coats, keep to themselves and follow shock rocker Marilyn Manson."[120] They were "loners, outcasts, and 'satanic individuals'" and "called themselves the trench coat mafia."[121] In discussing a broader pattern of school shootings, *Time* created a graph outlining the shooters' crimes, mental health status, and cultural influences such as Marilyn Manson and the video game *Doom*.[122] The framing of the tragedy in these terms demonstrated how central the logic of culture critics like Tipper Gore had become, and, no matter how the portrayal was nuanced, that framing prepared the reader to understand the motives and actions of Klebold and Harris as the logical outcome of deranged cultural influences that poor parenting had allowed to reach them.

Others went further in spelling out the "connections" more directly between those influences and what happened at Columbine High School. *USA Today* explicitly used the logic of the 1980s culture wars to argue that those dangerous media persisted and were now aided by other sources, such as violent video games and internet chat rooms, while *New York Post* columnist Steve Dunleavy argued the "blind could see it coming" because "these kids loved Marilyn Manson and his sick jive of destruction and self-destruction."[123] This thinking contributed to the widespread story of Cassie Bernal, who was reportedly killed for professing faith in God and being an evangelical Christian.[124] In fact, Bernal was not targeted, nor did the alleged incident preceding her death take place.[125] The narrative sprang from the cultural frame already central to making sense of teen tragedies—that the killers must be satanic outcasts exacting their revenge against their well-adjusted, God-fearing peers, a vengeance spurred on by the demonic exhortations of artists like Marilyn Manson.

Similarly, in the days after the attack, television news reporters and the experts they interviewed consistently cited the connections between the media consumed by Klebold and Harris and what happened at Columbine. In particular, cable and nightly news continually raised the specter of the dark influences of goth culture and artist Marilyn Manson as the origin of the shooters' evil. On April 21, the ABC newsmagazine *20/20* aired a special report on the phenomenon of the "gothic movement," which it called a "a growing, and, to many, troubling trend in suburban America."[126] Correspondent Brian Ross interviewed Steve Rickard of the Denver Police Department, who discussed at length the emergence of suburban gangs of gothic teens like those who committed the massacre at Columbine. When Ross finally asked him where it all comes from, Rickard responded, "I think in this case, you can trace it back to Marilyn Manson." Near the end of the segment, Ross linked the gothic subculture and its propensity for suburban violence to other incidents around the country, giving parents a sense of what to look for to prevent another attack.

Other experts, such as Los Angeles Unified School District psychologist Richard Lieberman, mixed their messages about teen boys.[127] He explained that kids in distress show a number of recognizable and consistent warning signs. However, he and a UCLA psychologist both emphasized that "children learn violence as a way of resolving problems. And music, movies and video games reinforce that view." Video games, in particular, seemed to be the new ingredient leading to violent teen behavior. On CNN's *Inside Politics*, James Fox, dean of the College of Criminal Justice at Northeastern University and a member of the President's Advisory Committee on School Shootings, reasoned, "The difference between video games and other forms of entertainment around us is that it's so active participation. Rather than just sitting on a couch and watching a massacre on television, which is passive, a kid can learn to enjoy killing cybernetically."[128] Fox represented the view of many experts that participatory video game violence was qualitatively different from other games or forms of entertainment and that the Columbine massacre was the evidence.[129] In a direct parallel to the cases of suicide and other violence in the 1980s, law enforcement officers, culture warriors, and reporters saw the malign influence of popular culture as the cause. Instead of heavy metal and *Dungeons & Dragons*, they now spotlighted Manson and violent video games like those vilified by Joe Lieberman in 1993.[130] This framing served similar purposes. News programs like those just described strongly suggested a simple, private solution to the problem of suburban teen violence, a producer and the product of the conservative politics and culture of that moment.

Some attempted to leverage the massacre at Columbine to highlight the need for stricter gun laws. President of New Line Cinema Michael DeLuca, in defending media industries, fused parenting concerns with the access to guns: "Bad home, bad parenting, having guns in the home, parents fighting and drinking. Kids need direction and guidance."[131] Similarly, Marc Klaas, a father turned policy advocate whose daughter was kidnapped and murdered in 1994, argued on the Fox News show *Hannity and Colmes*, "This isn't a kind of a situation that would have occurred in this country just twenty or thirty years ago, but now we live in a culture where we have somewhere between 200 million and 240 million guns adorning our cupboards, hiding in our drawers."[132] Yet Klaas also returned to the problem of popular culture as part of this dangerous mix: "We are a culture that waits in line for the latest Hollywood pyrotechnic extravaganza, where the hero goes away and blows away 30 or 40 people." Despite their efforts and that of their congressional supporters, the Senate failed even to pass popular restrictions on gun show sales, instead looking to parents to solve the problem of school shootings and teen gun violence.[133]

Yet the second part of Klaas's comments are what most viewers, including politicians of both parties, took away about the causes of the Columbine massacre.[134] Demonstrating the centrality of this cultural logic, they raced to blame popular culture and reinforce the role of parents in battling these hazards. President Bill Clinton implored parents to "take this moment to ask what else they can do to shield our children from violent images and experiences that warp young perceptions and obscure the consequences." His wife and future senator, secretary of state, and presidential nominee, Hilary Rodham Clinton, echoed this message: "We can no longer shut our eyes to the impact that the media is having on all of our children."[135] Signifying the consensus on the dangers of popular culture and media, conservative Christian presidential candidate Gary Bauer repeated a similar sentiment, "We've got a culture right now out of Hollywood that glorifies death. It's in the movies, it's in the music our kids here. You know, if you're a parent out there, and you haven't actually sat down and listened to some of the music that talks about killing cops, and glorifies violence against women and so forth, you need to do that; you need to take a closer look at what your kids are listening to."[136] Colorado governor Bill Owens succinctly summed up the conventional wisdom, "This is a cultural virus."[137]

In response to this virus, many called on the culture industries to take more responsibility for their products, and some even sued video game and film companies for helping contribute to the Columbine attack. As with the Judas Priest and AC/DC cases, however, the companies were not found culpable in the courts. Instead, critics unerringly called for a focus on the culture of the family to prevent further tragedies like these. In the aftermath, Vice President Al Gore lobbied internet service providers to give tools to parents to better police online activities.[138] Psychologist Michael Gurian exemplified the commonsense politics of increased parental involvement on CNN: "They [parents] need to make sure that they have a plan for the boy's adolescence, and that that plan includes a lot of the parents, a lot of the grandmas, grandpas, extended family or a lot of other friends of the family, so that the boy has this sort of safety net around him, this community, so that when he starts pulling away from the parents, he's got the safety net." Later in the interview Gurian made clear why this kind of intervention was so important: "Starting with the drive-by shootings in the inner city, then it has moved to the rural areas, and, it is, you know, to outer cities, suburbia."[139] Gurian's urgency stemmed in large part from his belief that the crisis of the family was causing violence in the suburbs.

In the face of this view, parents, mental health experts, and other teens did attempt to contextualize the behavior of Klebold, Harris, and other teens drawn to video games, Marilyn Manson, and goth culture. One mother who hosted goth dance nights for teens said, quite simply, "They're just trying to find their own identity, to fit in, experiment. They're good kids, kids just like anybody's kids. They are anybody's kids."[140] She reiterated the sense held by many that experimenting with dress and identity was a normal part of growing up. Hundreds of teens seemed to say a similar thing about Klebold and Harris. They were different in dress and demeanor but killed for their own reasons. Recent Columbine High School graduate Tasha E. Kelter exemplified this view in her college newspaper: "I'm not blaming the 'jocks' of Columbine High School, the kids' parents or Marilyn Manson. I'm blaming Klebold and Harris. To do anything else would be absurd—that's settled."[141] A student in Florida explained that she felt safe around goths because they "have their own group and are really nice."[142] Some mental health advocates, too, swatted away media explanations and looked toward the private and social lives of teens as the root causes.[143] Harold S. Koplewicz of the Child Study Center at New York University pleaded in the *New York Times*: "The true tragedy is that America refuses to recognize there are millions of teens and children with psychological illnesses, which are as real as physical illnesses."[144] Marilyn Manson himself eschewed media appearances but did pen an editorial for *Rolling Stone* in May 1999 titled "Columbine: Whose Fault Is It?"[145] In addressing this question, he followed the line of thinking of others who looked beyond popular culture to explain Columbine. "Throw a rock and you'll hit someone who's guilty. We're the people who sit back and tolerate children owning guns, and we're the ones who tune in and watch the up-to-the-minute details of what they do with them." Still, Manson, like Frank Zappa when he testified about porn rock in 1985, pointed not to artists like himself but to the larger culture of violence in America that must be addressed. However, these efforts did little to shape the view of Columbine or teen violence.

Instead, the aftermath of Columbine signified how news media and culture warriors drew a simple and misguided connection between violent video games and musical lyrics on one hand and the spate of teen violence during the 1990s on the other, a connection that continued the notion of the suburban home under siege and empowered parents as the best defense.[146] In his book *Columbine*, Dave Cullen provides the definitive explanation of what happened at Columbine High School and why making clear that so much of what the public thinks they know is wrong in just the way noted above. "We remember Columbine," he writes, "as a pair of outcast Goths from the Trench Coat Mafia snapping and tearing through their high school hunting down jocks to settle a long-running feud. Almost none of that happened. No Goths, no outcasts, nobody snapping. No targets, no feud, and no Trench Coat Mafia."[147] Yet politicians, culture critics, and parents continued to see incidents like this as a result of a cultural formula. Blaming the media and families buttressed culturally conservative politicians' power and authority in American culture to insist on family values and cultural solutions, not social programs and regulatory measures for addressing things like school shootings, depression, and teen pregnancy. Columbine did call forth activists calling for those kinds of policy solutions. However, as John King of CNN noted, despite the push for gun control, "the president's overriding message was that the cure to this recurring national nightmare would not be found in Washington."[148]

The dominant and enduring mode for understanding this tragedy and how to prevent another one was the conservative cultural politics of parental empowerment, family values, and eventually faith-based programs, not sweeping legislation. This was no more evident than in the values-centric campaign of George W. Bush. The suburban culture wars not only made possible Bush's election but facilitated his faith-based agenda for schools coping with substance abuse, teen pregnancy, and suicide. His approach opened the door to a wider assault on government, expertise, and science that often exacerbated the problems it was seeking to solve. This worldview, and the limited set of government programs facilitating it, also reinforced the primacy of the suburban household in American culture. When understood in context, this frame, which focused on family solutions and market choices in response to social ills, involved the valorization and empowerment of white suburbanites and, at the same time, further marginalized those already on the edge of the frame for understanding American families.

In many ways, the recommendations of parenting experts and the PMRC did not seem appropriate to the job of combating a threat promoted as ruining lives and destroying families. When the Columbine attacks occurred, it appeared those tactics had indeed failed, as the massacre seemed to represent the worst-case scenario feared by 1980s culture critics. This individualistic, piecemeal approach should have helped suburban parents just like those in Littleton to identify and address the dark influences of goth culture and Marilyn Manson (or, more productively, identify and act on their children's possible disorders). Of course, as Dave Cullen and others have shown, that tragedy and others had almost nothing to do with the media and popular culture habits of teens, and placing blame also on parents elided the many structural failures that paved the way for the massacre.

However, the scourge of supposedly hazardous media entering the home culture was important in other ways for critics and parents. It helped many suburban parents reassert authority over their homes and restore a sense of sanctity that would not have been possible without the victimization these products effected by coming right in the front door. With nothing less than their children's lives at stake, parents were empowered to re-regulate that space according to their own prerogatives with hardly any interference from the state or judgment from politicians. In adopting this private, family-centered approach to teen social problems, culture critics and the parents they empowered facilitated and were facilitated by the conservative attack on government and valorization of mythic family values. Indeed, the concerned parent and their fears of popular culture and new media outlets became essential to mainstream cultural politics as the United States headed into the twenty-first century. Politicians across the ideological spectrum leveraged the notion of a presumably innocent white suburban populace ruthlessly targeted by amoral culture industries to further valorize a nostalgic vision of family located in the suburban home. The consequences of this conventional political wisdom were experienced quite differently across race and gender lines, setting the terms of the culture wars for the new century as movements for equality like gay marriage and Black Lives Matter gathered steam. However, the legacy of the twentieth century meant they still faced stiff opposition from people who relied on nostalgic visions of a "traditional" suburban family and the innate innocence of its members, who must be protected or reformed. These were powerful visions that, in turn, politicians and culture critics used to marginalize and dehumanize those civil rights activists who did not fit that image.

Epilogue

By the turn of the twenty-first century, the tenor of American suburban life had changed. News media, popular culture representations, everyday practices, and lived experiences demonstrated that a postwar world of expected privilege had become one of crisis turned to advantage. Beginning in the mid-1970s, environmental, criminal, and moral hazards continuously emerged in everyday suburban life. Toxic contamination, home invasions, kidnappings, and occult-inspired violence, among other hazards, appeared visible, real, and pervasive on the suburban landscape. The result of postwar suburban development, these newly discernible local hazards produced an increasingly fraught and contested landscape unlike the one homeowners expected to inherit. However, their materialization did not simply endanger lives and property or create a sense of hazard. Their existence engendered a new form of power through productive victimization whereby the realistic endangerment of home and family, as detailed in the preceding chapters, gave suburbanites a reasonable justification to defend themselves. In response, they enacted measures that went beyond mere defense to expand cultural and spatial power. Those legitimate threats, then, actually worked to empower individual suburbanites and facilitate the consolidation of their authority over their families, homes, and neighborhoods, marking a new era in the history of American suburbs.

The battles over privilege and power fought by suburbanites played an essential role in the rightward turn of American culture and politics. The mainstreaming of conservative values about government and family enabled suburban actions in response to local threats. In turn, suburbanites made real calls for privatism, localism, and a return to "family values," giving evidence to both the need for and the success of these ideologies.

When faced with environmental and criminal threats, suburban residents blamed inept, incapable, and unwilling government entities for not protecting them from existential harm. In response, they credibly acted in their own defense within and beyond the state. To stop seemingly dangerous public projects like nuclear power plants, they cried "Not in my backyard!" to persuade corporations and government to shape land use around their parochial fears. Similarly, rather than be passive victims of criminals and the justice system, suburbanites took action to protect themselves through private means. They installed security systems, hired security officers, erected gates and walls, and educated themselves and their children about how to navigate an increasingly dangerous suburban landscape. Although suburbanites premised these actions on imperilment caused in some way by the failure of the state, they also leveraged state power to legitimate their actions and functionally regulate space. Elected officials and corporate leaders heeded the exclamations of fearful homeowners—their constituents and consumers—often by displacing projects to locales with less powerful or visible populations. Law enforcement also came to work with homeowners, neighborhood watch programs, and private security in order to better police suburban space. Urban space, meanwhile, was in the midst of the Wars on Drugs and Crime. In these ways, suburbanites could both understand government as broadly dysfunctional and call on government intervention to defend and affirm class, race, and homeowner privilege as manifested in suburban culture. In this era, the state did not so much pull back from American life as more selectively intervene in ways that favored suburban homeowners.

The rightward turn was also attended by a conservative cultural movement that played out most prominently in the suburbs. In responding to the foundational changes in sex, gender, and the family after World War II, many decried a crisis of the family as evidenced by increasing divorce rates, teen misbehavior, and popular culture that promoted "liberal" values. In response, conservatives called for a return to "traditional" family values—a nostalgic, largely false vision of earlier suburban life—in order to restore the morality of the family and the nation.

Heading into the 1980s, culture warriors highlighted the role that popular culture and the media played in supposedly destroying the family from the inside by corrupting the morals of young consumers and enticing them into dangerous behavior. To recapture and restore those mythic family values, their champions raised consciousness about the threats from popular occulture while emphasizing the role of parents—not government—in protecting children and teens. The ascendance of this worldview empowered suburban parents and clearly suggested which kinds of families were worth defending, particularly as seen in the different responses to urban versus suburban populations by both the state and culture critics.

To address these moral dangers symbolized by the "satanic panic," the rise in teen suicide and substance abuse, and the massacre at Columbine High School, culture warriors figured suburban teens as innocent victims of amoral culture industries leading them to these violent outcomes. By tracing the cause and solution to these dangers to consumer choices, culture critics, and the suburban parents they empowered, largely eschewed medicine, science, education, and public policy in addressing teen social ills. Concerned parents, then, were able to more strictly regulate their children's media consumption and discipline them, largely without reliance on or intervention by family services, police, or schools. And, in seeing the threats in these ways and responding through private action, suburbanites facilitated a turn away from broad-scale social policy. By further undermining the notion of effective state intervention, they slowed or stopped the implementation of policies that would more broadly and more effectively have addressed teen social problems.

Through these measures, suburbanites largely succeeded in eliminating, defusing, or marginalizing many of the environmental, criminal, and moral hazards that appeared so threatening. Even so, the values and practices of late-twentieth-century suburbanites remain with us today because they are persuasive and powerful. This persistence is due in large part to the coincidence of the suburb-under-siege's emergence with the concomitant rightward shift in American politics and culture that is now mainstream. Indeed, the story of the suburban neighborhood of fear shows not just how this shift occurred but also why it persists and the terms on which suburban power and privilege are being challenged today.

The excessive localism of Nimbyism, though successful at stopping many projects, became by the late 1990s an epithet labeling suburbanites not as justified home defenders but as privileged localists uninterested in the public good.[1] Branded as antigrowth by pro-business conservatives and as exclusionary by environmental justice groups on the left, Nimby protection of middle-class suburban neighborhoods carried less and less cultural heft.[2] Moreover, Nimbyism was often no longer necessary as suburbanites' successes at slowing, stopping, or moving projects suggested to government and industry that suburban opposition was usually not worth the risk. Instead, government and industry first handled suburbanites as legitimate stakeholders rather than staunch obstructionists so as to avoid costly battles.[3]

Still, suburbanites of the twenty-first century have taken their cues from their late-twentieth-century predecessors by developing and pursuing a privileged, middle-class consumerist environmentalism. Legitimated by the emergence of toxic America, suburbanites now express their fears of chemicals and additives by opposing genetically modified foods and those enriched with high-fructose corn syrup. And, in its most extreme form, they support the antivaccination movement, which is, at its core, an expression of privilege and self-determination and not an argument based on science or civic duty. Armed with the whiff of fact and the communicative power of the internet, suburban parents have leveraged unsupportable "scientific" claims into a powerful movement, one supported by celebrities and politicians, including President Donald Trump.[4] The claims and actions of antivaxxers amplify those of suburbanites who began suffering from multiple chemical sensitivities and environmental illness in the 1980s and '90s. However, those with MCS and EI experienced observable pain and ill effects even if the causes were not clear, in contrast to antivax supporters, who lack evidence to support their claims. Shunned by the medical establishment but firm in their beliefs, MCS and EI sufferers leveraged cultural and spatial privilege to attempt to protect themselves from the chemicals that they believed were destroying their lives. And yet, then as now, these expressions of privilege endangered and marginalized those without such power to protect themselves. As suburbanites pursue a varied and multipronged approach to protect the environment and ameliorate their suffering, the citizens of Flint and other cities still suffer from toxic chemical exposure through tainted drinking water, while many other urban apartment dwellers are exposed to lead paint.[5] Similarly, children of privilege forego vaccinations while increasing numbers of people die from diseases preventable by vaccine each year.[6] This worldview buttressed a broader attack on science and expertise that, at this writing (spring 2020), appears to have had dangerous consequences for the battle against the COVID-19 virus spreading across the United States. The focus on private interests at the expense of the body politic is part of the cultural heritage of late-twentieth-century suburban environmentalism detailed in this book.

Suburban crime culture of the late twentieth century, too, has proven powerful in shaping contemporary America. The continued expansion of private home security strategies and apparatuses, including the proliferation of gated communities, is a logical outgrowth of suburban security culture that operates under the notion of constant threat. While not new, technologically advanced, internet-connected smart homes and surveillance devices have expanded the carceral suburb, where homeowners feel both reassured and endangered through the implementation of security practices. New innovations like the Amazon-owned Ring smart doorbell continue to produce this suburban sensibility. It allows a homeowner to surveil their front door, speak to visitors, and generally mind their home even when not there all under the supposition that something could (or likely will) go wrong. As one Ring commercial demonstrates, its sales are premised on the same fears harbored by 1980s and '90s suburbanites. In the ad, as the viewer watches a white man in a hoodie approach a house, the inventor, Jamie Siminoff, explains that most burglaries are perpetrated during the day.[7] The man attempts to ascertain if someone is home before he breaks in in broad daylight. Hewing closely to the themes and imagery of 1990s ADT home security commercials, this ad reiterates the earlier notion of invisible, lurking burglars waiting to strike in the suburbs. Like other internet-connected devices and apps, the Ring-connected Nextdoor app, and its competitors Citizen and Neighbor, expand and enhance suburban paranoia as homeowners share information about strange characters, unfamiliar vehicles, and shifty deliverymen. As in the late twentieth century, homeowners today are using these powerful tools to protect homes and families. Yet their use is more likely to sow fear and skepticism of strangers, outsiders, or anyone who appears out of place, even as the crime rate continues to fall.[8]

In this way, suburban crime culture continues to facilitate and be facilitated by tough-on-crime culture and politics that produced disproportionate outcomes for people of color as seen in the "new Jim Crow" and the "golden gulag."[9] During this era, progressively militarized urban policing practices increasingly scrutinize populations of color subjecting them to strict regimes of surveillance and incarceration while suburbanites work with law enforcement and choose to monitor themselves.[10] Today, this difference can be seen as Ring has partnered with dozens of police departments to work with homeowners in installing the devices to prevent home invasions and assist police in catching invaders.[11] The ramifications of suburban crime culture can most clearly be seen in the incidents of homeowner violence committed against supposedly threatening individuals who seem out of place in their suburban communities, almost always young people of color. From George Zimmerman's murder of Trayvon Martin in his gated community to the hundreds of legally defensible shootings justified by expansions of the Castle Doctrine, the homeowner's right to use violence against perceived threats exists because of the suburban crime culture forged over the previous forty-five years, as detailed in chapter 3.

This understanding of the suburban neighborhood as essentially dangerous has had other ramifications as well. Across the country, police and neighbors have accused parents of neglect for letting their children walk to school alone or play without supervision in public space. As these cases demonstrate, the coding of suburban space as inherently dangerous and requiring vigilant surveillance lest a tragedy occur is now dominant.

This understanding of space has also buttressed the failure of many enclosed suburban malls. By most accounts, the shopping mall of the twenty-first century is dying or dead as many malls close while few are being built to replace them. The rise of e-commerce and the expense of renting brick-and-mortar locations are clearly significant contributors to this decline. As Josh Sanburn of *Time* Magazine notes, however, the failure of the shopping mall is about more than shopping.[12] The increased policing of the 1980s and '90s shopping center and the policies that effectively drove out teenage patrons to protect profits negatively affected the bottom line while destroying the notion of the shopping center as an open, civic space. Experts estimate that 25 to 35 percent of malls will fail by 2030. Though a considerable rate of closure, that still leaves a large percentage of malls still operating. However, these will largely be luxury malls with even stricter security to protect customers who desire a nearly privatized consumer experience for purchasing products from high-end retailers like Gucci and Louis Vuitton.[13] Indeed, upscaling and adding amusements has offered a way for many centers to survive in the era of Amazon. Centers like The Grove in Los Angeles run a mall trolley and host a summer concert series, suggesting that pure shopping experiences are not enough to sustain the mall. Some of the malls that have closed, so-called "dead malls," are being reimagined as different kinds of capitalist spaces, chiefly workspaces for tech companies, rather than serving as suburban town squares.[14] Others are simply being bulldozed to make way for new kinds of development, such as mixed-use open-air centers that hark back to the early visions of the shopping mall modeled on urban downtowns. Nonetheless, 80 percent of malls are considered healthy, but these have largely hewed to the luxury shopping model that perfectly articulates the privatized world of suburban living born of 1980s and '90s understandings and regulations of public space.[15]

Frequenting the mall less, suburban teens have further receded into the home, their retreat facilitated in no small part by the expansion of residential high-speed internet into their communities, while many low-income places lag behind in internet availability.[16] As teenagers have returned, the idealization of the home as a safe social hub for suburban children and teens has persisted. Similarly, the notion of dangerous popular culture products sneaking into the home has not only persisted but grown stronger, as has the elaboration of cultural explanations for tragedies with more viable social or medical justifications. The need to explain these tragedies and address their causes has become ever more urgent as an epidemic of shootings has occurred in the United States since the 1999 attack at Columbine High School. The mass shootings at Sandy Hook Elementary, Stoneman-Douglas High School, and Orlando's Pulse nightclub, to name but a few, found wild media speculation over the pop cultural habits of the perpetrators. While Satan and the occult have largely receded as explanations, there continues to be a framing of mass tragedies as caused in some part by cultural influences. Post-9/11, these have included violent media, as well as Middle Eastern heritage or Islamic worship, even as activists highlight other, more plausible causes, such as easy access to the high-powered weapons central to these tragedies. In this way, our contemporary calamities look much like those of the 1980s and '90s. In those instances, structural causes of and responses to tragedies were marginalized in favor of simpler and more reassuring but ultimately ineffective cultural explanations, paving the way for George W. Bush's compassionate conservatism and faith-based initiatives for addressing, in particular, teen social issues.

The era of the neighborhood of fear also fundamentally shaped domestic responses to the 9/11 terrorist attacks. In a suburban world characterized by the ongoing pursuit of security in a hazardous world, the attacks brought new urgency to the security consciousness of suburbanites. However improbable, they could envision another terror attack in their own backyard, particularly as the daily trip to the mailbox took on increased anxiety after the discovery of anthrax sent to politicians and media figures.[17] This preparedness to see the world as not just dangerous but locally hazardous facilitated the political and national security responses to terrorism. Suburbanites were ready to see increased communications surveillance and travel security as reasonable measures to achieve a sense of security, because they felt scared but were confident they were unlikely to be targets of such measures. When asked to reenter the marketplace in response to the attacks, suburbanites did as they had before. They worked to protect themselves by purchasing plastic sheeting, safety masks, emergency radios, weapons, and bunkers. Lastly, with other threats seemingly less urgent, suburbanites turned back the clock to register increasing skepticism of people, beliefs, and practices that seemed out of place. Knowing that many of the hijackers lived, studied, and worked in suburban locales, residents believed they were manning the front lines against another attack and must turn their security apparatus to that task by practicing the racial profiling clearly in use by homeland security. In total, these responses both to the attacks and the Bush administration's actions sprang from previous decades of suburban history and culture in which residents learned to address a catastrophic disaster through private security practices and marketplace consumption in order to achieve a sense of safety in a world tailored to their needs and desires and yet seemingly beyond their control.

Notes

Introduction

1. Linda Saslow, "Once upon a Time in the Safety of the Suburbs," *New York Times*, June 27, 1982.

2. Elaine Tyler May, *Homeward Bound: American Families in the Cold War Era* (New York: Basic Books, 1988); Lizabeth Cohen, *A Consumer's Republic: The Politics of Mass Consumption in Postwar America* (New York: Alfred A. Knopf, 2003).

3. Stephanie Coontz, *The Way We Never Were: American Families and the Nostalgia Trap* (New York: Basic Books, 1992); David M. P. Freund, *Colored Property: State Policy and White Racial Politics in Suburban America* (Chicago: University of Chicago Press, 2007); Kevin M. Kruse, *White Flight: Atlanta and the Making of Modern Conservatism* (Princeton, NJ: Princeton University Press, 2005); Kevin Kruse and Thomas Sugrue, eds., *The New Suburban History* (Chicago: University of Chicago Press, 2006); Matthew Lassiter, *The Silent Majority: Suburban Politics in the Sunbelt South* (Princeton, NJ: Princeton University Press, 2006); Lisa McGirr, *Suburban Warriors: Origins of the New American Right* (Princeton, NJ: Princeton University Press, 2001); Robert Self, *American Babylon: Race and the Struggle for Postwar Oakland* (Princeton: Princeton University Press, 2003); Becky M. Nicolaides, *My Blue Heaven: Life and Politics in the Working Class Suburbs of Los Angeles* (Chicago: University of Chicago Press, 2002); Becky M. Nicolaides and Andrew Wiese, eds., *The Suburb Reader* (New York: Routledge, 2006); Andrew Wiese, *Places of Their Own: African American Suburbanization in the Twentieth Century* (Chicago: University of Chicago Press, 2004).

4. Kruse, *White Flight*. Kruse argues that these were the push-pull values of "white flight." He persuasively shows how moving to the suburbs was about not only leaving behind urban problems but also moving toward the enticements of suburban living.

5. May, *Homeward Bound*, 208–9. May argues that the suburban family ideal was key to a powerful political consensus valorizing domestic and foreign containment.

6. Robert Bruegmann, *Sprawl: A Compact History* (Chicago: University of Chicago Press, 2005); Owen D. Guttfreund, *Twentieth-Century Sprawl: Highways and the Reshaping of the American Landscape* (Oxford: Oxford University Press, 2005); Louise Mozingo, *Pastoral Capitalism: A History of Suburban Corporate Landscapes* (Cambridge, MA: MIT Press, 2011); Adam Rome, *The Bulldozer in the Countryside: Suburban Sprawl and the Rise of American Environmentalism* (Cambridge: Cambridge University Press, 2001).

7. Rome, *Bulldozer in the Countryside*; Christopher Sellers, *Crabgrass Crucible: Suburban Nature and the Rise of Environmentalism in Twentieth-Century America* (Chapel Hill: University of North Carolina Press, 2012).

8. Frank Hobbs and Nicole Stoops, *Demographic Trends in the 20th Century*, US Census Bureau, Census 2000 Special Reports, Series CENSR-4 (Washington, DC: Government Printing Office, 2002), http://www.census.gov/prod/2002pubs/censr-4.pdf, 1, 8. This study defines *suburban* as the metropolitan population living outside central cities. Hayden, *Building Suburbia*, 10.

9. Jefferson Cowie, *Stayin' Alive: The 1970s and the Last Days of the Working Class* (New York: The New Press, 2010), 303–4; Elizabeth Hinton, *From the War on Poverty to the War on Crime* (Cambridge, MA: Harvard University Press, 2016), 1–26; Michael W. Flamm, *Law and Order: Street Crime, Civil Unrest, and the Crisis of Liberalism in the 1960s* (New York: Columbia University Press, 2005), 3–4.

10. Nancy E. Cohen, *America's Marketplace: The History of Shopping Centers* (Lyme, CT: Greenwich, 2002); L. Cohen, *A Consumer's Republic*; M. Jeffrey Hardwick, *Mall Maker: Victor Gruen, Architect of an American Dream* (Philadelphia: University of Pennsylvania Press, 2004).

11. Robert Self, *All in the Family: The Realignment of American Democracy since the 1960s* (New York: Hill & Wang, 2012), 9–10; Coontz, *The Way We Never Were*, 23–41.

12. David Hajdu, *The Ten-Cent Plague* (New York: Picador, 2008).

13. Self, *All in the Family*, 9–10, 361–65.

14. Natasha Zaretsky, *No Direction Home: The American Family and the Fear of National Decline, 1968–1980* (Chapel Hill: University of North Carolina Press, 2007), 2–5, 9–20; Matthew Lassiter, "Inventing Family Values," in Bruce J. Schulman and Julian Zelizer, eds., *Rightward Bound: Making America Conservative in the 1970s* (Cambridge, MA: Harvard University Press, 2008), 13–15.

15. Lassiter, "Inventing Family Values," 15; Whitney Strub, *Perversion for Profit: The Politics of Pornography and the Rise of the New Right* (New York: Columbia University Press, 2010), 146–78.

16. Daniel K. Williams, *God's Own Party: The Making of the Christian Right* (Oxford: Oxford University Press, 2010), 172–73.

17. McGirr, *Suburban Warriors*, 3–19.

18. Bruce J. Schulman, *The Seventies: The Great Shift in American Culture, Society, and Politics* (New York: Da Capo, 2002), 3; Ronald Reagan, "First Inaugural Address," January 20, 1981, Ronald Reagan Foundation and Institute, https://www .reaganfoundation.org/programs-events/webcasts-and-podcasts/podcasts/words-to-live -by/1981-inaugural-address/.

19. Corey Robin, *The Reactionary Mind: Conservatism from Edmund Burke to Sarah Palin* (Oxford: Oxford University Press, 2011), 246–48.

20. Kevin Kruse and Julian Zelizer, *Fault Lines: A History of the United States since 1974* (New York: W. W. Norton, 2019), ch. 6.

21. Lily Geismer notes this view in her study of suburban Massachusetts: "The desire of affluent suburbanites to preserve their individual quality of life and property and values bolstered another traditionally liberal cause: environmentalism." Lily Geismer, *Don't Blame Us: Suburban Liberals and the Transformation of the Democratic Party* (Princeton, NJ: Princeton University Press, 2015), 175.

22. Michelle Alexander, *The New Jim Crow: Mass Incarceration in the Age of Color-blindness* (New York: New Press, 2010); Matthew Lassiter, "Impossible Criminals: The

Suburban Imperatives of America's War on Drugs," *Journal of American History* 102, No. 1 (June 2015): 126–40; Ruth Wilson Gilmore, *Golden Gulag: Prisons, Surplus, Crisis, and Opposition in Globalizing California* (Berkeley: University of California Press, 2006).

23. Alexander, *The New Jim Crow*, 8; William J. Clinton Presidential Library, "President Clinton Signing the 'Crime Bill'" (1994), available on YouTube, https://www .youtube.com/watch?v=cOYoxSpt6IA. In his remarks upon signing the 1994 crime bill, President Clinton frequently referred to the massive wave of crime being experienced by average Americans as the impetus for the legislation. This law instituted punitive laws such as the three strikes provision, created new federal death penalty offenses, outlawed higher education Pell grants for federal inmates, and incentivized the building of new correctional facilities,

24. James Gilbert, *A Cycle of Outrage: America's Reaction to the Juvenile Delinquent in the 1950s* (Oxford: Oxford University Press, 1986); Frederick Wertham, *Seduction of the Innocent* (1954; reprint, Port Washington, NY: Kennikat Press, 1972); May, *Homeward Bound*; Jon Lewis, *The Road to Romance and Ruin: Teen Films and Youth Culture* (London: Routledge, 1992).

25. Andrew Hartman, *A War for the Soul of America: A History of the Culture Wars* (Chicago: University of Chicago Press, 2015), 171–200; Robin D. G. Kelley, *Yo' Mama's Disfunktional! Fighting the Culture Wars in Urban America* (New York: Beacon Press, 2001); Marisa Chappell, *The War on Welfare: Family, Poverty, and Politics in Modern America* (Philadelphia: University of Pennsylvania Press, 2009); Julilly Kohler-Hausmann, *Getting Tough: Welfare and Imprisonment in 1970s America* (Princeton, NJ: Princeton University Press, 2017).

26. Hartman, *A War for the Soul of America*, 177–83; Kelley, *Yo' Mama's Disfunktional!*; Eithne Quinn, *Nuthin' but a 'G' Thang: The Culture and Commerce of Gangsta Rap* (New York: Columbia University Press, 2005); Tricia Rose, *The Hip Hop Wars: What We Talk About When We Talk about Hip Hop—And Why It Matters* (New York: Basic Books, 2008), 33–42.

27. McGirr, *Suburban Warriors*; Rick Perlstein, *Before the Storm: Barry Goldwater and the Unmaking of American Consensus* (New York: Hill & Wang, 2002); Rick Perlstein, *The Invisible Bridge: The Fall of Nixon and the Rise of Reagan* (New York: Simon & Schuster, 2014).

28. Geismer, *Don't Blame Us*, 1–2.

29. Geismer reinforces this pragmatic orientation of suburbanites in Massachusetts: "Suburban activists along Route 128 proved equally effective at navigating the political culture of their own communities, adopting a strategy that couched issues to align with and complement privileges and priorities of suburban residency." Geismer, *Don't Blame Us*, 13.

30. In a further irony, David Freund notes that during the immediate postwar era the federal government itself diminished its role in creating the suburbs by positing their development as a manifestation of the free market. Freund, *Colored Property*, 33.

31. For a history of Stand Your Ground in America, see Caroline E. Light, *Stand Your Ground: A History of America's Love Affair with Lethal Self-Defense* (Boston: Beacon Press, 2017).

32. See Kruse and Sugrue, *The New Suburban History*; Wiese, *Places of Their Own*; Wendy Cheng, *The Changs Next to the Diazes: Remapping Race in Suburban California* (Minneapolis: University of Minnesota Press, 2013); and Mary Patillo-McCoy, *Black Picket Fences: Privilege and Peril among the Black Middle Class* (Chicago: University of Chicago Press, 2000).

33. Nancy A. Denton and Joseph R. Gibbons, "Twenty-First-Century Suburban Demography: Increasing Diversity Yet Lingering Exclusion," in Christopher Niedt, ed., *Social Justice in Diverse Suburbs* (Philadelphia: Temple University Press, 2013), 19–20, 27–28; Geismer, *Don't Blame Us*, 195–97; Richard Rothstein, *The Color of Law: A Forgotten History of How Our Government Segregated America* (New York: Liveright, 2015), 203–4; Wiese, *Places of Their Own*, 255, 270–81.

34. Andrea S. Boyles, *Race, Place, and Suburban Policing: Too Close for Comfort* (Berkeley: University of California Press, 2015), 10–11; Jodi Rios, "Everyday Racialization: Contesting Space and Identity in Suburban St. Louis," in John Archer, Paul J. P. Sandul, and Katherine Solomonson, *Making Suburbia: New Histories of Everyday America* (Minneapolis: University of Minnesota Press, 2015), 183–207.

35. Douglas S. Massey, Jonathan Rothwell, and Thurston Domina, "The Changing Bases of Segregation in the United States," *Annals of the American Academy of Political and Social Science* 626 (2009): 74–90; Mary Pattillo, *Black Picket Fences: Privilege and Peril among the Black Middle Class*, 2nd ed. (Chicago: University of Chicago Press, 2013), 1–3; Wiese, *Places of Their Own*, 258. Wiese argues, "Despite growing access to newer, more economically dynamic suburban areas, most black suburbanites in 1990 lived in older inner-ring suburbs, which exhibited a variety of fiscal shortcomings, such as high taxes, mediocre services, low-performing schools, commercial disinvestment, and anemic rates of property appreciation." Wiese, *Places of Their Own*, 285.

36. Rachel Heiman, *Driving after Class: Anxious Times in an American Suburb* (Berkeley: University of California Press, 2015). In her ethnographic study of a New Jersey suburb, Heiman argues that suburbanites experienced a heightened sense of anxiety in the late 1990s as they struggled for the appearance and feeling of class security as they sought to create "a little security in an insecure world." Ibid., 180.

37. Anna Clark, *The Poisoned City: Flint's Water Crisis and the American Urban Tragedy* (New York: Metropolitan Books, 2018); Christian Warren, *Brush with Death: A Social History of Lead Poisoning* (Baltimore: Johns Hopkins University Press, 2001).

38. German Lopez, "1,000 People Sent Me Their Addiction Stories: Here's What I Learned," *Vox*, December 30, 2009, https://www.vox.com/policy-and-politics/2019/12/30/21004923/drug-rehab-racket-addiction-treatment-survey-2019-review.

39. Coontz, *The Way We Never Were*, ch. 2; and Self, *All in the Family*, 9–10. The use of quotation marks around *traditional* is intended to signal the fiction of the middle-class, nuclear family as traditional in US history.

CHAPTER ONE: **Age of the Nimby**

1. Kent E. Portney, *Siting Hazardous Waste Facilities: The Nimby Syndrome* (New York: Auburn House, 1991), 10.

2. William Glaberson, "Coping in the Age of Nimby," *New York Times*, June 19, 1988.

3. John Graham, "NIMBY Politicking," *Nuclear News*, September 1982; Leon Daniel, "Town Unites to Fight Selection as Site for Nuclear-Waste Dump," *United Press International*, February 7, 1984; William K. Stevens, "Philadelphia Trash: Too Much and Nowhere to Go," *New York Times*, March 9, 1986; John Hanrahan, "Nuclear Power: The Dream Dims—Nuclear Waste Disposal: The 'Not In My Back Yard' Syndrome," *New York Times*, April 21, 1987; Sam Roberts, "Metro Matters: Growing Reply to Society's Ills: 'Not in My Yard,'" *New York Times*, June 25, 1987; Philip S. Gutis, "1987: A Year of City Problems on L.I.," *New York Times*, December 27, 1987; Warren R. Ross, "The Right to Protect Our Own Backyards," *New York Times*, July 24, 1988; Joshua Hammer, with Elizabeth Bradburn, "The Haul in Toxic Waste," *Newsweek*, October 3, 1988; David Arnold, "Distrust Creates the NIMBY Syndrome," *Boston Globe*, January 25, 1989; Bella English, "Child's Play Isn't Always," *Boston Globe*, February 6, 1989; "NIMBY?* But Trash Woes Are Ours to Cure," editorial, *Post-Standard* (Syracuse, NY), February 21, 1989; Richard Andrews, "Not in My Backyard," *Vermont Business Magazine*, April 1989; Bill Barol, "Big Fun in a Small Town," *Newsweek*, May 29, 1989; Donna Schaper, "Long Island Opinion: Yes in My Backyard," *New York Times*, June 18, 1989; Joseph P. Shapiro, "Uncle Sam's NIMBY Attack," *U.S. News & World Report*, September 18, 1989; John M. Endries, "'Not in My Backyard': Curing a Syndrome," *Public Utilities Fortnightly*, October 12, 1989; Mickey Baca, "What's It All About, NIMBY?" *New Hampshire Business Review*, September 8, 1989; Marianna Riley, "Homeless Can Be Us, Even in Suburbs, Students Find," *St. Louis Post-Dispatch*, May 28, 1990; Anne Carey, "Not in My Backyard!" *USA Today*, July 19, 1990; Debera Carlton Harrell, "Neighbors Opposing New Day-Care Center in Issaquah," *Seattle Post-Intelligencer*, September 19, 1990.

4. Carey Goldberg defined "affluenza," that particularly suburban affliction, as "the spiritual and environmental ills brought on by American-style overconsumption." Goldberg, "'Buy Nothings' Discover a Cure for Affluenza," *New York Times*, November 29, 1997.

5. Bella English, "The NIMBY Syndrome," *Boston Globe*, November 16, 1988.

6. David Gergen, "'Not in My Back Yard,' " *U.S. News & World Report*, July 22, 1991.

7. Self, *American Babylon*, 25.

8. Leo Marx, *The Machine in the Garden: Technology and the Pastoral Ideal in American History* (Oxford: Oxford University Press, 2000).

9. George Nash, *The Conservative Intellectual Movement in America since 1945* (Wilmington, DE: Intercollegiate Studies Institute, 2006), 331; Philip Mirowski, *Never Let a Serious Crisis Go to Waste: How Neoliberalism Survived the Financial Meltdown* (London: Verso, 2013), 39.

10. Walter Truett Anderson, "Environmentalists Come in All Stripes," *Oregonian*, December 22, 1989.

11. Robert D. Bullard, *Dumping in Dixie: Race, Class, and Environmental Quality* (New York: Routledge, 2000); Steve Lerner, *Sacrifice Zones: The Front Lines of Chemical Toxic Exposure in the United States* (Cambridge, MA: MIT Press, 2012); Dorceta Taylor, *Toxic Communities: Environmental Racism, Industrial Pollution, and Residential Mobility* (New York: New York University Press, 2014).

12. Sandy Tolan, "Revenge of the Nimby," *Arizona Trend*, March 1988.

13. Andrew Needham, *Power Lines: Phoenix and the Making of the Southwest* (Princeton, NJ: Princeton University Press, 2014), 80–83.

14. Carl A. Zimring, *Clean and White: A History of Environmental Racism* (New York: New York University Press, 2015), 215–16.

15. Kruse and Zelizer note: "Reagan took the same approach with environmental regulations, seeking to undermine the significant reforms undertaken in the 1970s. The administration did little to enforce existing laws and had no interest in giving support to environmentalists who called on the government to do more to combat issues such as pollution, acid rain, or toxic waste." Kruse and Zelizer, *Fault Lines*, 121.; see ch. 6 generally.

16. Dolores Hayden, *Building Suburbia: Green Fields and Urban Growth, 1820–2000* (New York: Vintage Books, 2003), 46–96.

17. Andrew Jackson Downing, *Cottage Residences; or, A Series of Designs for Rural Cottages and Cottage Villas, and their Gardens and Grounds Adapted to North America* (New York: Wiley & Putnam, 1844), available at *Internet Archive*, https://archive.org /details/cottageresidence00down_1. The planning and promotion of Llewellyn Park in New Jersey reflected these priorities. Its "Country Homes for City People" were sold with rules that prohibited fences and commercial land use in order to ensure the suburb remained a respite from urban life.

18. Robert Fogelson, *Bourgeois Nightmares: Suburbia, 1870–1930* (New Haven, CT: Yale University Press, 2005), 4, 22–24. Fogelson calls these suburbs "bourgeois nightmares" as they featured legal mechanisms for maintaining the class and race identity of the suburb as wealthy and white.

19. Rome, *The Bulldozer in the Countryside*, 87–119; Sellers, *Crabgrass Crucible*.

20. "Superfund History," US Environmental Protection Agency, https://www.epa .gov/superfund/superfund-history.

21. Hill, "Midpoint of 'Environmental Decade': Impact of National Policy Act Assessed."

22. Self, *American Babylon*, 1–2.

23. Kruse, *White Flight*.

24. Zachary J. S. Falck, *Weeds: An Environmental History of Metropolitan America* (Pittsburgh: University of Pittsburgh Press, 2010), 138–42.

25. Andrew Hurley, *Environmental Inequalities: Class, Race, and Industrial Pollution in Gary, Indiana, 1945–1980* (Chapel Hill: University of North Carolina Press, 1995), 54.

26. Meg Jacobs, *Panic at the Pump: The Energy Crisis and the Transformation of American Politics in the 1970s* (New York: Hill & Wang, 2017); David E. Nye, *Consuming Power: A Social History of American Energies* (Cambridge, MA: MIT Press, 1998), 200–203. Nye notes that overall energy consumption increased throughout the postwar era, and that consumer electronics likely to be found in suburban America, such as television sets and air conditioners, contributed significantly to this growth.

27. Rick Eckstein, *Nuclear Power and Social Power* (Philadelphia: Temple University Press, 1996), 41.

28. Eugene A. Rosa and Riley E. Dunlap note three stages in the shift in public opinion about nuclear power: "an early stage in the 1970s when Americans were

enthusiastic about the growth of nuclear power; a second stage of ambivalence following TMI when a less enthusiastic plurality of citizens consistently supported nuclear growth; and a third stage—emerging in the early 1980s—when a decisive majority of Americans opposed building more nuclear power plants." Rosa and Dunlap, "The Polls—Poll Trends: Nuclear Power: Three Decades of Public Opinion," *Public Opinion Quarterly* 58, No. 2 (summer 1994), 295–324. See also Margot Hornblower, "In the Trenches of the 'Nuclear' Battle," *Washington Post*, February 20, 1977.

29. Hayden, *Building Suburbia*, ch. 9.

30. Gene Smith, "Nuclear Power Hits a New Snag," *New York Times*, November 13, 1966. The Fermi accident was barely covered in the news and went largely unnoticed by customers and had no lasting impact on the popular associations of nuclear power or the growth of the industry.

31. Bett Pohnka and Barbara C. Griffin, *The Nuclear Catastrophe* (New York: Ashley Books, 1977); Billy Hale, dir., *Red Alert* (Paramount Television and CBS Television, 1977). Though fodder for popular entertainment, science fiction and pulp novels such as *The Nuclear Catastrophe* (1977) and televisions movies like *Red Alert* (1977) foreshadowed the risks of building plants and failures of communication and regulation.

32. Pat Squires, "The Nuclear Issue Becomes Suburban," *New York Times*, May 20, 1979.

33. Gary Arnold, "'Syndrome': The Nuclear Plant as Bogeyman in a Doomsday Thriller," *Washington Post*, March 16, 1979.

34. According to the article, "Controversy also has engulfed the movie 'The China Syndrome,' which opponents say greatly exaggerates the dangers involved in operation of nuclear power plants. Defenders, however, claim that the Three Mile Island reactor accident in Pennsylvania proved that makers of the film were right." "Do TV 'Docu-Dramas' Distort History?" *U.S. News & World Report*, May 21, 1979.

35. Sue Reilly, "A Disaster Movie Comes True," *People*, April 16, 1979.

36. William K. Knoedelseder Jr. and Ellen Farley, "When Fate Follows Fiction—The 'Syndrome' Fallout," *New York Times*, March 30, 1979; "A Nuclear Nightmare," *Time*, April 9, 1979.

37. Tom Mathews, with Susan Agrest, Gloria Borger, Mary Lord, William D. Marbach, and William J. Cook, "Nuclear Accident," *Newsweek*, April 9, 1979.

38. Dennis A. Williams, with Martin Kasindorf, Gerald C. Lubenow, and Ron LaBrecque, "Beyond 'The China Syndrome,'" *Newsweek*, April 16, 1979.

39. "The Credibility Meltdown," *New York Times*, March 30, 1979.

40. Conspiracy and paranoia about American institutions was rampant in American film of the 1970s. Just a few examples are: *The Parallax View* (1973), *Serpico* (1973), *The Conversation* (1974), *Hearts & Minds* (1974), *The Stepford Wives* (1975), *Three Days of the Condor* (1875), *Black Sunday* (1979), and *Winter Kills* (1979).

41. "A Nuclear Nightmare."

42. "The Credibility Meltdown."

43. Williams, "Beyond 'The China Syndrome.'"

44. Regarding the operators on duty the morning of March 28, the presidential commission that investigated the accident wrote that "each was a product of his training—training that did not adequately prepare them to cope with the accident at

TMI-2. Indeed, their training was partly responsible for escalating what should have been a minor event into a potentially devastating accident." John G. Kemeny, Chairman, "The Need for Change: The Legacy of TMI," in *Report of the President's Commission on the Accident at Three Mile Island*, October 1979, 13.

45. "A Glossary of Nuclear Terms: Cladding to Zircaloy," *New York Times*, April 1, 1979; B. Drummond Ayres Jr., "Reporter's Notebook: Nuclear Event," *New York Times*, April 3, 1979.

46. *New York Times*, "The Credibility Meltdown."

47. "Radiation: Who Said What?" *Patriot News*, March 30, 1979.

48. "Radiation: Who Said What?"; "Three Mile Island, 1979, 1981" Video Collection, Dick Thornburgh Papers, University of Pittsburgh, http://www.library.pitt.edu /thornburgh/collection/series19.html. The press conferences held on the first day of the crisis by William Scranton Jr., lieutenant governor of Pennsylvania and the officer charged with overseeing the Pennsylvania Emergency Management Agency (PEMA), were emblematic of the failure to manage not just the emergency but also the public's perception of it. The contrast in the quality of information and pure stagecraft between the early press conferences and those conducted later by Nuclear Regulatory Commission scientist Harold Denton and Governor Richard Thornburgh is marked. The later conferences were more informative, direct, and controlled than the chaotic scenes featuring Scranton and Met Ed officials.

49. Roger Quigley, "Goldsboro: Tranquility and Anger," *Patriot News*, March 30, 1979.

50. Kemeny, "The Need for Change," 8.

51. Kemeny, "The Need for Change," 8.

52. Sound and Hudson against Atom Development (SHAD) Alliance activists noted the accident at TMI as part of a longer track record of mismanagement and regulation of the nuclear power industry. The group's flyer promoting the documentary *Paul Jacobs and the Nuclear Gang* read, "They lied to us about Viet Nam! They lied to us about Watergate! This film shows how they lied to us about RADIATION." SHAD Alliance Papers, Peace and Conflict Studies Archive, Box 1, Swarthmore College.

53. *ABC Nightly News*, March 30, 1979, available on YouTube, accessed February 18, 2020, https://www.youtube.com/watch?v=2VRdkTvv878.

54. Kemeny, "The Need for Change," 19.

55. Kemeny, "The Need for Change," 19.

56. Kemeny, "The Need for Change," 18.

57. "Chapter 4: The Tough Fight to Contain the Damage," *Washington Post*, April 8, 1979.

58. Dickinson College, "Interview with College Employee #2," conducted July 16, 1979, *Three Mile Island*, Dickinson University, http://tmi.dickinson.edu/wp-content /uploads/2017/08/399.pdf.

59. Gilbert D. Thompson, "Three Mile Island: The Initial Reaction," *Washington Post*, April 4, 1979); "Letters: Reverberations of a Nuclear Accident," *New York Times*, April 6, 1979.

60. McKinley C. Olson, "Middletown Revisited: After T.M.I.—A Meltdown of Trust," *Nation* (April 19, 1980), 465–68.

61. Olson, "Middletown Revisited," 465–66.

62. "Chapter 14: Inhabitants Wonder What to Believe," *Washington Post*, April 11, 1979.

63. Adam Clymer, "Poll Shows Sharp Rise since '77 in Opposition to Nuclear Power Plants," *New York Times*, April 10, 1979.

64. Williams, "Beyond 'The China Syndrome'" (first quote); A. O. Sulzberger, "Nuclear Critics Plan Political Moves and Mass Protests," *New York Times*, April 7, 1979 (second).

65. Brown quoted in Tom Wicker, "Irony and Tragedy," *New York Times*, April 6, 1979.

66. "A Nuclear Nightmare."

67. Vance L. Sailor, "The High Cost of Gadflies," *New York Times*, April 9, 1978. Nuclear power supporter Vance L. Sailor, a nuclear physicist at the Brookhaven National Laboratory, said of these gadflies in 1978 that they clothed themselves in good citizenship but their delays were costing Long Island residents upward of a billion dollars. See Kenneth F. McCallion, *Shoreham and the Rise and Fall of the Nuclear Power Industry* (New York: Praeger, 1995), 25.

68. National Environmental Policy Act of 1969, Pub. L. No. 91–190, 42 U.S.C. §§ 4321–47 (1970), available at US Fish and Wildlife Service, https://www.fws.gov/r9esnepa/RelatedLegislativeAuthorities/nepa1969.PDF. One of the major regulatory changes that hindered the building of the Shoreham and many other plants was the passage of the National Environmental Policy Act of 1969, which required companies to consider the likely environmental effects of any major or significant project and publish those findings in an environmental impact study (EIS). Although the act did not mandate that companies do anything about potential problems found during the study, the law helped bring about transparency in the building process. Third parties, or "intervenors" as they were known, used the information gleaned from the impact reports to pressure companies to take environmental concerns seriously and perhaps change plans lest they incur protests.

69. "What is SHAD?" leaflet, 1978, SHAD Alliance Papers, Peace and Conflict Studies Archive, Box 1, Swarthmore College.

70. Williams, "The No Nuke Movement"; Kirk Victor, 'The Nuclear Turn-On," *National Journal* (September 9, 1989), 2196.

71. Carter B. Horsley, "Nuclear Plant Hearings Near an Exhaustive End," *New York Times* March 21, 1971.

72. Vance L. Sailor, "The High Cost of Gadflies," *New York Times*, April 9, 1978.

73. Carter B. Horsley, "Little Community on L.I. Welcomes Big Neighbor," *New York Times*, October 1, 1970. John Bellport, a town councilman in nearby Brookhaven, Long Island, and president of the Shoreham Civic Association, said in 1970 that the Lloyd Harbor Group protest was using scare tactics and ignoring the very real reduction in tax rates from 30 dollars for every 100 of assessed value to 6 for every 100. The Atomic Energy Council made essentially this point in a staff report on LILCO's bid for the Shoreham plant in 1972 writing that the "need for the power is said to outweigh any damage to the environment." David A. Andelman, "A.E.C. Staff Report Backs Nuclear Plant for LILCO," *New York Times*, December 5, 1972.

74. "What is SHAD?" 1978.

75. The authors wrote of their mission that they "seek to expose interrelation of economic and political institutions that sustain nuclear energy." "Outline of Manhattan Project Task Force Report," SHAD Alliance Papers, Peace and Conflict Studies Archive, Box 2, Swarthmore College.

76. "Vigil for Karen Silkwood" flyer, late 1978 or early 1979, SHAD Alliance Papers, Peace and Conflict Studies Archive, Box 1, Swarthmore College.

77. Spencer R. Weart, *Nuclear Fear: A History of Images* (Cambridge, MA: Harvard University Press, 1988), 301; SHAD Alliance Letter to Residents Soliciting Volunteers, January 10, 1979, SHAD Alliance Papers, Peace and Conflict Studies Archive, Box 1, Swarthmore College. As SHAD noted in its January 10 letter, before the accident at Three Mile Island, the groups struggled to attract new members beyond the hardcore antinuclear opponents already in their ranks.

78. Mark Harrington, "Saga behind the Shoreham Nuclear Plant Retold," *Newsday*, June 9, 2009.

79. Kyle Harvey, *American Anti-nuclear Activism, 1975–1990: The Challenge of Peace* (New York: Palgrave Macmillan, 2014), 6–7.

80. A. O. Sulzberger Jr., "Nuclear Critics Plan Political Moves and Mass Protests," *New York Times*, April 7, 1979 (quote); SHAD Alliance Letter, April 27, 1979, SHAD Alliance Papers, Peace and Conflict Studies Archive, Box 1, Swarthmore College; John T. McQuiston, "Shoreham Action Is One of Largest Held Worldwide," *New York Times*, June 4, 1979; Stoler, "Pulling the Plug."

81. Francis Brady, "The Shoreham Getaway," *New York Times*, January 31, 1982. The *Times* even noted in the author information section that "Francis Brady lives on the Island, but not too close to Shoreham," indicating a growing sense that being anywhere on Long Island was already too close to the plant.

82. "Shoreham Impasse: Suggested Solutions," *New York Times*, January 1, 1989.

83. Stanley S. Smilan, "Nuclear Power at Shoreham: Who Makes the Decisions?" *New York Times*, April 8, 1979.

84. Greco quoted in James Barron, "Doubts Voiced on Shoreham A-Plant," *New York Times*, April 16, 1982.

85. Edward Werth, "Nuclear Power: The 'Wool Over Our Eyes," *New York Times*, May 20, 1979.

86. "Sizing Up the Counties," *New York Times*, December 26, 1982.

87. Michael Winerip, "Cohalan's Opposition to Nuclear Plant Is Seen as Boon to Re-election," *New York Times*, June 3, 1983.

88. "Long Island Goes Nuclear or Bust," *New York Times*, February 27, 1983.

89. Sailor, "The High Price of Gadflies"; Thomas J. Burke, "Shoreham and the New Gadflies," *New York Times*, August 6, 1978.

90. Burke, "Shoreham and the New Gadflies."

91. Winerip, "Cohalan's Opposition"; Frank Lynn, "Narrow Victory Puts a Damper on Cohalan Plan," *New York Times*, November 13, 1983. Cohalan was narrowly elected, in part because a third-party conservative candidate siphoned off votes in a largely Republican county. All three candidates for county executive opposed Shoreham, though they differed on what to do if it was not opened.

92. "Excerpts," *New York Times*, March 11, 1983.

93. "Nuclear Power: Is It the Best Choice—Or the Worst?" *New York Times*, June 1, 1980.

94. "Carney Won't Seek Reelection to House due to Nuclear Issue," *Wall Street Journal*, May 23, 1986; Frank Lynn, "Stakes Are High in Suffolk House Race," *New York Times*, October 26, 1986. Closing the Shoreham plant was a key demand in the subsequent elections of the 1980s. In 1986, Republican leaders persuaded Representative William Carney to step aside because he did not oppose the plant strongly enough.

95. Frank Lynn, "Maverick Ending a Career," *New York Times*, April 26, 1987

96. Frank Lynn, "Shoreham Dispute Claims Carney as Latest Political Casualty," *New York Times*, June 1, 1986.

97. Michael Oreskes, "Shoreham Is Issue in Suffolk Races," *New York Times*, September 8, 1985; "Shoreham Foe Wins Easily," *New York Times*, September 11, 1985; "The '85 Elections: Major Incumbents Win on L.I. and in Rockland," *New York Times*, November 7, 1985; Frank Lynn, "Anti-LILCO Party an Election Force," *New York Times*, November 17, 1985; John Rather, "Howard Challenged for Post," *New York Times*, December 1, 1985; John Rather, "Proxy Showdown for LILCO," *New York Times*, December 8, 1985; John Rather, "State and LILCO in Clash on Power Outlook for Long Island," *New York Times*, December 29, 1985; "The State of the Governor," *New York Times*, January 9, 1986; Frank Lynn, "Shoreham Key to Special Vote," *New York Times*, March 23, 1986; Josh Barbanel, "Cuomo and Legislators Announce Accord on Takeover Plan for LILCO," *New York Times*, July 3, 1986; Irwin Stelzer, "American Account: Falling Out with Nuclear Power," *New York Sunday Times*, July 27, 1986; Frank Lynn, "Politics of Shoreham Pushes Suffolk Chief into Race for Judgeship," *New York Times*, September 17, 1986; Paul Taylor, "Cuomo: A Fighter Finds New Ways to Win," *Washington Post*, September 29, 1986; Clifford D. May, "Debate on Shoreham: Who Opposed It First?" *New York Times*, October 16, 1989; Frank Lynn, "Stakes Are High in Suffolk House Race," *New York Times*, October 26, 1986; Mary McGrory, "An Issue Whose Time Has Come," *Washington Post*, November 9, 1986; Philip S. Gutis, "Suffolk Politicians Brace for Battle on Executive," *New York Times*, November 10, 1986; Frank Lynn, "Appeal of Cuomo in Suburbs Is Noted," *New York Times*, December 7, 1986; Michael Oreskes, "Nuclear Plant Openings Threatened by Politics," *New York Times*, February 8, 1987; Eric Schmitt, "Suffolk Race Reflects Nation's Suburban Concerns," *New York Times*, June 8, 1987; Philip S. Gutis, "A-Plant Plays Major Role in L.I. Race," *New York Times*, October 27, 1987; Frank Lynn, "Lauder Prepares to Run for Congress in Suffolk," *New York Times*, March 23, 1988; Thomas B. Edsall, "New York's Local Issues May Dominate Its Primary," *Washington Post*, April 16, 1988.

98. Victor, "The Nuclear Turn-On"; "Lights Off on Long Island," *Economist*, April 29, 1989.

99. William Glaberson, "Coping in the Age of Nimby," *New York Times*, June 19, 1988.

100. James Barron, "Nuclear Power Foes Go on But the Ranks Are Thinner," *New York Times*, October 23, 1980. Barron noted that antinuclear activists' numbers were dwindling even though the residents of Long Island continued to oppose the Shoreham.

101. Robert Gottlieb, *Forcing the Spring: The Transformations of the American Environmental Movement* (Washington, DC: Island Press, 2005), 3; Hurley, *Environmental Inequalities*, 57.

102. Perry L. Norton, "Fine—But Not in My Backyard," *New York Times*, June 7, 1987.

103. Gottlieb, *Forcing the Spring*, 168, 176.

104. John T. McQuiston, "In the Suburbs Backyard Politics Comes Naturally," *New York Times*, June 10, 1984; Ross, "The Right to Protect Our Own Backyards" (quote).

105. Perlstein, *Before the Storm*.

106. Schulman, *The Seventies*, xvi; Nash, *The Conservative Intellectual Movement*, 331.

107. Nash contrasts earlier conservative movements that focused on national issues and politics, with the New Right, which "was essentially the product of traumas experienced by ordinary people in their everyday lives." This concentration on the everyday and the local encouraged suburban homeowners to see themselves as both victims of bureaucracies but also useful tools for shaping their local world. Nash, *The Conservative Intellectual Movement*, 331.

108. One contemporary newspaper article noted that the New Right came from "a 'conservative majority' of blue-collar workers and 'ordinary' people who are frustrated over rising taxes and the largess of costly federal programs." "'For a Broader Constituency,'" *Washington Post*, January 29, 1978.

109. John W. Freece, *Sprawl and Politics: The Inside Story of Smart Growth in Maryland* (Albany: State University of New York Press, 2005), 7. Freece notes that even in Maryland, which pioneered smart growth in the late 1990s, voters rejected a 1991 proposal to return the power of local land regulation to the state. This demonstrates that, even in pursuing progressive ideals, suburbanites still preferred local decision making; Ross, "The Right to Protect."

110. Diane Greenberg, "Firefighters Wary of Shoreham Plant," *New York Times*, April 6, 1980.

111. David Arnold, "Distrust Creates Nimby Syndrome," *Boston Globe*, January 25, 1989.

112. Glaberson, "Coping in the Age of Nimby."

113. Ross, "The Right to Protect Our Own Backyards."

114. Charlotte Libov, "Nimby Takes Hold," *New York Times*, August 16, 1987.

115. Gilmore, *Golden Gulag*. During the same era that Nimbys rejected jails in their local communities, Gilmore shows, the surveillance and prosecution of urban criminals increased to mammoth proportions, necessitating the construction of new jails.

116. Ross, "The Right to Protect Our Own Backyards."

117. Portney, *Siting Hazardous Waste Facilities*, 14–16.

118. Matt Yancey, "Delay Seen in Narrowing List of Nuclear Waste Sites," Associated Press, February 29, 1984; "Issues Guideline for Choosing Site," Associated Press, December 6, 1984.

119. Robert Sangeorge, "Everybody Wants Nuclear Waste Sites but 'Not in my Back Yard,'" United Press International, March 24, 1984.

120. John Hanrahan, "Nuclear Waste Disposal: The 'Not in My Back Yard' Syndrome," United Press International, April 21, 1987.

121. Jordana Hart, "Neighbors' Fears Stall New Homes for Mentally Ill," *Boston Globe*, April 11, 1989.

122. Kean quoted in Sam Roberts, "Growing Reply to Society's Ills: 'Not in My Yard,'" *New York Times*, June 25, 1987.

123. Henry D. Royal, "Nuclear Policy Driven by Fear, Not Facts," *St. Louis Post-Dispatch*, February 24, 1989.

124. "A Sterling Nuke Site Could Threaten Water Supply," *Syracuse (NY) Post-Standard*, December 21, 1988.

125. Frank DeLoache, "Hillsborough Residents Worry about Power Lines in Yard," *St. Petersburg Times*, April 28, 1987; Larry Lange, "Neighbors Protest Power Station," *Seattle Post-Intelligencer*, May 6, 1991.

126. See, for example, Paul Brodeur, *The Great Power-Line Cover-Up: How the Utilities and the Government Are Trying to Hide the Cancer Hazard Posed by Electromagnetic Fields* (New York: Little, Brown, 1995); William Leiss and Christina Chociolko, *Risk and Responsibility* (Montreal: McGill University Press, 1994); Mark S. Dworkin, *Cases in Epidemiology: A Global Perspective* (Sudbury, MA: Jones & Bartlett Learning, 2011); and Jeff Hect, "Cell Tests Suggest Link between Cables and Cancer," *New Scientist* (December 3, 1987), 28.

127. Lerner, *Sacrifice Zones*, 4–6.

128. Michael Pousnerhousing, "Not In My Back Yard . . . ," *Atlanta Journal and Constitution*, April 21, 1991.

129. John T. McQuiston, "In the Suburbs, Backyard Politics Comes Naturally," *New York Times*, June 10, 1984.

130. Richard Cohen, "The Truth and Lies about Nuclear Power," *Washington Post*, April 1, 1979.

131. "Springfield Nuclear Power Plant," *Simpsons Wiki*, accessed February 23, 2020, https://simpsons.fandom.com/wiki/Springfield_Nuclear_Power_Plant.

132. "Two Cars in Every Garage and Three Eyes on Every Fish," *The Simpsons* (Fox Television, November 1, 1990).

133. "US Approves First New Nuclear Reactor in a Generation," Reuters, February 12, 2012; Matthew L. Wald, "Nuclear Renaissance Is Short on Largess," *New York Times*, December 7, 2010, http://green.blogs.nytimes.com/2010/12/07/nuclear-renaissance-is-short-on-largess.

134. Peter Stoler, "Bracing for the Fallout," *Time*, May 12, 1986.

135. "Viewpoints: The Old Town Entertainment Center," *Riverside (CA) Press Enterprise*, February 15, 1995; Terry Nelson, "Don't Burst the Building Boom," *St. Louis Post-Dispatch*, March 14, 1995; Alida C. Silverman, "Tell Us What You Think," *Atlanta Journal and Constitution*, February 29, 1996; David Friedman, "Global Conflict Is in Our Back Yard," *Oregonian*, November 2, 1997.

136. Gottlieb, *Forcing the Spring*, 3–4.

137. Lassiter, *Silent Majority*, 13–14, 120–70.

138. Howard Kunreuther, "Please! Choose My Backyard!" *Christian Science Monitor*, September 19, 1990.

139. Environmental Protection Agency, "Key Dates in Superfund," http://www.epa.gov/superfund/action/law/keydates.htm.

140. Nancy Vogel, "Is California Bursting at Its Seams?" *California Journal*, July 1, 1991; Joyce Murdoch, "In Bethesda, Low-Income Housing With All the Extras," *Washington Post*, April 5, 1993; Terry Nelson, "Don't Burst the Building Boom," Editorial, *St. Louis Post-Dispatch*, March 14, 1995; and Dan Kalb, letter to the editor, *San Francisco Chronicle*, November 6, 1995.

141. Jack Rosenthal, "On Language: Acronym Power," *New York Times*, August 5, 1990; and "NIMBY*? But Trash Woes Are Ours to Cure" *Syracuse (NY) Post-Standard*, February 21, 1989.

142. Ross, "The Right to Protect Our Own Backyards."

CHAPTER TWO: **Neighborhood of Fear**

1. "Carter Proposes 'Super Fund' for Hazardous Cleanup," *National Journal* (June 23, 1979), 1055.

2. Elaine Tyler May, *Fortress America: How We Embraced Fear and Abandoned Democracy* (New York: Hachette Books, 2017), 1–56.

3. "The Neighborhood of Fear," *Time*, June 2, 1980.

4. "The Poisoning of America," *Time*, September 22, 1980.

5. Peter Gwynne, with Mark Whitaker, Elaine Shannon, Mary Hager, and Sharon Begley, "The Chemicals around Us," *Newsweek*, August 21, 1978.

6. "A Nightmare in Niagara," *Time*, August 14, 1978.

7. Self, *All in the Family*, 365–69.

8. Estelle Freedman, *No Turning Back: The History of Feminism and the Future of Women* (New York: Ballantine, 2002), 132–33; Alison Lefkovitz, *Strange Bedfellows: Marriage in the Age of Women's Liberation* (Philadelphia: University of Pennsylvania Press, 2018), 9–10.

9. Herman Staudenmayer, preface to *Environmental Illness: Myth and Reality* (Boca Raton, FL: Lewis, 1999).

10. "The Toxicity Connection," *Time*, September 22, 1980.

11. Julie Passanante Elman, *Chronic Youth: Disability, Sexuality, and U.S. Media Cultures of Rehabilitation* (New York: New York University Press, 2014), 169; Ruth Rosen, *The World Split Open: How the Modern Women's Movement Changed America* (New York: Viking, 2000), 314–20; Peter Conrad, The Medicalization of Society: On the Transformation of Human Conditions into Treatable Disorders (Baltimore: Johns Hopkins University Press, 2014), 4–10.

12. Gregory J. Seigworth and Melissa Gregg, "An Inventory of Shimmers," in Gregory J. Seigworth and Melissa Gregg, eds., *The Affect Theory Reader* (Durham, NC: Duke University Press, 2010), 1–28; Julie Passanante Elman, "'Find Your Fit': Wearable Technology and the Cultural Politics of Disability," *New Media and Society* 20 (October 2018): 3760–77.

13. Jasbir K. Puar, *The Right to Maim: Debility, Capacity, Disability* (Durham, NC: Duke University Press, 2017), 15–16.

14. Lisa Jones Townsel, "Symptoms Are 'All over the Map,'" *St. Louis Post-Dispatch*, July 24, 1999.

15. Evelyn Todd, *The Invisible Prison: A Handbook for Multiple Chemical Sensitivity* (United Kingdom: Troubadour, 2015), epigraph.

16. May, *Homeward Bound*; Coontz, *The Way We Never Were*.

17. Ruth Schwartz Cowan, *More Work for Mother: The Ironies of Household Technology from the Open Hearth to the Microwave* (New York: Basic Books, 1985), 192–210.

18. Linda Nash, *Inescapable Ecologies: A History of Environment, Disease, and Knowledge* (Berkeley: University of California Press, 2006), 195.

19. Lois Marie Gibbs, *Love Canal and the Birth of the Environmental Health Movement* (Washington, DC: Island Press, 2011), 1.

20. Richard S. Newman, *Love Canal: A Toxic History from Colonial Times to the Present* (New York: Oxford University Press, 2016), 103.

21. *Time*, "A Nightmare in Niagara."

22. Newman, *Love Canal*, 102–7.

23. *Time*, "Neighborhood of Fear."

24. Peter Gwynne, with Mark Whitaker, Elaine Shannon, Mary Hager, and Sharon Begley, "The Chemicals around Us," *Newsweek*, August 21, 1978.

25. *Time*, "Neighborhood of Fear."

26. Gwynne, "The Chemicals Around Us."

27. Glenn Jordan, dir., *Lois Gibbs and the Love Canal* (Filmways Television, 1982).

28. Fred Rothenberg, "Fighting-the-Establishment Stories on CBS and PBS Tonight," Associated Press, February 17, 1982.

29. *New York Times* television critic Tony Schwartz derisively said of this television movie, and the genre: "Life is more complex than the film's pat solutions suggest, and if you're looking for 'Crime and Punishment,' you won't find it here. But what you will get is an entertaining story about a tenacious woman who triumphed." This didactic tendency, though artistically maligned, did work to give a straightforward account of a complicated issue and story and to more directly communicate the existential threats to the suburban environment. Tony Schwartz, "Lois Gibbs Fights the Battle of Love Canal," *New York Times*, February 17, 1982.

30. Steve LaRue, "Region Copes with Toxics Risk," *San Diego Union-Tribune*, December 1, 1985.

31. Gwynne, "Chemicals All around Us."

32. Richmond quoted in Ed Magnuson, "The Poisoning of America," *Time*, September 22, 1980.

33. Natalie Angler, "Hazards of a Toxic Wasteland," *Time*, December 17, 1984.

34. Angler, "Hazards of a Toxic Wasteland."

35. Michael Weisskopf, "Toxic Waste Sites Awash in Mismanagement," *Washington Post*, November 16, 1986.

36. "Canal Cleanup," *Time*, July 26, 1982.

37. Maureen Dowd, "Superfund, Supermess," *Time*, February 21, 1983.

38. Angler, "Hazards of a Toxic Wasteland."

39. Melinda Beck, with Mary Lord, "A Caustic Report on Chemical Dumps," *Newsweek*, October 22, 1979.

40. "Part 3: Yesterday's Toxics: Superfund," *Newsweek*, July 24, 1989.

41. Lawrence Buell, *Writing for an Endangered World: Literature, Culture, and Environment in the U.S. and Beyond* (Cambridge, MA: Harvard University Press, 2001), 30–31.

42. Don DeLillo, *White Noise* (New York: Viking, 1985), 4.

43. *New York Times* book critic Christopher Lehman-Haupt offered his interpretation of the title of the novel: "'White Noise,' the title of Don DeLillo's ninth and latest novel, refers to death," which, like a constant sound, is ever present in postmodern life. Christopher Lehman-Haupt, "Books of the Times," *New York Times*, January 7, 1985.

44. Ursula K. Heise, "Toxins, Drugs, and Global Systems: Risk and Narrative in the Contemporary Novel," *American Literature* Vol. 74, No. 4 (2002): 747–78.

45. DeLillo, *White Noise*, 198.

46. DeLillo, *White Noise*, 41–43.

47. DeLillo, *White Noise*, 103.

48. DeLillo, *White Noise*, 139, 205.

49. Joanne Ostrow, "Rockville's Mock Disaster Develops a Few Disasters of Its Own," *Washington Post*, June 30, 1983.

50. DeLillo, *White Noise*, 129.

51. Other films of the era that took for granted the pervasive practice of illegal toxic waste dumping and its deleterious effects include *Prophecy* (1979), *The Children* (1980), *Modern Problems* (1981), *The Living Dead Girl* (1982), *The Being* (1983), *Mutant* (1984), *State Park* (1984), *Choke Canyon* (1986), *Night Trackers* (1987), *Street Trash* (1987), *Killer Crocodile* (1989), *Think Big* (1989), *Men at Work* (1990), and *Alligator II: The Mutation* (1991).

52. "The Movie Channel," *Washington Post*, October 13, 1988; "Showtime," *Washington Post*, October 30, 1988. These films got significant exposure in the predominantly suburban outlets of cable television and home video. After limited theatrical runs in the New York metro area, where the films were produced, *Class of Nuke 'Em High* and *The Toxic Avenger* played on pay cable movie channels like the Movie Channel and Showtime in the fall of 1987 and throughout 1988. *Class of Nuke 'Em High* was listed as playing for ten weeks on either Showtime or the Movie Channel between October 1987 and November 20, 1988.

53. Vincent Canby, "Screen: 'Class of Nuke 'Em High,'" *New York Times*, December 12, 1986.

54. Sangeorge, "Everybody Wants Nuclear Waste Sites But 'Not In My Back Yard.'"

55. Cindy Skrzycki, "Twentieth Century Anxieties: Accidents Waiting to Happen," *U.S. News and World Report*, May 19, 1986; "Close-Up: The Killing Ground," *ABC News*, March 29, 1979; Angler, "Hazards of a Toxic Wasteland."

56. Foster Church, "Dump Site Selection All Politics," *Portland Oregonian*, December 20, 1987.

57. Chris Chrystal, "Surveys Show Nation Fears Risks of Nuclear Dump," United Press International, January 18, 1989.

58. Hilary Sigman, "Midnight Dumping: Public Policies and Illegal Disposal of Used Oil," *RAND Journal of Economics* 29, No. 1 (spring 1998): 157–78.

59. "The Killing Ground."

60. Rochelle L. Stanfield, "Because It Can Happen Here, Localities Want Tougher Rules on Dangerous Cargo," *National Journal*, February 23, 1985.

61. Staudenmayer, *Environmental Illness*, 12–13.

62. "The Toxicity Connection."

63. Conrad calls this process "medicalization," whereby "nonmedical problems become defined and treated as medical problems." Conrad, *The Medicalization of Society*, 4.

64. Susan Abod, dir., *Homesick: Living with Multiple Chemical Sensitivity* (Dual Power Productions, 2013).

65. Robert Reinhold, "When Life Is Toxic," *New York Times*, September 16, 1990.

66. Jean Marbella, "No Breathing Space," *St. Louis Post-Dispatch*, May 5, 1990.

67. Kathy Boccella, "Inside Pollutants May Be Riskier than Outside Ones," *Philadelphia Inquirer*, April 2, 1995.

68. Steve Kroll-Smith and H. Hugh Floyd, *Bodies in Protest: Environmental Illness and the Struggle over Medical Knowledge* (New York: New York University Press, 1997), 2.

69. Bonnye L. Matthews, *Chemical Sensitivity: A Guide to Coping with Hypersensitivity Syndrome, Sick Building Syndrome, and Other Environmental Illnesses* (Jefferson, NC: McFarland, 1998).

70. Matthews, *Chemical Sensitivity*, 82.

71. Matthews, *Chemical Sensitivity*, xi.

72. Matthews, *Chemical Sensitivity*, 71.

73. John C. Burnham, *Health Care in America: A History* (Baltimore: Johns Hopkins University Press, 2015), 446–47; Paul Starr, *Remedy and Reaction: The Peculiar American Struggle over Health Care Reform* (New Haven, CT: Yale University Press, 2011), 63–64.

74. Todd, *The Invisible Prison*, xv.

75. Todd, *The Invisible Prison*, 13.

76. Susan Abod and Lisa Pompopidam, dirs., *Funny, You Don't Look Sick: Autobiography of an Illness* (Dual Power Productions, 1995).

77. Susan Greenhalgh, *Under the Medical Gaze: Facts and Fictions of Chronic Pain* (Berkeley: University of California Press, 2001); Robert A. Aronowitz, *Making Sense of Illness: Science, Society, and Disease* (Cambridge: Cambridge University Press, 1998), 19–39.

78. Robert Gioielli, *Environmental Activism and the Urban Crisis: Baltimore, St. Louis, Chicago* (Philadelphia: Temple University Press, 2014); Zimring, Clean and White.

79. Terr Al, "Environmental Illness: A Clinical Review of 50 Cases," *Archives of Internal Medicine* 146, No. 1 (January 1986): 145–49; Paul Berg, "California Doctors Discredit Clinical Ecology Theory," *Washington Post*, February 26, 1986.

80. Thomas Orme and Paul Benedetti, "Multiple Chemical Sensitivity," American Council on Science and Health, February 1, 1994, https://www.acsh.org/news/1994/02/01/mcs-multiple-chemical-sensitivity.

81. Staudenmayer, preface to *Environmental Illness*.

82. Donna E. Stewart, "Environmental Illness and Patients with Multiple Unexplained Symptoms," *Archives of Internal Medicine* 146, No. 7 (1986): 1447; C. M. Brodsky, "Multiple Chemical Sensitivities and Other 'Environmental Illness': A Psychiatrist's View," *Occupational Medicine* 2, No. 4 (October–December 1987): 695–704; Ephraim Kahn and Gideon Letz, "Clinical Ecology: Environmental Medicine or Unsubstantiated Theory?" *Annals of Internal Medicine* 111, No. 2 (July 1989): 104–6; G. E. Simon, W. J. Katon, and P. J. Sparks, "Allergic to Life: Psychological Factors in Environmental

Illness," *American Journal of Psychiatry* 147, No. 7 (July 1990): 901–6; Donald W. Black, Ann Rathe, and Rise B. Goldstein, "Environmental Illness: A Controlled Study of 26 Subjects with '20th Century Disease,'" *Journal of the American Medical Association* 264, No. 24 (December 1990): 3166–70; Donald W. Black, "Environmental Illness and Misdiagnosis—A Growing Problem," *Regulatory Toxicology and Pharmacology* 18, No. 1 (August 1993): 23–31; J. E. Salvaggio, "Psychological Aspects of 'Environmental Illness,' 'Multiple Chemical Sensitivity,' and Building-Related Illness," *Journal of Allergy and Clinical Immunology* 94, No. 2, Part 2 (August 1994): 366–70; R. Sergio Guglielmi, Daniel J. Cox, and Daniel A. Spyker, "Behavioral Treatment of Phobic Avoidance in Multiple Chemical Sensitivity," *Journal of Behavior Therapy and Experimental Psychiatry* 25, No. 3 (September 1994): 197–209; Rebecca L. Gomez, Roger W. Schvaneveldt, and Herman Staudenmayer, "Assessing Beliefs about 'Environmental Illness/Chemical Sensitivity,' " *Journal of Health Psychology* 1, No. 1 (January 1996): 107–23; Herman Staudenmayer, "Clinical Consequences of the EI/MCS 'Diagnosis': Two Paths," *Regulatory Toxicology and Pharmacology* 24, No. 1 (August 1996): 96–100; Stephen Barrett and Ronald Gots, *Chemical Sensitivity: The Truth about Environmental Illness* (New York: Prometheus Books, 1998); Arthur J. Borsky and Jonathan F. Borus, "Functional Somatic Syndromes," *Annals of Internal Medicine* 130, No. 11 (June 1999): 910–21.

83. Catriona Sandilands, "Sexual Politics and Environmental Justice: Lesbian Separatists in Rural Oregon," in Rachel Stein, ed., *New Perspectives on Environmental Justice: Gender, Sexuality, and Activism* (New Brunswick, NJ: Rutgers University Press, 2004), 109–26; Nancy C. Unger, *Beyond Nature's Housekeepers: American Women in Environmental History* (London: Oxford University Press, 2012), 163–87. Carol's choice to move to Wrenwood mirrored a tactic practiced by marginalized communities of the 1970s in response to their own environmental endangerment. In Carol's case, however, she leverages privilege in choosing to leave. She can afford to stay at the Wrenwood Center and not be forced to live off the land as many women's groups did in the 1970s.

84. Marlene Simons, "Concern Rising over Harm from Pesticides in Third World," *New York Times*, May 30, 1989. It seemed, according to the *New York Times* that outside the United States, people were largely exposed to toxins, often exported from that country, while American suburbanites chose to be around them, or at least to tolerate them, for other benefits.

85. Steve Lerner, *Sacrifice Zones: The Front Lines of Chemical Toxic Exposure in the United States* (Cambridge, MA: MIT Press, 2010).

86. Colman McCarthy, "The Chemical Refugees," *Washington Post*, January 23, 1988.

CHAPTER THREE: **"Fear Stalks the Streets"**

1. William L. Chaze, "Fear Stalks the Streets," *U.S. News & World Report*, October 27, 1980.

2. Judith Valente, "Bucolic Burglary Wave," *Washington Post*, April 7, 1978.

3. "Burglar Alarms," *Consumer Reports* (August 1981), 436–42.

4. Lassiter, *The Silent Majority*, 2; Self, *American Babylon*, 256–90. According to Self, California suburbanites in the 1970s crafted a narrative of victimization that belied the

great power they held, a vision in which government and inner-city minorities attempted to deprive them of the benefits of suburban living, including home ownership and local sovereignty. Lassiter, too, asserts that a suburban culture of political exclusion emerged around race and civil rights that attempted to exempt suburban areas from collective responsibility and encouraged a privatist ethic. In the midst of battles over busing, taxation, school control, and racial integration during the 1960s and '70s, suburbanites imagined themselves as aggrieved and sought to combat their victimization through locally directed actions to protect their power and privilege. This chapter follows these scholars' lines of thinking about the power of suburban victimization to see how they mobilized new fears as part of this privatist ethic centered on local power and spatial exclusivity.

5. National Sherriff's Association, "Neighborhood Watch Manual," Bureau of Justice Assistance, Office of Justice Programs, U.S. Department of Justice, https://www.bja.gov /Publications/NSA_NW_Manual.pdf. In the wake of urban unrest in the 1960s and the apocryphal story of bystander inaction in the Kitty Genovese murder in 1969, the National Sherriff's Association created the neighborhood watch program in 1972 to empower citizens to assist local law enforcement. Despite its urban origins, it was suburbanites who largely implemented the neighborhood watch program as the twentieth century wore on.

6. Alexander, *The New Jim Crow*; Gilmore, *Golden Gulag*, 22.

7. Charles H. Levine, "Police Management in the 1980s: From Decrementalism to Strategic Thinking," *Public Administration Review* 45 (1985): 691–700; William P. Browne, "Resource Needs and Attitudes toward Financial Allocation: A Study of Suburban Police Chiefs," *Public Administration Review* 34, No. 4 (July–August 1974): 397–99; Stuart A. Scheingold, "Politics, Public Policy, and Street Crime," *Annals of the American Academy of Political and Social Science* 539 (May 1995): 163; Albert J. Reiss Jr., "Police Organization in the Twentieth Century," *Crime and Justice* 15 (1992): 63–64. Reiss notes that small police forces were predominant in the 1980s; in New Jersey, for example, 77 percent of all departments had fewer than forty officers.

8. This relationship to law enforcement experienced by people of color in American cities differed in the sense that it directly expressed the privilege of suburban living even in a moment of seeming imperilment. As Elizabeth Hinton observes of urban policing, "National law enforcement programs introduced various forms of surveillance into social welfare programs, labeled entire groups of Americans as likely criminals and targeted them with undercover and decoy squads, ran sting operations that created underground economies, and combated gangs with militarized police forces and severe sentencing guidelines." Conversely, the state empowered residents of suburbs under siege to surveil and police spaces as adjuncts to law enforcement. Hinton, *From the War on Poverty to the War on Crime*, 10–11. See also Victor Rios, *Punished: Policing the Lives of Black and Latino Boys* (New York: New York University Press, 2011); Max Felker-Kantor, *Policing Los Angeles: Race, Resistance, and the Rise of the LAPD* (Chapel Hill: University of North Carolina Press, 2018), 1–3.

9. Gilmore, *Golden Gulag*. At the same moment when suburbanites were pursuing private solutions to perceived criminal threats, Gilmore persuasively argues, the prison industry and the surveillance and prosecution of urban criminals expanded to

mammoth proportions, further highlighting the spatial and political privilege of suburban life, buttressed by racial inequality, articulated in the criminal justice system, and mapped onto space.

10. Edward J. Blakely and Mary Gail Snyder, *Fortress America: Gated Communities in the United States* (Washington, DC: Brookings Institution Press, 1999), 7.

11. Steven Macek, *Urban Nightmares: The Media, the Right, and the Moral Panic over the City* (Minneapolis: University of Minnesota Press), 32–35. In arguing for a more city-centric view of suburban security measures, Macek shows that these safety innovations simply heightened fear of the central city by further stigmatizing it as being outside the zone of safety. While urban criminal threats remained visible during this period, his argument does not account for the ways in which suburbs themselves were understood as dangerous, specifically because of security measures that served as everyday reminders of danger.

12. "Voices from the Suburbs," *Christian Science Monitor*, May 24, 1983.

13. "Fear Drives to Suburbs," *New York Times*, June 8, 1982.

14. Hugh A. Mulligan, "Thieves Rush In," Associated Press, October 31, 1980; "When Fear is the Burglar," *New York Times*, March 2, 1982; Bureau of Justice Statistics, "1973–1982 Trends: Criminal Victimization in the United States," United States Department of Justice, Washington, DC, September 1983, 2.

15. Andree Brooks, "Adapting to the Rise in Suburban Crime," *New York Times*, February 7, 1982.

16. James K. Stewart, "Public Safety and Private Police," special issue, "Law and Public Affairs," *Public Administration Review* 45 (November 1985): 758–65.

17. "The People's War against Crime," *U.S. News & World Report*, July 13, 1981; Thomas McCarroll, Richard Woodbury, and John Greenwald, "The New Fortress America," *Time*, September 13, 1983.

18. Bruce Hager, "Burglar-Alarm Fines for Faulty Devices," *New York Times*, September 21, 1980.

19. Patricia Yoxall, "Here's How—Short of a Moat—to Protect Your Castle," *Chicago Tribune*, June 13, 1981.

20. Bob Vila, "Old House Restoration," *Popular Mechanics* (July 1986), 45–46.

21. Linda B. Martin, "Another Myth Crumbles: Crime Is Marching In," *New York Times*, October 30, 1980.

22. Jeanne Lesem, "Burglar-Proofing Your Home: Tips from a Retired Detective," United Press International, April 8, 1983.

23. Louise Cook, "Consumer Scorecard: Locking Burglars Out," Associated Press, March 21, 1980.

24. Stewart, "Public Safety and Private Police," 760. See also Louise Cook, "Part I: The Problem," Associated Press, May 17, 1977; Julia Malone, "Crime: Neglected Issue," *Christian Science Monitor*, February 19, 1981.

25. Hinton, *From the War on Poverty to the War on Crime*, 291–99.

26. Felker-Cantor, *Policing Los Angeles: Race, Resistance, and the Rise of the LAPD*, 17.

27. Saslow, "Once Upon a Time."

28. Saslow, "Once Upon a Time"; Rosalyn Baxandall and Elizabeth Ewen, *Picture Windows: How the Suburbs Happened* (New York: Basic Books, 2001); Jessica Grose,

"Parents Are Now Getting Arrested for Letting their Kids Go to the Park," *Slate*, July 15, 2014, http://www.slate.com/blogs/xx_factor/2014/07/15/debra_harrell_arrested_for _letting_her_9_year_old_daughter_go_to_the_park.html; Mark O'Mara, "Does Leaving Kids Alone Make Parents 'Criminals'?" *CNN*, January 30, 2015, http://www.cnn .com/2014/07/31/opinion/omara-parents-children-unattended/index.html?hpt=hp_t3. The fear of what might happen to children left alone in public spaces has become a norm in today's suburbs, sometimes even enforced as law. From South Carolina to Florida to Ohio, parents have been accused of child endangerment for letting their son or daughter walk home alone or play in a park unsupervised. The cultural logic of such laws has its origins in the emerging view of crime and public space voiced and made material by 1980s suburbanites.

29. Steven J. Marcus, "Home Barriers against Theft," *New York Times*, October 13, 1983.

30. Cook, "Part I: The Problem."

31. Carol Krucoff, "Keeping Burglars Away While You're Off to Play," *Washington Post*, July 10, 1979; Louise Cook, "Consumer Scorecard: Locking Burglars Out," Associated Press, March 21, 1980; Tom Zito, "The Saga of Superthief: Pranks, Gadgets, and the Big Payoff," *Washington Post*, April 29, 1980; Bill Gold, "Is Your House Protected by a Burglar Alarm?" *Washington Post*, May 27, 1980; Diana Shaman, "As Daytime Burglaries Rise, Homeowners Add Alarm Systems," *New York Times*, October 5, 1980; Louise Cook, "Make Sure Protection Keeps Pace with Prices," Associated Press, October 6, 1980; "Burglar Alarm Buyers Must Get $25 Permit," *New York Times*, January 21, 1981; Lorrie DeRose, "Burglaries: Cause for Alarm," *Washington Post*, October 6, 1981; Ron Scherer, "Home Alarms Ring Profits," *Christian Science Monitor*, October 23, 1981; Hugh A. Mulligan, "Crime Turns Back Civilization's Clock," *New York Times*, November 20, 1981; "When Fear Is the Burglar," *New York Times*, March 2, 1982; Peter Kerr, "Essentials for Security in the Home," *New York Times*, April 15, 1982; Bernard Gladstone, "The Essentials for Maintaining Security at Home," *New York Times*, April 15, 1982; James T. Yenckel, "Sounding the Alarm," *Washington Post*, November 11, 1982; James T. Yenckel, "What to Do When Help Is Not on the Way," *Washington Post*, November 28, 1982; "Strengthen Home Alarm System," United Press International, December 29, 1982; Larry Neumester, "Fear Spreads as Third Morris County Woman Found Murdered," Associated Press, January 6, 1983; Andrew Pollack, "Bell and G&W Offer Talking Alarm System," *New York Times*, June 2, 1983; Samuel G. Freedman, "Tapping the Security Market," *New York Times*, June 12, 1983; Bernard Gladstone, "Ways to Make Your Home More Secure While You're Away," *New York Times*, July 10, 1983; "Man Fatally Shoots Wife After Burglar Alarm Goes Off," Associated Press, September 26, 1983; Tom Shea, "Grab Bag of Devices Helps Control Homes," *InfoWorld*, October 31, 1983; Fred Bayles, "Part I: America's Changing the Way It Fights Crime," Associated Press, August 12, 1985. Bayles estimated that half a million alarms were installed in 1984.

32. Steven J. Marcus, "Home Barriers against Theft," *New York Times*, October 13, 1983.

33. Diana Shaman, "Long Island Housing: As Daytime Burglaries Rise, Homeowners Add Alarms," *New York Times*, October 5, 1980.

34. Norman Black, "Wiring America IV: News and Information Services," Associated Press, July 9, 1981. See also Pat Bauer, "Free Shares of Cable TV Costs Its Users," *Washington Post*, September 14, 1980; Margaret Shapiro, "2-Way Cable TV Channels Urged for P.G.," *Washington Post*, October 2, 1980; Pat Bauer, "Cable Television: Area Communities Fret over Electronic Snooping," *Washington Post*, November 18, 1980; Tom Jory, "Wiring America I: Cable's Dizzying Growth," Associated Press, July 5, 1981; Matthew L. Wald, "Towns Eye Future of Cable TV Net," *New York Times*, July 5, 1981; Thomas Rizzo, "Columbus: America's Cable Capital," Associated Press, July 6, 1981; and Thomas Rizzo, "Home Security Systems—A New Frontier for Cable," Associated Press, July 9, 1981.

35. Susan Chira, "A Crackdown on False Burglar Alarms," *New York Times*, October 2, 1983.

36. "False Alarm Law Studied," *Washington Post*, August 6, 1978; Linda Wheeler, "Burglar Alarm Sound Usually a False Note," *Washington Post*, August 3, 1980; Bruce Hager, "Burglar-Alarm Fines for Faulty Devices," *New York Times*, September 21, 1980; Judy Glass, "False Burglar Alarms Set Off Controversy," *New York Times*, June 27, 1981; "Keeping Up with Burglar Alarms," *New York Times*, July 28, 1981; McCarroll, Woodbury, and Greenwald, "The New Fortress America."

37. Chira, "A Crackdown on False Burglar Alarms."

38. ADT, "We're Home Even When You're Not" (1989), YouTube, https://www.youtube.com/watch?v=ekL9TpMY7NE.

39. ADT, "Sound Advice" (1990), YouTube, https://www.youtube.com/watch?v=PQ792Ls4t8U.

40. ADT, "Burglar Confessions" (1992), YouTube, https://www.youtube.com/watch?v=CIwPNWwpDZo.

41. ADT, "Prized Possessions" (1993), YouTube, https://www.youtube.com/watch?v=QsR9JH4GOkg.

42. ADT, "Security for Life" (1999), YouTube, https://www.youtube.com/watch?v=zQJGsVYgl9o.

43. National Crime Prevention Council, Office of Justice Programs, United States Department of Justice, *Are We Safe? The 2000 National Crime Prevention Survey*, NCJ 186729 (Washington, DC, 2001). This survey estimates that, by the year 2000, 41 percent of all homes in the United States were under the protection of neighborhood watch programs.

44. Black, "Wiring America IV: News and Information Services."

45. Molly Moore, "Burglars Beware: Neighbors on Duty," *Washington Post*, December 10, 1981.

46. Richard M. Titus, "Residential Burglary and the Community Response," in Ronald Clarke and Tim Hope, eds., *Coping with Burglary* (Boston: Kluwer-Nijhoff, 1984), 114.

47. Katy Holloway, Trevor Bennett, and David P. Farrington, "Does Neighborhood Watch Reduce Crime?" *Crime Prevention Research Review* (Office of Community Oriented Policing Services, US Department of Justice), No. 3 (2013).

48. Holloway, Bennett, and Farrington, "Does Neighborhood Watch Reduce Crime?"

49. Kathryn Tolbert, "Keeping Crime at Bay: Lookouts, Block Watch Groups Make Homes Seven Times Safer," *Washington Post*, April 23, 1981; Holloway, Bennett, and Farrington, "Does Neighborhood Watch Reduce Crime?" 8. Studies show that community policing efforts are largely difficult to evaluate in terms of the extent to which they prevent crime or lower crime rates, though some studies conclude they are mostly ineffectual.

50. "When Fear Is the Burglar"; Henry Fairlie, "It's Time to Stop Letting Criminals Imprison Us," *Washington Post*, January 11, 1981.

51. Saslow, "Once Upon a Time."

52. Susan Ladov, "Speaking Personally: Our Homes Have Become Our Castles under Siege," *New York Times*, January 18, 1981.

53. Ladov, "Speaking Personally."

54. Setha Low, *Behind the Gates: Life, Security, and the Pursuit of Happiness in Fortress America* (New York: Routledge, 2003); Blakely and Snyder, *Fortress America*, 3.

55. Despite the high profile of the crime and the efforts of law enforcement, the case remained unsolved for many years. However, on December 16, 2008, Hollywood police announced that, after a review of the case, they were confident that Otis Toole, convicted murderer and confidante of child molester and murderer Henry Lee Lucas, was responsible for Adam's murder.

56. Etan's story was retold in the 1983 film *Without a Trace*. However, at the end of that filmic retelling, a heroic detective discovers the Etan character living with another family.

57. Susan D. Greenbaum, *Blaming the Poor: The Long Shadow of the Moynihan Report on Cruel Images of Poverty* (New Brunswick, NJ: Rutgers University Press, 2015); Daniel Geary, *Beyond Civil Rights: The Moynihan Report and Its Legacy* (Philadelphia: University of Pennsylvania Press, 2015); Self, *American Babylon*, 26–37; and James T. Patterson, *Freedom Is Not Enough: The Moynihan Report and America's Struggle over Black Family Life—from LBJ to Obama* (New York: Basic Books, 2010).

58. Bernard D. Healey, *The Atlanta Youth Murders and the Politics of Race* (Carbondale: Southern Illinois University Press, 1998), 3.

59. John Erman, dir., *The Atlanta Child Murders* (Rafshoon Communications et al., 1985); Paul Renfro, "'The City Too Busy to Care': The Atlanta Youth Murders and the Southern Past, 1979–81," *Southern Cultures* 21, No. 4 (2015): 43–66.

60. Paul Renfro, "Milk Carton Kids: Endangered Childhood and the Carceral State," in Susan Eckelmann, Sara Fieldston, and Paul Renfro, eds., *Growing Up America: Youth and Politics since 1945* (Athens: University of Georgia Press, 2019), 256.

61. "Still No Sign of 6-Year-Old Boy Who Vanished from Toy Department," United Press International, July 29, 1981; "Head Identified as That of Missing Youth," Associated Press, August 11, 1981.

62. "Action on Lost Children Urged," *New York Times*, November 22, 1981.

63. David Gelman, Susan Agrest, John McCormick, Pamela Abramson, Nikki Finke Greenberg, Marsha Zabarsky, Holly Morris, and Tessa Namuth, "Stolen Children," *Newsweek*, March 19, 1984.

64. Phillip Jenkins, *Decade of Nightmares: The End of the Sixties and the Making of the Eighties* (New York: Oxford University Press, 2006), 111. Jenkins argues that 1977 was

the year of the child because that was when a movement against molestation, abuse, and child pornography appeared on the political agenda. This emerging conception of children as particularly endangered helped pave the way for fears of stranger abductions to become culturally powerful.

65. Gelman, Agrest, McCormick, Abramson, Greenberg, Zabarsky, Morris, and Namuth, "Stolen Children"; Neal Karlen, with Nikki Finke Greenberg, David L. Gonzalez, and Elisa Williams, "How Many Missing Kids?" *Newsweek*, October 7, 1985. In the latter article, experts from the Department of Health and Human Services, FBI, and National Center for Missing and Exploited Children disagreed about the number of missing children, especially those abducted by strangers. FBI statistics revealed only sixty-seven stranger abductions in 1984, which, in light of later studies, seems much more likely than the higher figures cited in the mid-1980s.

66. David F. Whitman, "Missing Children: What Makes Search So Tough," *U.S. News & World Report*, August 19, 1985.

67. Eugene Kraybill, "Scaring Our Kids," *U.S. News & World Report*, February 10, 1986. Kraybill, a father of three, wrote that though it is a tragedy when any child is abducted, relatively few are actually abducted by a stranger. Instead, he suggested the public should focus on broken homes, which, he argued, spurred most runaways and child abductions by family members.

68. Judd Pilot, dir., *How to Raise a Street Smart Child* (Home Box Office, 1987), available on YouTube, https://www.youtube.com/watch?v=9-IDpPBj6pk.

69. John Walsh, *Tears of Rage: From Grieving Father to Crusader for Justice; The Untold Story of the Adam Walsh Case* (New York: Pocket Books, 1997), 103.

70. Juvenile Justice, Runaway Youth, and Missing Children's Act Amendments of 1984: Hearing on H.R. 4971 before the House Subcommittee on Human Resources of the Committee on Education and Labor, 98th Cong., 45, 47 (April 9, 1984) (statement of John Walsh).

71. Judy Mann, "From Caution to Hysteria," *Washington Post*, April 9, 1986.

72. Mann, "From Caution to Hysteria."

73. Lawrence Kilman, "Child Protection Game Endorsed by Adam Walsh Center," Associated Press, June 12, 1986.

74. Barbara Kantrowitz and Connie Leslie, "Teaching Fear," *Newsweek*, March 10, 1986.

75. *Awareness Series: No Thanks, Stranger* (playEd Games, 1986).

76. Vivian Kramer Fancher, *Safe Kids: A Complete Child-Safety Handbook and Resource Guide for Parents* (New York: John Wiley & Sons, 1991).

77. *Strangers Dangers* (MiTi, 1985).

78. Jerry Buck, "Television's 'Wanted' Gets Its Man," Associated Press, May 17, 1988. This article compared three new crime-focused reality shows: *America's Most Wanted*, *Cops*, and *Unsolved Mysteries*. Premiering in 1987, *Cops* focused more on the tasks of beat officers on the street than on asking for help from the viewing audience to catch criminals. Debuting in 1988, *Unsolved Mysteries* did ask for help from the audience, but the show ranged widely from asking for information on murder cases to exploring UFO sightings and the paranormal. Earlier incarnations of the reality genre appeared mostly

on the Public Broadcasting Service. The most successful series was *An American Family*, which premiered in January 1973. The show followed the lives of the Loud family while parents Pat and Bill were filing for divorce and son Lance emerged as the first openly gay character on television.

79. Monica Collins, "Broadcast Crime Busters; 'Wanted' Captures Its Audience," *USA Today*, March 2, 1989; "Full Capture List," *America's Most Wanted Fans*, https://amwfans.com/thread/16/full-capture-list. According to the show's fansite, amwfans.com, since the show started airing, law enforcement has captured 1,202 fugitives because of viewer intervention. After moving from Fox to the Lifetime network, the show was canceled in October of 2012.

80. Anna Williams notes in her analysis of the show that "the spectacle of the imperiled white nuclear family is crucial to AMW's definition of crime," including a focus on "violent crimes, the majority of whose victims are women and children." Williams, "Domestic Violence and the Aetiology of Crime in *America's Most Wanted*," *Camera Obscura* 31 (January–May 1993): 99.

81. Phil McCombs, "John Walsh's Pursuit, and 'America's Most Wanted' One Year Later," *Washington Post*, April 25, 1989. Other people considered for the job of the show's host were author Joseph Wambaugh and former Marine Corps commandant Paul X. Kelley, but they did not bring the same gravitas to the role as the aggrieved father John Walsh.

82. Peter Farrell, "Sniping Crimestoppers Recruit Viewing Posse," *Portland Oregonian*, September 19, 1988.

83. Steven Erlanger, "Manhunting in an Armchair," *New York Times*, February 2, 1988.

84. Farrell, "Sniping Crimestoppers Recruit Viewing Posse."

85. Farrell, "Sniping Crimestoppers Recruit Viewing Posse."

86. Bob Niedt, "Crime Stopper: John Walsh and America's Most Wanted," *Syracuse (NY) Post-Standard*, August 2, 1988.

87. Niedt, "Crime Stopper."

88. Frank J. Prial, "Freeze! You're on TV," *New York Times Magazine*, September 28, 1988.

89. Donna Gable, "'AMW' Honors 200th Capture," *USA Today*, May 7, 1992.

90. For news articles and reviews that tied *AMW* to the tragedy that befell Walsh's family in a suburban shopping mall, see Catherine Shahan, "Fox Television Unveils Show Searching for 'Most Wanted' Criminals," United Press International, February 2, 1988; David Briscoe, "TV Show Credited with Capturing Some of America's 'Most Wanted,'" Associated Press, March 28, 1988; Buck, "Television's 'Wanted' Show Gets Its Man"; Collins, "Broadcast Crime Busters"; Greg Joseph, "'Wanted' A Huge Neighborhood Watch," *San Diego Union-Tribune*, June 16, 1989; Jim Sullivan, "'Most Wanted' Least Wanted by Felons," *Boston Globe*, April 14, 1990; Amy Ellis, "Host Is Caught Up in 'Most Wanted' Show," *St. Petersburg Times*, July 7, 1990; Robert P. Laurence, "Crusade to Catch Culprits," *San Diego Union-Tribune*, February 7, 1991; Peter Farrell, "Here's a Guide to TV's Version of the Real World," *Oregonian*, March 3, 1991; David L. Shaw, "'Wanted' Host to Speak in Auburn," *Syracuse (NY) Post-Standard*,

April 11, 1991; Dan Sewell, "'America's Most Wanted' Host Gets 'Sad Satisfaction' from Major Arrest," Associated Press, April 26, 1991; Deborah Hastings, "Using Television to Capture Criminals," Associated Press, April 27, 1991; Ed Siegel, "It's Not Fiction; It's Not News; It's Not Reality; It's Reali-TV," *Boston Globe*, May 26, 1991; Janis D. Froelich, "Drama in Real Life," *St. Petersburg Times*, June 5, 1991; Sean Piccoli, "Living on the Edge: There's No Hiding from Fear," *Washington Times*, February 19, 1992; Brian Donlon, "Hosting Real-Life Dramas: Narrators Set the Tone," *USA Today*, March 9, 1992; Donna Gable, "Missing Children Are 'Most Wanted' in '92," *USA Today*, September 11, 1992; and Brian Donlon, "'Most Wanted' Still Hard at Work," *USA Today*, November 19, 1992. Beyond those otherwise noted, there were numerous instances in the press of Adam's story being connected to the mission and success of *America's Most Wanted*.

91. Erlanger, "Manhunting in an Armchair."

92. It was announced prominently on the show that it was produced with cooperation from federal and local enforcement, including the Bureau of Alcohol, Tobacco, and Firearms and the Federal Bureau of Investigation. So it likely did not behoove Walsh or others to be overtly critical of law enforcement.

93. Tom Shales, "Fox's 'Most Wanted' A Worrisome Success," *Oregonian*, May 20, 1988.

94. Prial, "Freeze! You're on TV."

95. This was also the premise of late 1980s board game *Security Watch* from Tinker Games. Players acted as adjuncts to police, accumulating points for criminals they help apprehend.

96. Shahan, "Fox Television Unveils Show."

97. Stephanie Mann, with M. C. Blakeman, *Safe Homes, Safe Neighborhoods: Stopping Crime Where You Live* (Berkeley: Nolo Press, 1993), 3, 7.

98. Laura E. Quarantiello, *On Guard! How You Can Win against the Bad Guys* (Lake Geneva, WI: Tiare, 1994).

99. Vincent Canby, "'Death Wish' Exploits Fear Irresponsibly," *New York Times*, August 4, 1974; Macek, *Urban Nightmares*, 203–13. The first urban vigilante films emerged in the early 1970s around the time that President Richard Nixon called for a return to "law and order." They featured the righteous vigilante defending white middle-class victims on urban landscapes filled with minorities and criminals. These images were intended to be visceral reminders of the supposed failures of the liberal state in decaying urban centers; as such, they helped pave the way for the suburban iterations analyzed in this chapter.

100. Richard Maxwell Brown, *No Duty to Retreat: Violence and Values in American History and Society* (Norman: University of Oklahoma Press, 1991). Brown argues that standing your ground as a legally endorsed American value has a history dating back to the Civil War.

101. Michael Winner, dir., *Death Wish* (Dino De Laurentiis Company and Paramount Pictures, 1974); Don Siegel, dir., *Dirty Harry* (Malpaso Company and Warner Brothers Pictures, 1971). *Dirty Harry*, the original modern vigilante film, demonstrated these essential elements. Harry Callahan (Clint Eastwood) eschews protocol and the law to catch the Scorpio killer terrorizing San Francisco. The tagline for the film

exaggerated not only the single-mindedness of the vigilante but also his righteousness: "You don't assign him to murder cases. You just turn him loose." Harry Callahan doesn't need to be told to stop crime, no matter the method. Other films in the genre include the other films in the *Dirty Harry* series, *Magnum Force* (1973), *The Enforcer* (1976), and *Sudden Impact* (1983), as well as *Outrage* (made for television, 1973), *Walking Tall* (1973), *The Death Squad* (television, 1974), *The Psychopath* (1975), *Deadbeat* (1976), *Breaking Point* (1976), *Taxi Driver* (1976), *The One Man Jury* (1978), *Exterminator* (1980), *Fighting Back* (1982), *Young Warriors* (1983), *Vigilante* (1983), *The Executioner, Part II* (1984), *Exterminator 2* (1984), *The Annihilators* (1985), *Sudden Death* (1985), and *The Ladies Club* (1986).

102. Vincent Canby, "Film: 'Impact,' with Clint Eastwood," *New York Times*, December 9, 1983.

103. Deana Poole, "Gun Bill Could Mean: Shoot First, Ask Later," *Palm Beach Post*, March 23, 2005; Jim Haug, "Bill Allows Freer Use of Deadly Force," *Daytona Beach News Journal*, March 24, 2005; "Deaths Nearly Triple since 'Stand Your Ground' Enacted," *CBS Miami*, March 3, 2020, https://miami.cbslocal.com/2012/03/20/deaths-nearly-triple-since-stand-your-ground-enacted/; Josh Sanburn, "Florida's 'Stand Your Ground' Law Linked to Homicide Increase," *Time*, November 16, 2016; David K. Humphreys, Antonio Gasparrini, and Douglas J. Wiebe, "Evaluating the Impact of Florida's 'Stand Your Ground' Self-Defense Law on Homicide and Suicide by Firearm," *Journal of the American Medical Association* 177, No. 1 (January 2017): 44–50; Shankar Vedantam, "'Stand Your Ground' Linked to Increase in Homicides," *All Things Considered*, National Public Radio, January 2, 2013.

104. Spencer's explanation of the modern criminal justice system in America eerily mirrors the words of President Bill Clinton upon signing the 1994 Crime Bill: "Every day we read about somebody else who has literally gotten away with murder. The American people have not forgotten the difference between right and wrong, but the system has." "President Clinton Signing the 'Crime Bill' (1994)," posted to YouTube by William J. Clinton Presidential Library, December 11, 2012, https://www.youtube.com/watch?v=cOYoxSpt6IA.

105. "Attorney General Barr Presents Justice Department Awards," U.S. Newswire, December 14, 1992.

106. Erlanger, "Manhunting in an Armchair"; Collins, "Broadcast Crime Busters; "'Wanted Captures Its Audience."

107. Michael W. Flamm, *Law and Order: Street Crime, Civil Unrest, and the Crisis of Liberalism in the 1960s* (New York: Columbia University Press, 2005), 4–5.

108. Flamm, *Law and Order*, 4–5.

109. Stuart Hall, *Policing the Crisis: Mugging, the State, and Law and Order* (London: Macmillan, 1978); Macek, Urban Nightmares.

110. Osha Gray Davidson, *Under Fire: The NRA and the Battle for Gun Control* (Iowa City: University of Iowa Press, 1998), 29.

111. Donald Baer, Ted Gest, and Lynn Anderson Carle, "Guns," *U.S. News & World Report*, May 8, 1989.

112. Alexander, *The New Jim Crow*, 9–11. Alexander argues that white Americans usually managed to avoid the complex web of social control through mass incarceration

because of the disparities in enforcement of laws and the sentencing of those convicted, particularly as part of the war on drugs.

113. Robert Spitzer, *Guns across America: Reconciling Gun Rules and Rights* (London: Oxford University Press, 2015), 105–6.

114. Wyatt Holliday, "The Answer to Criminal Aggression Is Retaliation: Stand-Your-Ground Laws and the Liberalization of Self-Defense," *University of Toledo Law Review* (Winter 2012): 407–436; Christine Catalfamo, "Stand Your Ground: Florida's Castle Doctrine for the Twenty First Century," *Rutgers Journal of Law and Public Policy* (fall 2007): 504–45.

115. Alan Gomez, "House Passes NRA-Backed Gun Proposal," *Palm Beach Post*, April 6, 2005.

116. Holliday, "The Answer to Criminal Aggression," 418; Catalfamo, "Stand Your Ground."

117. Haug, "Bill Allows Freer Use of Deadly Force"; "Go Ahead; Pass This Bill," *Palm Beach Post*, March 27, 2005; Lloyd Dunkelberger, "Self-Defense Bill Gets Early Senate OK" *Lakeland (Fla.) Ledger*, March 23, 2005; Deana Pool, "Gun Bill Could Mean: Shoot First, Ask Later," *Palm Beach Post*, March 23, 2005; "'Make My Day' Law Won't Do Anything for Tourism," *Palm Beach Post*, April 29, 2005; Patrik Jonsson, "Is Self-Defense Law Vigilante Justice?" *Christian Science Monitor*, February 26, 2006.

118. Deana Poole, "Deadly Force Bill Moving on a Fast Track," *Palm Beach Post*, March 24, 2005.

119. Poole, "Deadly Force Bill Moving on a Fast Track."

120. Latisha R. Gray, "Gun Critics Fear State Law Will Become O.K. Corral," *Sarasota Herald Tribune*, October 1, 2005.

121. Jonsson, "Is Self-Defense Law Vigilante Justice?"

122. Adam Liptak, "15 States Expand Right to Shoot in Self-Defense," *New York Times*, August 7, 2006.

123. Alexander, *The New Jim Crow*, 99–109.

124. According to the National Crime Victimization Survey, a phone survey of American households, the number of households per 1,000 reporting a violent crime remained steady between 1973 and 1985, with a high of 52.3 in 1981 and a low of 45.2 in 1985. Between 1986 and 1990, the rate dropped to an average of 43.5, followed by an upswing through 1995. However, the total crime index—i.e., "the estimated number of homicides of persons age 12 and older recorded by police plus the number of rapes, robberies, and aggravated assaults from the victimization survey whether or not they were reported to the police"—reported an uptick in violent crime in 1982 and a slow decline through 1986, followed by another increase through 1993, and then a continued reduction into the new millennium. Bureau of Justice Statistics, United States Department of Justice, "Key Facts at a Glance: Four Measure of Serious Violent Crime," Office of Justice Programs, March 25, 1998, https://www.bjs.gov/content/pub/pdf/sckfg.pdf; idem, "Key Facts at a Glance," Office of Justice Programs, accessed March 17, 2020, http://www.ojp.usdoj.gov/bjs/glance/cv2.htm; idem, "National Crime Victimization Survey Violent Crime Trends, 1973–2005," Office of Justice Programs, accessed March 17, 2020, https://www.bjs.gov/index.cfm?ty=dcdetail&iid=245; and "Violent

Crime," Office of Justice Programs, accessed March 17, 2020, https://www.bjs.gov/index.cfm?ty=tp&tid=31.

125. Janet. L. Lauritsen and Maribeth L. Rezey, *Measuring the Prevalence of Crime with the National Crime Victimization Survey*, NCJ 241656 (Washington, DC: Bureau of Justice Statistics, Office of Justice Programs, US Department of Justice, September 2013), https://www.bjs.gov/content/pub/pdf/mpcncvs.pdf; Bureau of Justice Statistics, "Criminal Victimization in the United States, 1995," NCJ 171129 (Washington, DC: Office of Justice Programs, US Department of Justice, May 2000), https://www.bjs.gov/content/pub/pdf/cvus95.pdf. The overall burglary rate declined by 63 percent between 1993 and 2010, while white households experienced lower rates of burglary than black households.

126. Alexander, *The New Jim Crow*, 1–19; Gilmore, *Golden Gulag*, 5–30.

CHAPTER FOUR: **Punks, Mallrats, and Out-of-Control Teenagers**

1. I use the term *public space* in this chapter in its generic sense to refer to space seemingly open to all but not necessarily collectively owned or regulated. So, in addition to spaces like streets and parks, the shopping mall functioned as de facto public space, central to cultural, political, and social life, in the use and discourses of suburban life in the era under review. Shopping malls performed this function despite the fact that they were privately owned and operated and that state courts have taken different approaches to interpreting the constitutional rights of free speech and assembly in these spaces.

2. Zaretsky, *No Direction Home*, 12. Zaretsky argues persuasively that existential fears about familial and national decline were intertwined following the cultural revolutions of the 1960s. By the 1980s, then, parents and children—including the teens discussed in this chapter—were the focus of both anxiety and regulation; Hartman, *A War for the Soul of America*, 87. See also Cohen, introduction to *A Consumer's Republic*.

3. Jonathan Kaplan, dir., *Over the Edge* (Orion Pictures, 1979; Warner Home Video, 2005).

4. "Suburb's Teen Center Deserves 2nd Chance," *Milwaukee Sentinel*, September 16, 1977; Amelia Davis, "Largo Teens Want to Keep Pool Room, Center As Is," *St. Petersburg Times*, May 16, 1987.

5. Amy Heckerling, dir., *Fast Times at Ridgemont High* (Universal Pictures, 1982).

6. Bob Levey, "Teens View Center as 'Their' Community," *Washington Post*, January 1, 1981; Mike Sager, "Malls—Hubs of Often Centerless Suburbia Become Home Away from Home," *Washington Post*, February 9, 1983.

7. Ted Gest, with Jeannye Thornton, "As More Crime Invades the Shopping Malls—," *U.S. News & World Report*, June 11, 1984.

8. Ray Pelosi, "Amusement Centers Change Again, but Profit Potential Is Still Strong," *Shopping Center World* (September 1983), 41.

9. Greydon Clark, dir., *Joysticks* (Jensen Farley Pictures, 1983).

10. Cohen, *A Consumer's Republic*, 257–89; Margaret Crawford, "The World in a Shopping Mall," in Michael Sorkin, ed., *Variations on a Theme Park: Scenes from the New American City and the End of Public Space* (New York: Hill & Wang, 1992).

11. Bruce Koon and James A. Finefrock, "Mouse Packs: Kids on a Crime Spree," *San Francisco Examiner*, November 11, 1973.

12. Joseph R. Mitchell and David Stebenne, *New City Upon a Hill: A History of Columbia, Maryland* (Charleston, SC: History Press, 2007); Nicholas Dagen Bloom, *Suburban Alchemy: 1960s New Towns and the Transformation of the American Dream* (Columbus: Ohio State University Press, 2001).

13. Roger Ebert, "Over the Edge" (review), *Chicago Sun-Times*, January 1, 1980.

14. Ebert, "Over the Edge."

15. Kerry Segrave, *Jukeboxes: An American Social History* (Jefferson, NC: McFarland, 2002), ch. 4.

16. Hinton, From the War on Poverty to the War on Crime, 218–49.

17. Bloom, Suburban Alchemy.

18. "Shorttakes," *Christian Science Monitor*, January 28, 1982.

19. Julie Brossy, "Reaching Out to Community: Community Center Fills Void for Seniors, Teens," *San Diego Tribune*, December 5, 1988; Terry Rodgers, "Oceanside to Turn Building into Community Center," *San Diego Tribune*, March 30, 1990.

20. "Suburb's Teen Center Deserves 2nd Chance."

21. Valeria M. Russ, "Recreation Center to Open Saturday," *St. Petersburg Times*, January 31, 1980.

22. Davis, "Largo Teens Want to Keep Pool Room, Center As Is."

23. For example, the Millwood Presbyterian Church outside Spokane, Washington, opened an "alternative recreation center" essentially to provide a safe place for teens to congregate, unlike other recreation centers. Tim Hanson, "Center for Teen-Agers Will Open Saturday," *Spokane Spokesman-Review*, February 16, 1985.

24. Anita Farel, "Planning After-School Activities for Young Adolescents: Parents' Preferences and Needs," *Children Today*, March 1, 1984.

25. Steve Waksman, "Suburban Noise: Getting Inside Garage Rock," in John Archer, Paul J. P. Sandul, and Katherine Solomonson, *Making Suburbia: New Histories of Everyday America* (Minneapolis: University of Minnesota Press, 2015), 329–42. Suburban hardcore punk's access to and use of the electric guitar appears to be a later manifestation of its emergence as an instrument used by young, suburban consumers in the 1960s. Waksman argues that the instrument and the garage bands formed because of its availability was a domesticated form of rock rebellion focused on the making and consumption of music in the liminal space of the garage. This forms a clear contrast with hardcore, which was public and against domestication and was largely uninterested in a musical career or the music industry.

26. Leerom Medevoi sees this same dynamic between rock-and-roll music and its suburban audiences of the 1950s. He argues that youth rebellion then was packaged and sold as an identity that was supposed to control actual teen rebellion, spurred by suburban life, which, he shows, was the worst of urban and rural life. Rather than an identity that could contain rebellion, hardcore was a direct articulation of suburban tensions that fomented rebellion and confrontation. Medevoi, *Rebel: Youth and the Cold War Origins of Identity* (Durham, NC: Duke University Press, 2005), 92–94.

27. Zaretsky, *No Direction Home*, 3–5.

28. For example, hardcore punk critiques were reminiscent of Pete Seeger's song "Little Boxes" and John Keats's book *The Crack in the Picture Window*.

29. Dick Hebdige, *Subculture: The Meaning of Style* (London: Routledge, 2002), 2.

30. Hebdige, *Subculture*, 3–4, 74–89.

31. Paul Rachman, dir., *American Hardcore* (AHC Productions and Envision Films, 2006); Steve Waksman, "California Noise: Tinkering with Hardcore and Heavy Metal in Southern California," *Social Studies of Science* 34, No. 5 (October 2004): 683.

32. Middle Class, "Out of Vogue," on *Out of Vogue* (Joke Records, 1978).

33. "The Middle Class," *Flipside*, No. 9 (August 1978).

34. Middle Class, "Out of Vogue."

35. "Interview with Middle Class," *Flipside*, No. 12 (December 1978).

36. McGirr, Suburban Warriors.

37. Self, *All in the Family*, 309–10, 328, 332.

38. David E. James, "Hardcore: Cultural Resistance in the Postmodern," in David E. James, ed., *Power Misses* (London: Verso, 1996), 224; Ryan Moore, *Smells like Teen Spirit: Music, Youth, and Social Crisis* (New York: New York University Press, 2010), 52; Lefkovitz, *Strange Bedfellows*; Self, *All in the Family*, 309–311. James argues that hardcore punks were "taking the anger, negativity and the anti-professionalism of English punk as a point of departure" to create suburban punk as "hundreds of bands sprang up in garages in the endless, homogenized cinder-block tracts."

39. Steven Blush, *American Hardcore: A Tribal History* (Los Angeles: Feral House, 2001), 12.

40. Self, *All in the Family*, 309–38.

41. Narratives of suburban imperfection have trafficked well in postwar American culture, with books, films, and television programs on the topic winning awards and critical praise. For example, 1980's *Ordinary People* and 1999's *American Beauty* were both awarded Best Picture at the Academy Awards. Other films on this topic include *Neighbors* (1981), *Pump Up the Volume* (1990), *The Brady Bunch Movie* (1995), Todd Solondz's *Welcome to the Dollhouse* (1995) and *Happiness* (1998), and Rian Johnson's *Brick* (2005). Novels include Richard Ford's suburban novels *The Sportswriter* (1986), *Independence Day* (1995), and *Lay of the Land* (2006) and John Updike's Rabbit novels, as well as novels turned into films such as Richard Yates's *Revolutionary Road* (1961; film, 2008), Ira Levin's *The Stepford Wives* (1972; film, 1975 and 2004), Jeffrey Eugenides's *The Virgin Suicides* (1993; film 1999), Rick Moody's *The Ice Storm* (1994; film, 1997), Tom Perrotta's *Little Children* (2004; film, 2006), and Alice Sebold's *The Lovely Bones* (2002; film, 2009). Award-winning television shows debunking the myth of suburban perfection include *The Simpsons* (1989–present), *Married . . . with Children* (1987–97), and *The Sopranos* (1999–2007).

42. Black Flag, "TV Party," on *Damaged* (SST, 1981).

43. Black Flag, "Six Pack," on *Damaged* (SST, 1981). Other bands, such as the Descendents, from Manhattan Beach, California, also created short, punchy songs about banal amusements. Their song "I Like Food" (on the album *Fat*, 1980) does little more than declare the band's love for eating food as opposed to "dining," but the song punctures the pretentiousness of bland suburban cuisine.

44. Christopher Lasch, *The Culture of Narcissism: American Life in an Age of Diminishing Expectations* (New York: W. W Norton, 1991).

45. Circle Jerks, "Mrs. Jones," on *Wonderful* (Combat Records,1985).

46. Youth Brigade, "You Don't Understand," on *Sink with Kalifornija* (Frontier Records, 1984).

47. Descendents, "Suburban Home," on *Milo Goes to College* (New Alliance, 1982).

48. Peter Belsito and Bob Davis, *Hardcore California: A History of Punk and New Wave* (Berkeley: Last Gasp of San Francisco, 1983), 11.

49. Moore, *Smells like Teen Spirit*, 55.

50. Gaines, *Teenage Wasteland*, 196.

51. Produced with little or no money, zines provided concert and album reviews, interviews, and scene reports. Zines, because fans made them, were irregularly produced, poorly constructed, and often lasted no more than a few issues. However, those with the largest readership, such as *MaximumRockNRoll*, *Flipside*, and *Suburban Voice*, lasted for many years and served to tie together places and audiences with the bigger scenes of greater Los Angeles, Boston, and Washington, D.C. In these zines, there was no pretense of objectivity. The reporting is matter-of-fact and the style gossipy as the writer recounts comings and goings of band members and scenesters, often using only first names. The intent, from reviews to scene reports, was to evaluate what was good and cultivate it through the production of a print public to parallel the experience of the scene.

52. Jack Rabid, "Punk Goes Hardcore," in Theo Cateforis, ed., *The Rock History Reader* (New York: Routledge, 2007), 198. Rabid's account of the Black Flag show was originally featured in his zine, *The Big Takeover*, No. 4 (1981).

53. "Intro," *Flipside*, No. 22 (December 1980),.

54. "Stop the Presses! Late Bulletin! RIOT ON THE SUNSET STRIP!!!" *MaximumRockNRoll*, No. 4 (January–February 1983).

55. "Stop the Presses!"

56. John Rockwell, "Disks That Clarify Los Angeles Rock," *New York Times*, April 4, 1982.

57. Stephen Braun, "Battle over Punk Rock Club Reflects Rift in Values," *Los Angeles Times*, February 12, 1984.

58. Belsito and Davis, *Hardcore California*, 62.

59. Craig Lee, "Four Teen-Metal Labels of Love," *Los Angeles Times*, November 8, 1981.

60. Blush, *American Hardcore*, 276.

61. Michael Azerrad, *Our Band Could Be Your Life: Scenes from the American Indie Underground, 1981–1991* (New York: Little, Brown, 2012), 16; Belsito and Davis, *Hardcore California*, 45.

62. Al Flipside, "Intro," *Flipside*, No. 16 (October 1979),.

63. "Flipside Interviews Black Flag," *Flipside*, No. 22 (December 1980),.

64. The hardcore scene did include venues that regularly hosted hardcore shows, but most stayed in business only for brief periods because of violent clashes with police outside the venue and difficulty in making money from the hardcore scene. According to show flyers and zines, some of the more frequent venues included the Starwood at

8151 Santa Monica Blvd. Hollywood, California; Mabuhay Gardens, 443 Broadway, San Francisco; Hong Kong Café, 425 Gin Ling Way, Los Angeles; Madame Wong's, Chinatown, Los Angeles; Masque, 1655 N. Cherokee, Los Angeles; and the Cuckoo's Nest, 1714 Placentia Ave., Costa Mesa, California. "Intro and Nooze," *Flipside*, No. 17 (December 1979). This issue of *Flipside* has a useful rundown of clubs that were hosting punk shows at the time. As the author indicates, lists like his were necessary to keep track of which clubs were open and friendly to hardcore.

65. "Punk Flyers Collection," Cornell University Digital Collections, Division of Rare and Manuscript Collections, accessed March 17, 2020, https://digital.library .cornell.edu/collections/punkflyers. These flyers were the lifeblood of promoting hardcore punk shows, because they directed fans and bands to shows in otherwise nondescript places. Donna Gaines also makes this point: "Participation in the scene was made possible only by word of mouth. Fliers, occasional street sheets, were the only clue." Gaines, *Teenage Wasteland*, 196.

66. For a concise history of the shopping mall, see Kenneth T. Jackson, "All the World's a Mall," *American Historical Review* 101, No. 4 (October 1996): 1111–21. For further reading on malls and public space, see Cohen, *A Consumer's Republic*, 257–89; and Crawford, "The World in a Shopping Mall." For general shopping center history see: Nancy E. Cohen, *America's Marketplace: The History of Shopping Centers* (Lyme, CT: Greenwich, 2002.). For a history of Victor Gruen and the indoor mall. see Hardwick, *Mall Maker*. On the history of American architecture and shopping, see Richard W. Longstreth, *City Center to Regional Mall: Architecture, the Automobile, and Retailing in Los Angeles, 1920–1950* (Cambridge, MA: MIT Press, 1997).

67. Bob Levey, "Teens View Center as 'Their' Community," *Washington Post*, January 1, 1981; Mike Sager, "Malls—Hubs of Often Centerless Suburbia Become Home Away from Home," *Washington Post*, February 9, 1983.

68. N. Cohen, *America's Marketplace*, 46. There were thirty-six thousand and five hundred by 1990.

69. Dan Kane and Cheryl Imelda Smith, "Mall Rats Bring Thefts, Fights, and Drugs," *Syracuse (NY) Post-Standard*, March 20, 1988.

70. Lynn Spiegel has persuasively argued that early television shows with a suburban setting emphasized simple family disputes and straightforward conflict resolution within the span of one episode. Lynn Spiegel, *Make Room for TV: Television and the Family Ideal in Postwar America* (Chicago: University of Chicago Press, 1992), 136–37. I would extend her argument to say that most family sitcoms, through the cancelation of *The Brady Bunch* in 1974, followed this format and presented tame subject matter compared to later incarnations. Further, more controversial material was usually relegated to shows with a distinctly urban setting, such as *All in the Family*. Suburban-set films of the postwar era also rarely delved into the lives of teens as straightforwardly as the films discussed in this chapter. This is not to say that film dealt with suburban life in quite the same way as sitcoms, but the emphasis on realism and darker subject matter remain fixed on the lives of adults in films such as William Wyler's *The Desperate Hours* (1955) or the sex comedy *Bob and Carol and Ted and Alice* (1969).

71. Levey, "Teens View Center as 'Their' Community."

72. Levey, "Teens View Center as 'Their' Community."

73. Larry Elkin, "The American Style: Suburban Mall Breeds New Species," Associated Press, July 31, 1981.

74. Leah Y. Latimer, "'Mall Rats': Idle Youths Become Street People of Shopping Center," *Washington Post*, February 21, 1983; Kane and Smith, "Mall Rats Bring Thefts, Fights, and Drugs."

75. Rochelle Slovin, "Hot Circuits," in Mark J. P. Wolf, ed., *The Medium of the Video Game* (Austin: University of Texas Press, 2001), 145. Slovin argues that video games "shifted from immersive, social experiences in arcades (where, according to some academic studies, more than half the time participants would watch, 'hang out,' and socialize rather than play) to solitary, home-based entertainment." See also Laura June, "For Amusement Only: The Life and Death of the American Arcade," *The Verge*, January 16, 2013, http://www.theverge.com/2013/1/16/3740422/the-life-and-death-of-the -american-arcade-for-amusement-only. June argues that, currently, arcades still exist only as family-friendly venues such as Chuck E. Cheese or as establishments geared toward nostalgic adults, such as the national chain Dave & Buster's and minichain Barcade, that rely on food and alcohol sales to make money.

76. In 1980, reporter Kathleen Ennis described the ubiquity of coin-operated video game players: "Videomaniacs can be found everywhere here: In singles bars, mingling around Asteroids; in arcades, spending the last quarter of their allowances to beat the high score on Space Invaders; in nightclubs, vying for a spot at Galaxian between acts, and in fast-food restaurants, grabbing a quick game of Astro Fighter before heading back to work. They're kids, businessmen in three-piece suits and unemployed writers. And, many of them will readily admit, playing electronic games is more than a mere pastime. It's a lifestyle." Kathleen Ennis, "Aargh! Swoosh! It's Video Games," *Washington Post*, Dec. 11, 1980.

77. Steven L. Kent, *The Ultimate History of Video Games: From Pong to Pokémon—The Story Behind the Craze That Touched Our Lives and Changed the World* (New York: Three Rivers Press, 2001), 5–7. Mayor Fiorello LaGuardia banned pinball in New York City in 1942 because he believed it encouraged gambling and fighting. The ban lasted until 1976, right before the emergence of the video game arcade.

78. Pelosi, "Amusement Centers Change Again, but Profit Potential is Still Strong," 36.

79. Jura Koncius, "Video Games: Regulating America's Latest Craze," *Washington Post*, October 8, 1981.

80. Koncius, "Video Games."

81. "Video Games Win in Arcades," *New York Times*, August 23, 1980.

82. "1981 Spaceport Employee Training Video, Parts 1 and 2," available on YouTube, http://www.youtube.com/.

83. Lynn Langway, with Pamela Abramson, David T. Friendly, Frank Maier, Marsha Zabarsky, and Linda R. Prout, "Invasion of the Video Creatures," *Newsweek*, November 16, 1981.

84. David Pauly, "Hard Times for Pizza Time," *Newsweek*, January 23, 1984.

85. Richard Brandt, with Cynthia Green, "How Do You Start a Craze? Ask Nolan Bushnell," *Business Week*, February 17, 1986.

86. "Videogames—Fun or Serious Threat?" *U.S. News & World Report*, February 22, 1982.

87. "Frequency of Coin-Op Videogame Releases," International Arcade Museum, accessed March 1, 2020, http://www.arcade-museum.com/members/statistics /videogame-title-frequency.php.

88. Shelagh Kealy, "Asteroids Machines Hook All Types and Ages; Home and Bars Now Sound Alike," United Press International, August 2, 1981.

89. *U.S. News & World Report*, "Videogames—Fun or Serious Threat."

90. Lola Sherman, "Council Gives Video Arcade a Replay: Carlsbad Vote Ignores Advice of Planners, Police on Teen Hangout," *San Diego Union-Tribune*, November 21, 1984.

91. Joseph Sargent, dir., *Nightmares* (Universal Pictures, 1983); Nick Castle, dir. *The Last Starfighter* (Lorimar Films and Universal Pictures, 1984); "Pac-Man Fever," *Time*, April 5, 1982.

92. "Pac-Man Fever"; Curt Suplee, "Video Game Vitality," *Washington Post*, February 6, 1983.

93. *Time*, "Pac-Man Fever."

94. "The Battle for America's Youth," *New York Times*, January 5, 1982.

95. Elkin, "The American Style."

96. George Mihalka, dir., *Pinball Summer* (Film Ventures International, 1982); Clark, *Joysticks*.

97. Black Randy and the Metrosquad, "I Slept in an Arcade," on *Pass the Dust, I Think I'm Bowie* (Dangerhouse Records, 1979).

98. *Bonito v. Bloomfield*, N.J. Super 390, LEXIS 1246 (1984). According to the briefs in this case, other states had similar provisions for regulating arcades or other businesses with coin-operated games, including New York, Illinois, Wisconsin, Pennsylvania, and California.

99. *Bonito v. Bloomfield*.

100. Paul Hodge, "Video-Games Limit Proposed in Vienna," *Washington Post*, January 26, 1983.

101. *Amusing Sandwich v. City of Palm Springs*, Court of Appeal of California, App. LEXIS 1796 (March 22, 1985).

102. *Kieffer v. Spencer*, Court of Appeal of California, App. LEXIS 1840 (March 29, 1984).

103. Besides those discussed below, other places where bans limiting access were attempted or instituted included Mesquite, Texas; Brookhaven, New York; Centereach, New York; Marlboro, Massachusetts; Oakland, California; Coral Gables, Florida; West Warwick, Rhode Island; Durham, New Hampshire; Plymouth, Massachusetts; and Hialeah, Florida. See Robert Sangeorge, "Supreme Court: Pool Halls to Video Arcades," United Press International, November 8, 1981; Ellen Mitchell, "Video Game Rooms Targeted by Towns," *New York Times*, December 13, 1981; "The Battle for America's Youth"; "Two Cities Ban Video Games for Youngsters," Associated Press, February 10, 1982; Hilary DeVries, "Pow! Bang! Towns Zap Video Games," *Christian Science Monitor*, May 27, 1982; "Mass. Town Zaps Space Invaders," United Press International, June 17,

1982; and Barry Klein, "Hialeah Plays for Keeps, Bans Video Games," *St. Petersburg Times*, May 11, 1988.

104. "Two Cities Ban Video Games for Youngsters."

105. Barbara Wierzbicki, "Video Arcades Meet Stiff Community Opposition," *InfoWorld*, December 6, 1983; Elsa Brenner, "Arcade Ban Ends," *New York Times*, April 26, 1998.

106. Phillippa K. Mezile, "Video Game Mania," *Washington Post*, March 11, 1982.

107. Mitchell, "Video Game Rooms Targeted by Towns"; DeVries, "Pow! Bang! Towns Zap Video Games."

108. "Shoplifting Is Number One Problem," *Shopping Center World* (November 1978), 39.

109. Dr. Harold Gluck, "Beating the Shoplifter," *Shopping Center World* (March 1979), 30.

110. Stephanie Dyer, "Designing 'Community' in the Cherry Hill Mall: The Social Production of a Consumer Space," in "Constructing Image, Identity, and Space," special issue, *Perspectives in Vernacular Architecture* 9 (2003): 263–75; Victor Gruen, with Larry Smith, *Shopping Town USA: The Planning of Shopping Centers* (New York: Van Nostrand Reinhold, 1960); Longstreth, *City Center to Regional Mall*, 324–25.

111. "Security . . . How to 'Defend' Your Investment," cover of *Shopping Center World* (November 1977); Charles J. Hura, "Fire Protection: 'Vital to Uninterrupted Operations,'" *Shopping Center World* (November 1977), 16; "Security Is Upgraded by Effective Use of Lighting," *Shopping Center World* (November 1977), 18; Anthony N. Potter, "Mall Security Field Changing to Meet Needs of the Industry," *Shopping Center World* (February 1983), 26.

112. Dr. Harold Gluck, "Burglars Are Professionals Trying to Make a Living," *Shopping Center World* (November 1977), 13.

113. William R. Brown, "Protecting Shoppers Means Protecting Profits," *Shopping Center World* (October 1984), 64.

114. Jeff Parsons, *Blue Skies: A History of Cable Television* (Philadelphia: Temple University Press, 2008), 98, 228, 316.

115. Leon A. Wortman, *Closed Circuit Television Handbook* (Indianapolis: Howard W. Sams & Co., 1974), 164–66.

116. Wortman, *Closed Circuit Television Handbook*, 183–87.

117. Government Accounting Office (hereafter GAO), "Report to the Chairman, Committee on Government Reform, House of Representatives: Video Surveillance," GAO-03-748 (June 2003), 7–8; Marcus Nieto, "Public Video Surveillance: Is It an Effective Crime Prevention Tool?" California Research Bureau, CRB-97-005 (1997), http://www.library.ca.gov/crb/97/05/.

118. GAO, "Report to the Chairman, Committee on Government Reform," 29–30.

119. A. Truett Ricks, B. G. Tillet, and Clifford W. Van Meter, *Principles of Security*, 3rd ed. (Cincinnati: Anderson, 1994), 170–71; Nieto, "Public Video Surveillance."

120. L. Cohen, *A Consumer's Republic*, 272–78. In tracing the battles over the legal definition of mall space as public or private through the postwar era, Cohen finds that the controlling Supreme Court decision, *PruneYard Shopping Center v. Robbins* (1980),

recognized limited free speech rights in malls but affirmed an earlier ruling that states should decide for themselves the protections and limits to free speech within shopping centers.

121. Robert Bond, "Feeling Safe Again," *Shopping Center World* (November 1989), 181.

122. Mike McCaffrey, with Larry Oxenham, "Find the Shoplifter—If You Can," *Shopping Center World* (May 1983), 160.

123. Ricks, Tillet, and Van Meter, *Principles of Security*, 203–11.

124. Art Levine, "Watch Those Watchdogs! The Security Business Is Booming, but So Are Crimes by Guards," *U.S. News & World Report*, July 11, 1988.

125. Levine, "Watch Those Watchdogs!"

126. Hardwick, *Mall Maker*, 4–5.

127. Gruen, *Shopping Town USA*, 257.

128. Gruen, *Shopping Town USA*, 264.

129. Mary Ellen Podmolik, "Malls Get Tough on Teenage Rowdies," *Chicago Sun-Times*, July 10, 1992.

130. William Clay Cunningham, John J. Strauchs, and Clifford W. Van Meter, *Private Security Trends, 1970–2000: The Hallcrest Report II* (McLean, VA: Butterworth-Heinemann, 1990), 203.

131. Levine, "Watch Those Watchdogs!"

132. Cunningham, Strauchs, and Van Meter, *Private Security Trends*, 163.

133. Lisa Benton-Short, *The National Mall: No Ordinary Public Space* (Toronto: University of Toronto Press, 2016), 5–6. Benton-Short provides a short but thorough discussion of contemporary definitions of public space.

134. "Malls for Shopping, Not Hanging Out," *USA Today*, September 11, 1996; Jeff Flock, "Mall of America Imposes Curfew on Teenagers," *CNN Early Prime*, October 4, 1996;

135. "Teen Spending Power," *Chain Store Age* 73, No. 4 (April 1997): 24; John T. Riordan, "Just One Child Arrested," *Chain Store Age* 73, No. 11 (November 1997): 160; Dan Hanover, "Child's Play," *Chain Store Age* 74, No. 5 (May 1998): 54–57.

136. Karl Vick, "Mall and Order in Minnesota: Rowdy Groups of Teens Prompt Huge Shopping Complex to Impose Weekend Curfew," *Washington Post*, September 18, 1996; Craig Wilson, "'Fight City' No Longer: Mall of America Teen Curfew Off to a Quiet Start," *USA Today*, October 7, 1996.

137. Maureen Busch, "Safety Is Our Top Priority," *USA Today*, September 10, 1996.

138. Connie Gentry, "Lost Prevention," *Chain Store Age* 77, No. 11 (November 2001): 121–24.

139. Brady C. Williamson and James A. Friedman, "State Constitutions: The Shopping Mall Cases," *Wisconsin Law Review*, No. 3 (May–June 1998): 883–904; Vick, "Mall and Order in Minnesota."

140. Meredith Robing, "Big Mall's Curfew Raises Questions of Rights and Bias," *New York Times*, September 4, 1996.

141. Robing, "Big Mall's Curfew Raises Questions of Rights and Bias."

142. "Many Teens Pay as Mall Punishes Sins of the Few," *USA Today*, September 10, 1996.

143. Neal Karlen, "Tapping 'Mom Power' to Police a Huge Mall," *New York Times*, December 19, 1996; "Parents Patrol Minnesota Mall to Enforce Teen Curfew," Associated Press, February 19, 2001.

144. Kenneth Adams, "The Effectiveness of Juvenile Curfews at Crime Prevention," *Annals of the American Academy of Political and Social Science* 587 (May 2003): 137–38; Deborah Sharp, "Cities Big, Cities Small, City's Mall Use Curfews," *USA Today*, October 4, 1996; Jennifer Newsom, "Curfew Is Bane for Teens, Boon for Parents," *St. Paul Pioneer Press*, July 8, 1996; Theresa C. Viloria, "By Their Own Rules in a World Perceived as Dangerous, Many Teens See Wisdom in Setting Some Limits," *San Jose Mercury News*, November 5, 1996; "Bensalem Adopts New Teen Curfew," *Philadelphia Inquirer*, May 25, 1999. In *Punished*, Victor Rios places urban curfew laws within the broader context of punitive social control targeted at young men of color and as a technique to more easily arrest and incarcerate this population.

145. Meredith, "Big Mall's Curfew Raises Questions of Rights and Bias"; Jeff Flock, "Morning News," *CNN*, October 4, 1996; Chuck Haga, "Commerce and Curfew Clash at a Mall," *Christian Science Monitor*, October 9, 1996; Chet Fuller, "Curfew Targets Teenagers at Minnesota Mall," *Atlanta Journal Constitution*, October 21, 1996.

146. Sally Apgar, "Megamall's Plan for Required Escorts Praised, Assailed," *Minneapolis Star-Tribune*, June 21, 1996.

147. Dirk Johnson, "Nice City's Nasty Distinction: Murders Soar in Minneapolis," *New York Times*, June 30, 1996.

148. Devah Pager and Hana Shephard, "The Sociology of Discrimination: Racial Discrimination in Employment, Housing, Credit, and Consumer Markets," *Annual Review of Sociology* 34 (2008): 181–209; Zachary W. Brewster and Sarah Nell Rusche, "Quantitative Evidence of the Continuing Significance of Race: Tableside Racism in Full-Service Restaurants," *Journal of Black Studies* 43, No. 4 (May 2012): 359–84; Jerome D. Williams, "Racial Discrimination in Retail Settings: A Liberation Psychology Perspective," in Mia Bay and Ann Fabian, eds., *Race and Retail: Consumption across the Color Line* (New Brunswick, NJ: Rutgers University Press, 2015), 263–77; Cohen, *Consumer's Republic*, 265.

149. Connie Gentry, "Security Is Marketing," *Chain Store Age* 74, No. 6 (June 1998): 121–24.

150. Wilson, "'Fight City' No Longer."

151. Gentry, "Security Is Marketing."

152. Riordan, "Just One Child Arrested."

153. Jim McCartney, "The Megamall's First Five Years," *St. Paul Pioneer Press*, August 3, 1997; Kimberly Hayes, "Mall of America Is Pleased with Its Teen Policy's Results," *Star Tribune*, October 5, 1997; "Mall Curfew Called a Success," *St. Paul Pioneer Press*, October 6, 1997.

154. Hayes, "Mall of America Is Pleased with Its Teen Policy's Results."

155. "Parents Patrol Minnesota Mall to Enforce Teen Curfew."

156. Tom Steadman, "Malls Limit Teens with Curfews, Rules," Associated Press, December 30, 1998; Jason Strait, "Mall Sets Teen Curfew to Curtail Rowdy Behavior,"

Associated Press, March 30, 2001; "Coastal Georgia Mall Mandates Weekend Chaperons for Teen Visitors," Associated Press, August 9, 2001.

157. Williamson and. Friedman, "State Constitutions"; Richard Epstein, "Takins, Exclusivity and Speech: The Legacy of *PruneYard v. Robins," University of Chicago Law Review* 64, No. 1 (winter 1997): 21–56; Cohen, "From Town Center to Shopping Center," 1070. In terms of the law, the nature of shopping mall space with regard to constitutional rights is largely determined at the state level per the decision in *PruneYard Shopping Center v. Robins* (1980). This has resulted in individual states treating that space differently. Some, including New Jersey and five others, see shopping centers as public space for the purposes of free speech and right of assembly, while the rest do not or have yet to make a determination.

158. Suzi Migrani, *Target Markets: International Terrorism Meets Global Capitalism in the Mall* (Bielefeld, Germany: Transcript Verlag, 2017), 81. Migrani calls this process of training mall patrons to spend more and loiter less "discipline and purchase."

159. N. R. Kleinfeld, "Video Games Industry Comes Back to Earth" *New York Times*, October 17, 1983.

160. One industry observer wrote of the late 1980s arcade, "In addition to featuring new, improved games in a more attractive setting, the new and overhauled arcades are being targeted more toward the family than they were in the past according to retailers and operators." Joe Morris, "Amusement Centers Are Winners Again," *Shopping Center World* (September 1987), 60.

161. John McCloud, "Fun and Games Is Serious Business," *Shopping Center World* (July 1989), 32.

162. McCloud, "Fun and Games Is Serious Business."

163. June Williamson, "Protest on the Astroturf at Downtown Silver Spring: July 4, 2007," in Niedt, *Social Justice in Diverse Suburbs*, 54–69. Williamson argues that this regulation of indoor malls led to new suburban forms that functioned outside strict surveillance as public space and were defended as openly accessible by local residents, as seen in her analysis of Silver Spring.

164. Evan McKenzie, *Privatopia: Homeowner Associations and the Rise of Residential Private Government* (New Haven, CT: Yale University Press, 1994). McKenzie calls this tendency "hostile privatism" and sees it in the movement toward privately owned communities governed by their residents, a movement that has upset the traditions of shared public space and government.

165. Teachers and psychologists were concerned with video game addictions and exposure to violent content that might spur adolescent players to adopt transgressive behavior. In 1981, the *New York Times* cited a Dr. Millman of New York Hospital who predicted a slippery slope from addiction to video games to more dangerous addictions: "The games present a seductive world. They offer a social structure, a system, a special language, something to relate around. There is the ritual of waiting on line, of being the predator in a violent game. From time immemorial kids have wanted to alter the way they felt—to be totally absorbed in an activity where they are out on an edge and can't think of anything else. That's why they try everything from gambling to glue sniffing." Glenn Collins, "Children's Video Games: Who Wins (or Loses)?" *New York Times*, August 31, 1981.

166. Edward J. Walsh, Rex Warland, and D. Clayton Smith, *Don't Burn it Here: Grassroots Challenges to Trash Incinerators* (University Park: Pennsylvania State University Press, 1997).

CHAPTER FIVE: **Parental Advisory—Explicit Content**

1. C. Everett Koop, "Raised on Rock 'n' Roll: The Sound and the Fury," address delivered at Parents' Music Resource Center symposium, October 26, 1987.

2. Both the PMRC and Koop were part of a broader antipornography movement and the pornography wars in the postwar United States, as explained in Whitney Strub, *Perversion for Profit: The Politics of Pornography and the Rise of the New Right* (New York: Columbia University Press, 2010).

3. Kruse and Zelizer, *Fault Lines*, ch. 7; William P. Putsis Jr., "Product Diffusion, Product Differentiation, and the Timing of New Product Introduction in the Television and VCR Market, 1964–85," *Managerial and Decision Economics* 10, No. 1 (March 1989): 37–50; Thomas Eisenmann, "The U.S. Cable Television Industry, 1948–1995: Managerial Capitalism in Eclipse," *Business History Review* 74, No. 1 (April 1, 2000): 19; Austan Goolsbee and Amil Petrin, "The Consumer Gains from Direct Broadcast Satellites and the Competition with Cable TV," *Econometrica* 72, No. 2 (March 2004): 351–81.

4. Parsons, *Blue Skies*, 452–77.

5. Koop, "Raised on Rock 'n' Roll," 3.

6. Koop, "Raised on Rock 'n' Roll," 5. Koop echoed the concerns of evangelical Christians who also located the moral problems of American culture in the home. See Eileen Luhr, *Witnessing Suburbia: Conservatives and Christian Youth Culture* (Berkeley: University of California Press, 2009), 27.

7. "'Missing Genius' Apparently Tried Suicide, Police Say," Associated Press, August 12, 1980; "Two Arraigned in 'Satanic' Slaying of 17-Year-Old," Associated Press, July 6, 1984; "Parents of Teen Who Killed Self Sue Singer Ozzy Osbourne," Associated Press, January 14, 1986; John Roll, "Whether Music Instigated Youth Suicide Pact Apparently Headed for Trial," Associated Press, December 4, 1986.

8. Kelley, *Yo' Mama's Disfunktional*, 4–9.

9. Rose, *Hip Hop Wars*, 40.

10. Hinton, *From the War on Poverty to the War on Crime*, 9–18.

11. Hinton, *From the War on Poverty to the War on Crime*; Kelley, *Yo' Mama' Disfunktional*, 78–103; Sanford F. Schram, *After Welfare: The Culture of Postindustrial Society* (New York: New York University Press, 2000), ch. 2. Tricia Rose writes, "Over the last three decades, the public conversation has decidedly moved toward an easy acceptance of black ghetto existence and the belief that black people themselves are responsible for creating ghettos and for choosing to live in them, thus absolving the most powerful segments of society from any responsibility in the creation and maintenance of them." Rose, *Hip Hop Wars*, 9.

12. Chappell, *The War on Welfare*, 11–15, 200–201; Julilly Kohler-Hausmann, "Guns and Butter: The Welfare State, the Carceral State, and the Politics of Exclusion in the Postwar United States," *Journal of American History* 102, No. 1 (June 2015): 87–99.

13. Chappell, *The War on Welfare*, 200.

14. Coontz, *The Way We Never Were*; Hartman, *A War for the Soul of America*, 2–3.

15. Lawrence Grossberg, *We Gotta Get Out of this Place: Popular Conservatism and Postmodern Culture* (New York: Routledge, 1992), 5–7; Strub, *Perversion for Profit*, 187–94; William Martin, *With God on Our Side: The Rise of the Religious Right in America* (New York: Broadway Books, 1996), 232; Sara Diamond, *Not by Politics Alone: The Enduring Influence of the Christian Right* (New York: Guilford Press, 1998), 63–66.

16. Self, *All in the Family*, 349.

17. Charles W. Phillips, "Focus on the Family," *Saturday Evening Post* (April 1982), 34–37, 121; Richard N. Ostling, "Jerry Falwell's Crusade," *Time*, September 2, 1985; Robert Ajemian, "Jerry Falwell Spreads the Word," *Time*, September 2, 1985; Richard N. Ostling, "A Jerry-Built Coalition Regroups," *Time*, November 16, 1987; "Falwell's Farewell," *National Review*, July 14, 1989; Diamond, *Not by Politics Alone*, 18–41.

18. Luhr, *Witnessing Suburbia*, 23, 46; Ronald Reagan, "Remarks at a White House Ceremony Honoring the Winners in the Secondary School Recognition Program and the Exemplary Private School Recognition Project," Ronald Reagan Presidential Library and Museum, October 1, 1985, https://www.reaganlibrary.gov/research/speeches /100185h.

19. Hartman, *A War for the Soul of America*, 2–3.

20. Hartman, *A War for the Soul of America*, 171–200; Kelley, *Yo Mama's Disfunktional*; Chappell, *The War on Welfare*; Kohler-Hausmann, *Getting Tough*.

21. Ronald Reagan, "Message to the Congress Transmitting the Annual Economic Report of the President," *The American Presidency Project*, February 1, 1982, http://www .presidency.ucsb.edu/ws/index.php?pid=42121.

22. Schulman, *The Seventies*, 235–36.

23. Gil Troy, *Morning in America: How Ronald Reagan Invented the 80s* (Princeton, NJ: Princeton University Press, 2005), 290.

24. Ronald Reagan, "Remarks on the Signing of the Proclamation of 'Just Say No' to Drugs Week," Pub. Papers 658, May 20, 1986.

25. Tom Adams and Hank Resnik, "Teens in Action: Creating a Drug-Free Future for America's Youth" (Washington, DC: U.S. Department of Health and Human Services, Public Health Service, Alcohol, Drug Abuse, and Mental Health Administration, 1985).

26. Hinton, *From the War on Poverty to the War on Crime*, 276–333; Scott O. Lilienfeld and Hal Arkowitz, "Why 'Just Say No' Doesn't Work," *Scientific American*, January 1, 2014.

27. Troy, *Morning in America*, 15, 267.

28. May, *Homeward Bound*, 16–37. This figuring of the suburban home was reminiscent of that during the heyday of the Cold War when, Tyler May argues, the suburban home was a bulwark against social change and the broader sense of imminent nuclear war—a domestic iteration of the Cold War strategy of containment of communism.

29. Margaret Hornblower, "Youths' Deaths Tied to Satanic Rite," *Washington Post*, July 9, 1984.

30. "Two Arraigned in 'Satanic' Slaying of 17-Year-Old," Associated Press, July 6, 1984.

31. Robert D. McFadden, "Youth Found Hanged in L.I. Cell after Arrest in Ritual Killing," *New York Times*, July 8, 1984.

32. Sara Rimer, "Northport Residents Express Disbelief at News of Slaying," *New York Times*, July 8, 1984.

33. "The Devil Worshippers," *20/20* (ABC News, May 16, 1985), available on YouTube, https://www.youtube.com/watch?v=UQuwxBgpAg.

34. Hornblower, "Youths' Deaths Tied to Satanic Rite"; Lindsay Gruson, "'Satanic Ritual' Is Now Ruled Out in June Slaying of Youth in L.I. Woods," *New York Times*, December 27, 1987; "Youth Charged in 'Satanic' Slaying Found Dead in Jail Cell," Associated Press, July 7, 1984.

35. "Teen Found Innocent in Killing," Associated Press, April 25, 1985.

36. Lasch, *The Culture of Narcissism*, 4–6.

37. Lynn Schofield Clark, *From Angels to Aliens: Teenagers, the Media, and the Supernatural* (New York: Oxford University Press, 2003), 27–28.

38. Stephanie Mansfield, "The Man in the Moon," *Washington Post*, January 23, 1982.

39. Sandra Salmans, "Fighting That Old Devil Rumor," *Saturday Evening Post* (October 1982).

40. Robert Walser, *Running with the Devil: Power, Gender, and Madness in Heavy Metal Music* (Middletown, CT: Wesleyan University Press, 1993), 10–13.

41. Eileen Luhr, "Metal Missionaries to the Nation: Christian Heavy Metal Music, 'Family Values,' and Youth Culture, 1984–1994," *American Quarterly* 57, No. 21 (March 2005): 103–28.

42. An urban legend from the 1970s held that KISS stood for Knights in Satan's Service.

43. Luhr, *Witnessing Suburbia*, 49.

44. Kevin Kruse, *One Nation Under God: How Corporate America Invented Christian America* (New York: Basic Books, 2015).

45. Divina Infusino, "Senators' Wives Aim to Revolutionize Disc Ratings," *San Diego Union-Tribune*, August 7, 1985.

46. "Heavy Metal," *20/20* (ABC News, May 21, 1987), available on YouTube, http://www.youtube.com/watch?v=orrgV_piHPA and http://www.youtube.com/watch?v=nZ4PTiL1RDs.

47. "Youth Charged in 'Satanic' Slaying Found Dead in Jail Cell."

48. Hornblower, "Youths' Deaths Tied to Satanic Rite."

49. Laurinda Keys, untitled article, Associated Press, February 26, 1982; Kenneth Stoffels, "TSR Sees Profits in Its Future following Austerity Measures," *Business Journal–Milwaukee*, January 27, 1986; Mary Austin, "The Assignment: Find Out about Dungeons and Dragons," *Christian Science Monitor*, February 9, 1981; Anne H. Oman, "Dungeons & Dragons: It's Not Just a Game, It's an Adventure," *Washington Post*, February 20, 1981.

50. Thomas Radecki, "Dungeons & Dragons Controversy," United Press International, January 15, 1985.

51. "Missing 'Genius' Apparently Tried Suicide, Police Say," Associated Press, August 12, 1980.

52. Tom Zito, "Dungeons and Dragons: In This Fantasy Land of Power and Treasure, You Don't Play Around," *Washington Post*, September 7, 1983.

53. Rona Jaffe, *Mazes and Monsters* (New York: Dell, 1981); Steven Hilliard Stern, dir., *Mazes and Monsters* (McDermott Productions et al., 1982).

54. Jaffe, *Mazes and Monsters*, 13.

55. Pat Pulling, with Kathy Cawthon, *The Devil's Web: Who Is Stalking Your Children for Satan?* (Lafayette, LA: Huntington House, 1989), 11–12.

56. Bothered About *Dungeons & Dragons* (hereafter BADD), "Introductory Letter to Supporters," 1984 (copy in author's possession).

57. BADD, "Introductory Letter to Supporters."

58. BADD, "Introductory Letter to Supporters."

59. Ed Bradley, "Dungeons & Dragons," *60 Minutes* (CBS), September 15, 1985.

60. Loren K. Wiseman and Michael A. Stackpole, "Questions & Answers about Role-Playing Games," pamphlet prepared for the Game Manufacturing Association, available at *Internet Archive*, https://web.archive.org/web/20160601032228/https://www.rpg.net/realm/critique/gama.html. The authors claim that in a 1991 study the Centers for Disease Control found no evidence of any causal links between RPGs and teen suicide.

61. "Parents of Teen Who Killed Self Sue Singer Ozzy Osbourne."

62. Roll, "Whether Music Instigated Youth Suicide Pact Apparently Headed for Trial."

63. Robert E. McKeown, Steven P. Cuffe, and Richard M. Schulz, "US Suicide Rates by Age Group, 1970–2002: An Examination of Recent Trends," *American Journal of Public Health* 96, No. 10 (2006): 1744–51.

64. *Jack McCollum et al., Plaintiffs and Appellants v. CBS, Inc., et al.*, Court of Appeal of California, Second Appellate District, Division Three, No. B025565, July 1988.

65. Roll, "Whether Music Instigated Youth Suicide Pact Apparently Headed for Trial."

66. *McCollum v. CBS*, 8; Sandra Chereb, "Lawyer: Judas Priest Album Sent 'Boys over the Edge to Eternity,'" Associated Press, July 16, 1990.

67. *McCollum v. CBS*, opinion of Judge Croskey, note 22, p. 12.

68. Tipper Gore, *Raising PG Kids in an X-Rated Society: What Parents Can Do to Protect Their Children from Sex and Violence in the Media* (Nashville: Abingdon Press, 1987; reprinted, New York: Bantam Press, 1988), 104.

69. Sandra Chereb, "British Rock Singer Expresses Relief, Concern over Ruling," Associated Press, August 24, 1990; *McCollum v. CBS*, 2–6.

70. Dionne Searcey, "Behind the Music: Sleuths Seek Messages in Lyrical Backspin," *Wall Street Journal*, January 9, 2006.

71. Jon Pareles, "Speed-Metal: Extreme, Yes; Evil, No," *New York Times*, September 25, 1988.

72. Richard Deatley, "Heavy Metal Singer Denies His Song Caused Suicide," Associated Press, January 21, 1986.

73. Deatley, "Heavy Metal Singer."

74. Ronald Reagan, "Youth Suicide Prevention Month," June 4, 1985, Pub. Papers, 737.

75. Melinda Cooper, *Family Values: Between Neoliberalism and the New Social Conservatism* (New York: Zone Books, 2017), 190–91.

76. James S. Newton, "Suicides Put 'Burnouts' in Spotlight," *New York Times*, March 13, 1987; Jane Gross, "Bergenfield Adults View Youths Who Lack Hope," *New York Times*, March 18, 1987; Larry Martz, with Peter McKillop, Andy Murr, and Ray Anello, "The Copycat Suicides," *Newsweek*, March 23, 1987.

77. Martz, "The Copycat Suicides"; Richard Harrington, "Bedeviling Rumors," *Washington Post*, November 20, 1985. The press characterized AC/DC as satanic based on the band's song titles, such as "Highway to Hell" and "Night Prowler," the latter supposedly about the serial killer Richard Ramirez, the "night stalker." Further, rumors persisted that the band's name was some sort of abbreviation or satanic code for "antichrist devil's crusade" or the like.

78. Gross, "Bergenfield Adults View Youths Who Lack Hope."

79. Lindsay Tanner, "Police Link Two Young Suicides with New Jersey Deaths," Associated Press, March 13, 1987.

80. Martz, "The Copycat Suicides."

81. "Teen's Suicide Linked to Six Others, Police Say," Associated Press, March 16, 1987; Michael Fleeman, "Young Couple Attempts Suicide in Same Garage Four Teen-Agers Used," Associated Press, March 17, 1987.

82. Julia Dolan, "Community Tries to Understand Teen-Agers' Suicides," Associated Press, March 12, 1987; Jane Gross, "Amid Grief, Classmates Fault Earlier Response," *New York Times*, March 12, 1987; Jane E. Brody, "Youth Suicide: A Common Pattern," *New York Times*, March 12, 1987; Malcolm Ritter, "Studies Suggest Suicide News Can Trigger More Elsewhere, But Questions Remain," Associated Press, March 13, 1987; Michael Dobbs, "After Suicides, Town Ponders How It Failed 4 Teen-Agers," *Washington Post*, March 13, 1987; Martz, "The Copycat Suicides"; Charles S. Taylor, "CDC Says Youth Suicides Still Increasing," United Press International, March 10, 1988; and Robert Byrd, "CDC Recommends 10 Steps for Handling 'Cluster' Suicides," Associated Press, August 25, 1988.

83. "Heavy Metal."

84. Walser, introduction to *Running with the Devil*. Walser argues that 1980s heavy metal was a particularly suburban genre of popular music.

85. Phillips said that Teaneck High School was known for academic excellence, but, like most high schools across America, it also had a group of metalheads. The implication was that Teaneck High was the "average" suburban high school with its requisite metalhead population. One of the kids says, "Not everyone has to go to college—I think I've had enough years of school."

86. Gaines, *Teenage Wasteland*, 237–61.

87. On the show, de-metaling consisted mostly of tearing down posters, purging music collections of heavy metal, and changing teenagers' wardrobes. Waksman, "Suburban Noise." Waksman tells a similar story about 1960s teenage suburban garage rockers forced to take down their posters and put away their instruments because of the negative influence of rock and roll.

88. Pat H. Broeske, "Deprivation and the Power of Punk," *Washington Post*, November 29, 1985.

89. Ellis E. Conklin, "Punk and Heavy Metal: Teen Rebellion or Something Darker?" United Press International, May 25, 1985.

90. Conklin, "Punk and Heavy Metal."

91. Gregory Bodenhamer, *Back in Control: How to Get Your Children to Behave* (New York: Prentice Hall, 1988), xii.

92. Parents Music Resource Council, *Rising to the Challenge*, 2nd ed. (Video Visions, 1988).

93. "Frank Zappa vs. Candy Stroud," *Nightwatch with Charlie Rose* (CBS, August 25, 1985), available on YouTube, http://www.youtube.com/watch?v=VTdTvK_d9lQ; George Varga, "Blackie of the W.A.S.P. Is a Bit Stung by All the Band's Critics," *San Diego Union-Tribune*, February 10, 1986; Lisa Leavitt Ryckman, "Violent Teens Often Obsessed with Heavy Metal Rock," Associated Press, February 13, 1988; Brian G. Bourke, "Anti-rock Beat Goes on for Campaigning Tipper," *Syracuse (NY) Post-Standard*, April 8, 1988; Roxie Smith, "Group Helps Parents and Children Decide Value of Music," *St. Petersburg Times*, February 17, 1990; Karen Haywood, "Parents Group in Middle of Debate over Warning Labels," Associated Press, July 10, 1990.

94. Gore, *Raising PG Kids*, 28.

95. Richard Harrington, "X-Rated Lyrics Bill on Maryland Slate," *Washington Post*, February 8, 1986; Richard Harrington, "Porno Wars, Part XXX," *Washington Post*, February 12, 1986; Jon Pareles, "A Case against Censoring Rock Lyrics," *New York Times*, May 3, 1987. Some legislative initiatives were considered that would have regulated who could buy records or go to concerts. The two best examples were considered by the Maryland House of Representatives and the San Antonio City Council. Maryland delegate Pauline Toth lost a vote to have her bill made into law, while the ordinance in San Antonio to restrict underage concertgoers was passed but proved largely irrelevant to curbing heavy metal concerts in the city.

96. US Senate, Committee on Commerce, Science, and Transportation, *First Session on Contents of Music and the Lyrics of Records, September 19, 1985* (Washington, DC: Government Printing Office, 1985), 11. S. Hrg. 99–529, 11.

97. Untitled article, Associated Press, June 5, 1985.

98. Allan Parachini, "'84 Youth Suicides a Blip in 7-Year Drop, Report Says," *Los Angeles Times*, November 20, 1986.

99. US Senate, *First Session on Contents of Music and the Lyrics of Records*, 1.

100. US Senate, *First Session on Contents of Music and the Lyrics of Records*, 56.

101. Gore, *Raising PG Kids*, 43.

102. Gore, *Raising PG Kids*, 12.

103. Gore, *Raising PG Kids*, 13.

104. Gore, *Raising PG Kids*, 117, 118. The focus on heavy metal and satanism spun off a group of "experts" who went into great detail about satanic cult activities. To a large degree, they imparted advice similar to the PMRC's, though the Satan experts' came from an overtly Christian perspective. Two examples of this genre that emerged in the late 1980s were Thomas W. Wedge with Robert L. Powers, *The Satan Hunter* (Canton,

OH: Daring Books, 1988); and Bob Larson, *Satanism: The Seduction of America's Youth* (Nashville: Thomas Nelson, 1989).

105. Gore, *Raising PG Kids*, 119.

106. Gore, *Raising PG Kids*, 114.

107. Gore, *Raising PG Kids*, 160–64. Gore provided twelve actions for parents carry out in the community—most of which follow the program of the PMRC. These approaches valorized the home, local action, and individual freedom and responsibility, as well as the exercise of consumer rights, including local boycotts, letter writing, sharing concerns with fellow parents, organizing community groups, and monitoring radio, television, movie theaters, and video rental stores.

108. Gore, *Raising PG Kids*, 157.

109. The narrator also noted that a hydraulic penis, reported to be twenty feet in length, was seen at Beastie Boys concerts. This fact is recited in such a way that it seems a ten- or fifteen-foot hydraulic penis would have been more appropriate.

110. Pat Pulling, with Kathy Cawthon, *The Devil's Web: Who Is Stalking Your Children for Satan?* (Lafayette, LA: Huntington House, 1989).

111. Pat A. Pulling, Pat Dempsey, and Mary Dempsey, "Dungeons and Dragons: Witchcraft, Suicide, Violence," n.d., available at Internet Archive, https://archive.org/details/dungeons_and_dragons-witchcraft_suicide_violence.

112. Pulling, *The Devil's Web*, x.

113. Pulling, *The Devil's Web*, 27.

114. Pulling, *The Devil's Web*, 12.

115. US Senate, Committee on Governmental Affairs and the Judiciary, *First Session on Contents of Music and the Lyrics of Records September 19, 1985* (Washington, DC: Government Printing Office, 1985), 11. S. Hrg. 99-529, 11.

116. Josef Adalian, "Coverage of Shootings Blankets TV," *Variety*, April 22, 1999.

117. Dave Cullen, *Columbine* (New York: Twelve, 2009), 107.

118. Eric Harris, "Manifesto," FBI Report on Columbine, Part 1, April 22, 1999, p. 32, available at Congressional and Federal Web Harvests, National Archives, https://www.webharvest.gov/peth04/20041019064809/http://foia.fbi.gov/columbine_high_school/columbine_%20high_school_part01.pdf.

119. Bill Hutchinson and K. C. Baker, with Virginia Breen, "Two Looked to Darkness," *Daily News*, April 22, 1999; Michael Fleeman, "Goth or Not? High School Massacre Puts Spotlight on Dark Sub-culture," Associated Press, April 22, 1999; "Our Children Too Often Hear That Violence Is the Solution," *Detroit News*, April 22, 1999; Jodi Wilgoren, "Society of Outcasts Began with a $99 Black Coat," *New York Times*, April 25, 1999.

120. Robin McDowell, "Colorado Suspects Called Outcasts," Associated Press, April 20, 1999.

121. Patrick O'Driscoll, "Shooting Suspects Seen as Outcasts," *USA Today*, April 21, 1999; Brent Pulley, "Terror in Littleton: The Trench Coat Mafia," *New York Times*, April 21, 1999.

122. John Cloud, "Special Report: Troubled Teens," *Time*, May 31, 1999.

123. Karen Thomas, "Surrounded by Sound and Fury: Whirlwind of Violence, Hate Sweeps Kids Online and Off," *USA Today*, April 22, 1999; Steve Dunleavy, "Blind Could See It Coming," *New York Post*, April 22, 1999.

124. Cullen, *Columbine*, 177–81, 222–24.

125. Cullen, *Columbine*, 227–28.

126. "Phenomenon of the Gothic Movement, *20/20* (ABC News, April 21, 1999).

127. Steve Carney, "Kids Who Kill: How to See the Warning Signs in Today's Kids," *Daily News of Los Angeles*, April 22, 1999.

128. CNN, "Columbine Shooting Leaves 15 Dead," *Inside Politics*, April 21, 1999.

129. Timothy Egan, "Violence by Youths: Looking for Answers," *New York Times*, April 22, 1999; Erica Goode, "When Violent Fantasy Emerges as Reality," *New York Times*, April 25, 1999; Patricia Hersch, "Life in the Lost Lane," *Washington Post*, April 25, 1999; Sarah Boxer, "When Fun Isn't Funny," *New York Times*, May 1, 1999; Chris Taylor, "Digital Dungeons," *Time*, May 3, 1999; Andrew Pollack, "Video Game Industry Gathers Under Siege," *New York Times*, May 14, 1999; "Video Battlers Stick by Their Games," *New York Times*, June 20, 1999.

130. *The O'Reilly Factor*, Fox News, April 21, 1999.

131. Thomas, "Surrounded by Sound and Fury."

132. "School Shootings," *Hannity and Colmes*, Fox News Channel, April 22, 1999.

133. Frank Bruni, "Senate Narrowly Rejects Plan to Restrict Gun-Show Sales," *New York Times*, May 13, 1999.

134. Andrew Ferguson, "What Politicians Can't Do," *Time*, May 3, 1999.

135. "Columbine Shooting Leaves 15 Dead," *Inside Politics*, CNN, April 21, 1999.

136. CNN, "Columbine Shooting Leaves 15 Dead."

137. James Brooke, "Terror in Littleton: The Overview," *New York Times*, April 20, 1999.

138. "Anti-violence Help for Parents," Associate Press, May 5, 1999.

139. "Shock and Horror Grip Littleton and the Nation in the Wake of Columbine High School Shooting," CNN, April 21, 1999.

140. Fleeman, "Goth or Not?"

141. Tasha E. Kelter, "No Answers," *Daily Nebraskan*, April 22, 1999.

142. Robert King and Amy Schatz, "Schools Focus on Safety," *St. Petersburg Times*, April 22, 1999.

143. Erica Goode, "Deeper Truths Sought in Violence by Youths," *New York Times*, May 4, 1999.

144. Ethan Bronner, "Experts Urge Swift Action to Fight Depression, Isolation and Aggression," *New York Times*, April 22, 1999.

145. Marilyn Manson, "Columbine: Whose Fault Is It?" *Rolling Stone*, June 24, 1999.

146. Cullen argues the first wave of reporting and commentary firmly set the narrative of what happened. Cullen, *Columbine*, 213.

147. Cullen, *Columbine*, 149.

148. CNN, "Columbine Shooting Leaves 15 Dead."

Epilogue

1. "NIMBY? Trash Woes Are Ours to Cure" editorial, *Post Standard*, February 21, 1989; Robert A. Hamilton, "The View from Preston: The Town That Won't Give Up Its Fight against an Incinerator," *New York Times*, April 16, 1989; Donna Schaper, "Yes in My Back Yard," *New York Times*, June 18, 1989; "Beating Back Nimby—Creativity Important in Siting Interim Jail," (editorial), *Seattle Times*, March 11, 1990; James Fink, "Nimbys Seen as Amherst's Grinch," *Business First-Buffalo*, March 25, 1991; Steven A. Holmes, "When Grass Looks Greener on Our Side of the Fence," *New York Times*, April 21, 1991; Kathryn Balint, "Nuclear Waste Piles Up While Dump Debated," *San Diego Union-Tribune*, July 26, 1991; Angela Logomasini, "Trashing the Nimby Syndrome," *Journal of Commerce*, July 6, 1992; Andrew L. Yarrow, "'Not in My Back Yard' and Repercussions," *New York Times*, October 4, 1992; Jeff Webb, "NIMBYs Will Pressure New Commissioners," *St. Petersburg Times*, November 22, 1992.

2. Rae Tyson, "USA's Backyard Backlash: Communities Want Projects Put Elsewhere," *USA Today*, July 19, 1990; Gottlieb, *Forcing the Spring*, 3.

3. Angela Logomasini, "Trashing the NIMBY Syndrome," *Journal of Commerce*, July 6, 1992.

4. Michael Kinch, introduction to *Between Hope and Fear: A History of Vaccines and Human Immunity* (New York: Pegasus Books, 2018); Andrea Kitta, *Vaccinations and Public Concern in History* (New York: Routledge, 2012), 58–90; Michael Willrich, *Pox: An American History* (New York: Penguin, 2011), 343.

5. Gioielli, *Environmental Activism and the Urban Crisis*; Andrew Zaleski, "The Unequal Burden of Lead," *CityLab*, January 2, 2020, https://www.citylab.com /environment/2020/01/lead-poisoning-toxic-paint-pipes-health-iq-crime-baltimore /604201/.

6. Kinch, *Between Hope and Fear*.

7. "Ring Video Doorbell Commercial," August 15, 2015, available on YouTube, https://www.youtube.com/watch?v=Zh6QqvuagMI.

8. Rani Molla, "The Rise of Fear-Based Social Media like Nextdoor, Citizen, and now Amazon's Neighbors," *Vox*, May 7, 2019; Michael Harriot, "App Developer Responds to 'The Racist Nextdoor,'" *The Root*, July 1, 2019.

9. Alexander, *The New Jim Crow*, 1–19; Gilmore, *Golden Gulag*, 5–30.

10. Davis, *City of Quartz*, 253–57.

11. Paresh Dave, "Ring Modernized the Doorbell, Then Its Inventor, Jamie Siminoff, Went to War Against Crime," *Los Angeles Times*, May 12, 2017.

12. Josh Sanburn, "Why the Death of Malls Is about More than Shopping," *Time*, July 20, 2017.

13. Sanburn, "Why the Death of Malls Is about More than Shopping."

14. Natasha Geiling, "The Death and Rebirth of the American Mall," *Smithsonian*, November 25, 2014.

15. Nelson D. Schwartz, "The Economics (and Nostalgia) of Dead Malls," *New York Times*, January 3, 2015; Amanda Kolson Hurley, "Shopping Malls Aren't Actually Dying," *CityLab*, March 25, 2015, https://www.citylab.com/design/2015/03/shopping -malls-arent-actually-dying/387925/.

16. James Witte, Marissa Kiss, and Randy Lynn, "The Internet and Social Inequalities in the U.S." in Massimo Ragnedda and Glenn W. Muschert, eds., *The Digital Divide: The Internet and Social Inequality in International Perspective* (London: Routledge, 2013), 67–84; Karl Vick, "The Digital Divide: A Quarter of the Nation Is without Broadband," *Time*, March 30, 2017.

17. Zelizer and Kruse, *Fault Lines*, ch. 12.

Index

Page numbers in *italics* refer to figures.

Lightning Source UK Ltd.
Milton Keynes UK
UKHW041842230223
417559UK00018B/131/J